RISKY BUSINESS

RISKY BUSINESS

The Political Economy of Hollywood

David F. Prindle

Westview Press

Boulder • San Francisco • Oxford

Chapter 6 is adapted from David F. Prindle and James W. Endersby, "Hollywood Liberalism," *Social Science Quarterly*, Volume 74, Number 1, March 1993, 136–149. Reprinted by permission.

Copyright © 1993 by Westview Press, Inc.

Published in 1993 in the United States of America by Westview Press, Inc., 5500 Central Avenue, Boulder, Colorado 80301-2877, and in the United Kingdom by Westview Press, 36 Lonsdale Road, Summertown, Oxford OX2 7EW

Library of Congress Cataloging-in-Publication Data
Prindle, David F. (David Forrest), 1948–
   Risky business : the political economy of Hollywood / David F. Prindle.
       p.   cm.
   Includes bibliographical references and index.
   ISBN 0-8133-1770-3
   1. Motion picture industry—Economic aspects—United States.
2. Motion picture industry—Political aspects—United States.
I. Title.
PN1993.5.U6P76   1993
388.4'779143'0973—dc20

                                                                                  93-2975
                                                                                  CIP

Printed and bound in the United States of America

   The paper used in this publication meets the requirements
   of the American National Standard for Permanence of Paper
   for Printed Library Materials Z39.48-1984.

10   9   8   7   6   5   4   3   2   1

Contents

ONE   Existential Truths

TWO   Economic Anxieties

THREE   Sociological Nightmares

FOUR   Political Paradoxes

Tables and Boxes

Acknowledgments

This book is my work, and I am responsible for it. Along the way, however, I have been helped by many people who deserve at least my public thanks.

My wife, Angalene, endured my absences from our home in Texas while I was conducting research in California. She also read the entire manuscript in its first draft and steered me away from several pitfalls. She deserves all the royalties that may come her way.

My father and mother, Elliott and Vivian Prindle; my brother Ken and his wife, Marilyn; and my friend William Alex Rennie all allowed me to stay with them in their homes and borrow their cars when I was in the Los Angeles area. Also, Deborah Rennie permitted me to house-sit for her for three weeks in the summer of 1990 while I was interviewing. I hope they all consider this book to be worth the trouble I caused them.

Thomas Schatz, of the Radio-Television-Film Department of the University of Texas at Austin, read eight of the chapters in the second draft and provided me with an exhaustive critique. His repeated insistence that I clarify my theme is at least partly responsible for whatever clarity it now possesses.

Dr. Thomas Backer of the Human Interaction Research Institute in Los Angeles read early drafts of Chapters 1 and 5 and made many useful suggestions. My colleague Mark Graber read my first draft of Chapter 9 and saved me from several rash pronouncements about constitutional law. An undergraduate at the University of Texas, Talal Hattar, read five chapters in the first draft; his comments helped me to understand how students might react to the book. James Endersby, who was then a graduate student in the Government Department at Texas and is now a professor in the Political Science Department of the University of Missouri at Columbia, performed the computer runs that made possible the statistical discussion of Hollywood opinion in Chapter 6. None of these people, of course, are responsible for any errors of fact or outrages to common sense that appear in this book.

Many others helped in a variety of ways. I am grateful to Ellen Benjamin, Doug Brantley, Robert Brigham, James Burshtyn, Barbara Crofford, Robert Easton, Paul Fairbrother, Augie Grant, John Higley, Joli Jensen, Carol

Lanning, Mark McIntire, Penny Marcus, Horace Newcomb, Rand Owen, Scott Packman, Larry Reed, James Roach, Joe Slate, Janet Staiger, Sharon Strover, and James Ulmer.

My greatest debt is to those busy people in the Hollywood industry who were willing to be interviewed by a college professor from Texas. Some of them fall into the category of "opinion leader" and thus participated in the data collection that forms the foundation for Chapter 6. Others were helpful in a more general way, offering information and opinions on the film and television industries. Some of them asked me not to name them in my book, on the grounds that it would encourage other importunate researchers to pester them as badly as I had. Unfortunately, the more important they were in Hollywood, the more likely they were to make this request. I therefore cannot name some of my most helpful respondents. I remain grateful to them all, named and unnamed.

Among those who were interviewed and who do not mind being named were Dr. Thomas Backer, Leo Chaloukian, Charles Champlin, Martha Coolidge, J. Nicholas Counter, Barry Diller, Charles Fitz-Simons, Barry Gordon, Ernest Harada, Sumi Haru, Charlton Heston, Arthur Hiller, Marvin Kaplan, Marcy Kelly, George Kirgo, Stephen Kolzak, Jonathan Lovin, Mark McIntire, Sydney Pollack, Thomas Pollock, Elaine Pounds, Vikki Powell, Marian Rees, Teri Ritzer, Alvin Rush, William Shields, Michael Silverman, Eliot Silverstein, Marcia Smith, Leonard Stern, Margery Tabankin, Marc Allen Trujillo, Jack Valenti, Robert Wise, and David Wolper.

In writing of the general psychological atmosphere in Hollywood and among actors in particular, I also made extensive use of the interviews I conducted for my previous book, *The Politics of Glamour: Ideology and Democracy in the Screen Actors Guild.* I will not repeat the names of those several dozen people here but nevertheless admit that I owe them a double debt.

David F. Prindle

PART ONE

Existential Truths

1

Why Hollywood Is Different

IN THE SUMMER OF 1986, Hollywood actors were in a panic. The Republican administration in Washington was negotiating with Congress over a reform of the income tax laws and seemed on the verge of dealing performers a crippling blow. Actors had always been able to deduct the 10 percent of their income that they paid their agents from the total on which they were required to pay federal taxes. Contrary to the popular image of performers as fabulously wealthy, the typical actor barely scraped by. Because actors experienced so many periods of unemployment, the average annual earnings for each was well below $2,000. Most actors couldn't live on what they made, even though they were taxed on only 90 percent of their earnings. The proposed change would slice still further into the already measly income that most actors derived from their profession.[1]

The solution to the problem would seem to have been obvious. Although most actors are poor and obscure, several hundred are rich and famous. Normally in the United States, such people are Republicans. Ordinarily, a threatened community of rich citizens has no trouble getting access to a Republican administration and little difficulty achieving a sympathetic hearing there. Hollywood actors might have been expected to send a delegation of prominent Republican campaign contributors to Washington, have them bend a few well-placed ears, and relax in safety. Since all actors were threatened by the change in the tax law, protecting a few hundred rich would also protect many thousand poor. All that would be necessary would be a little lobbying.

And yet the actors were in trouble. For in all their thousands, even among the rich only a tiny percentage were Republicans, and only a handful had any contacts within the administration, despite the fact that President Reagan was himself a former actor. One of the wealthiest and most celebrated communities in the United States had almost no influence over a government catering to the wealthy and the celebrated and that was headed by a former member of that community. Despite its riches, despite its fame, despite its power, it was a community of liberal Democrats.

But there was one connection—and that was enough. Charlton Heston, one of the very few political conservatives in Hollywood, one of the only Republicans among performers, and just about the only one who made it his business to keep close and cordial relations with the Reagan administration, took it upon himself to carry the actors' case to Washington. Making personal calls on the secretary of labor and several senators, he persuaded them to drop the proposed "reform" of the performer-agent relationship from the new tax bill. The actors were saved by a man whose political views most of them abhorred.

Four years later, in 1990, no one would have guessed that celebrity performers had ever had trouble finding volunteers to participate in a political activity. The occasion was a Hollywood fund-raising dinner for Nelson Mandela, leader of South Africa's African National Congress, an organization with impeccable radical credentials and no clear relevance to Hollywood. Among the almost one thousand entertainment glitterati happy to be seen with him and eager to contribute their share to the $1.2 million raised for his revolutionary organization were the heads of the major studios, the important talent agents, the most prominent producers, writers, and directors of motion pictures and television, and just about every star except Charlton Heston.[2]

In other words, these prominent people who could find almost no one in their group willing and able to influence public policy on an issue directly threatening their personal income could nevertheless summon a horde of supporters to raise funds for a man who had spent his life crusading in a far corner of the world for a cause having nothing to do with them.

In the everyday world of American politics, this juxtaposition would be too fantastic to be believed. In the special world of Hollywood, however, it is entirely unsurprising. For Hollywood politics is different. It is different because Hollywood's sociology is different, and its sociology is different because its economics is different. The purpose of this book is to explore these connections in detail.

THE RISKIEST BUSINESS

The Hollywood entertainment industry is a *business* whose product is *art,* and that causes the trouble. For art has several qualities that make it a less-than-ideal object of commerce. In the first place, although it is fairly easy to gauge the market for an art (say, movies) in general, it is nearly impossible to do so for a particular artistic product. Everyone knows that people love to see good movies; nobody knows which movies will be considered good by enough people to make them profitable. Many of the industry's huge box-office hits were originally turned down by various studios that thought they would be surefire failures: *Star Wars, Back to the Future,* and *Dances With Wolves,* to name only three.[3] Conversely, since no one will produce a film expected to fail, it can be presumed that the studios that released *Pennies From Heaven, Howard the Duck,* and *Ishtar* thought that these movies would make money. Instead, they lost a total of $83 million in domestic rentals.[4] Meanwhile, the large amount of judgment, testing, and improvement that goes into the creation of prime-time television series nevertheless results in a failure rate of over 75 percent. At the same time, great successes, such as "All in the Family" and "Hill Street Blues," are at first opposed by network executives and only make it to the screen by strokes of luck, after which they amaze their detractors with their popularity.[5]

In the second place, successful screen art is nearly impossible to replicate. When the Ford Motor Company introduced the first Mustang to general acclaim in 1965, it then produced and sold millions more of the identical car; when the Chrysler minivan proved popular in the 1980s, the company manufactured as many as possible. In a non-art commodity such as automobiles, firms can reproduce a successful product nearly indefinitely. Not so with entertainment. "Cheers" attracts millions of viewers, but it is impossible for NBC to duplicate it immediately and show it every night. *Driving Miss Daisy* fills the theaters, but Warner Brothers cannot release the same film every year under a different title. Once a work of screen art has been consumed, it is, with some exceptions, useless. The next time, the public will want something else. As director Sydney Pollack explains, "It's a totally irrational business. The problem is that you reinvent the art of picture-making every time you make a picture."[6] Producers employ an increasingly complicated repertoire of business strategies to attempt to overcome this problem, and sometimes they succeed. Much of what Hollywood does can be interpreted as a series of strategies to replicate the unreplicable. But even if producers succeed with an individual product, they always face the fact that their next offering cannot be exactly like their previous one.

These two aspects of the screen art industry—the difficulty of predicting public tastes and the impossibility of exactly duplicating a hit—make the enterprise of producing film and television extraordinarily risky. Every business contains a significant element of risk, of course. But for most executives or investors in the fairly stable market that characterizes most businesses, the relative probabilities of success are somewhat calculable. People in Hollywood, however, face the incalculable every day. Each choice is a stab in the dark, every decision a wager against unknown odds. In fact, the everyday speech of people in the business is replete with gambling metaphors, and nothing better captures the emotional texture of their lives than to compare them to Las Vegas tourists shooting craps or standing at a roulette wheel:

The odds in Vegas are better. Finding the chips to bankroll future film productions and television programming, as well as expansion or acquisitions, has become nothing more than a crap shoot for the industry.   —Judy Brennan[7]

Although Hollywood production has factory characteristics, the general atmosphere pervading the studios is no more that of a factory than it is of a creative human enterprise. Rather, it is that of the gamblers' den.
    —Hortense Powdermaker[8]

The business is a gamble, really.
    —Leonard Goldenson, president and founder of the ABC television network[9]

They loved to gamble. ... Gambling was a kind of therapy that cut through all the affectations and reduced everything to basic naked aggression. It tested the skills of bluff and nerve and judgement, which were the measure of a film executive, and it provided a small arena for tremendously competitive and insecure men to intimidate one another and prove themselves.
    —Neil Gabler (on the studio moguls of the 1930s)[10]

Hollywood is a technological crapshoot.   —John Gregory Dunne[11]

The place makes everyone a gambler. Its spirit is speedy, obsessive, immaterial. ... The action is everything, more consuming than sex, more immediate than politics; more important always than the acquisition of money, which is never, for the gambler, the true point of the exercise.   —Joan Didion[12]

All motion pictures are a gamble. Anything having to do with creating something that nobody's seen before, and showing it, and counting on 10 or 20 million people, individuals, to go into the theater to make or break that film—that's a gamble.   —Steven Spielberg[13]

A consequence of the high risk inherent in the business is the rate of failure. Most ideas for films never make it to celluloid: the few that are produced often lose money. Most television ideas are never turned into series, and those that are usually do not return for a second season. Similarly, because almost all executives in studios and networks are thus likely to have low batting averages in their decisions, they cannot but frequently displease their superiors. The tenure of top executives in studios can often be measured in months.[14] In other words, the riskiness of the Hollywood corporate world is expressed not only in financial uncertainty but also in job insecurity.

THE RISKIEST ART

If Hollywood is fraught with economic insecurity for executives, it is a mine field of psychological peril for artists. All artists placing their work before the public run the risk of rejection. But Hollywood artists, addressing the huge audience of entertainment consumers not only in the United States but all around the world, become vulnerable to rejection by almost literally everybody. The history of Hollywood is replete with stories of has-been and never-were actors, directors, and writers who missed their grab at the brass ring or, having grabbed it, somehow lost it again. Although no one keeps statistics for the industry, it probably has the highest suicide rate in the world (with the possible exception of Las Vegas, another town that has made an industry out of fantasy). Hollywood folklore is full of stories of old-time stars, once worshipped by the world, now alcoholic wrecks living on charity. Everybody knows these stories, and everybody draws the same correct conclusion: It could happen to me. The belief that all success in Hollywood is temporary intensifies the anxiety that accompanies every step up the ladder.

In the third place, however, the art of Hollywood is glamorous. This is true both because of the emotional magic that permeates the motion picture and television industries and because of the astounding fortunes that can be made in them. Stated simply, most people love Hollywood. They want to work in the industry; they want to know performers; they want to be rich, beautiful, admired, loved, desired; they want their dreams to come true. Hollywood exerts an attraction that is wholly independent of rational cost-benefit analysis.

On the financial side, hard-headed business people who have never made a rash decision with their money are willing to invest in film and television prospects that, examined in a cool and analytical manner, would be seen as foolish. Despite the risks, there are always plenty of pilots awaiting network approval, and there is seldom a shortage of investors willing to back even dubious film projects.

But the major impact of Hollywood's glamorous appeal is felt on the labor side. In most industries, the supply of workers adjusts over time to the number of available jobs. Unemployment in, for example, a steel plant in one part of the country tends to decline as the jobless move to another part of the country or go into another line of work. Over the long run, the number of people seeking employment in a particular industry tends to equal the number of opportunities. In the language of economists, labor markets tend toward equilibrium. Not so in Hollywood. Since the 1920s, hordes of people have converged on Los Angeles, attracted both by the hope of realizing themselves in cinematic expression and by the possibility of striking it rich. Despite the odds, despite the continuous rejection to which they are subjected, most of these people cannot be discouraged. It is a standing joke in Hollywood that if you stop any person at random on the street and ask, "How's your screenplay coming?" the answer will always be "It's making the rounds" or "I'm looking for an agent," never "What screenplay?" Go into any bar in the area and when the cocktail waitress serves you, look hard at her and ask, "Didn't I see you on stage somewhere?" The reply will be a list of minor parts in musicals at obscure theaters in Orange County and the San Fernando Valley. Eavesdrop on the conversation between waiters at any restaurant west of downtown and you will hear gossip about auditions. The official unemployment rate among members of the Screen Actors Guild is about 85 percent. (That figure does not even count the ambitious amateurs who have not been able to acquire a union card.) Yet more hopeful actors arrive every day.[15]

This insane oversupply of workers conditions the financial and emotional atmosphere of the industry. Almost every artist lives in a continuous pique of rejection and frustration. Not only are most unemployed, but even the chosen few who are working at any given moment can feel the hungry mob behind them, waiting for the slightest opportunity to shunt them aside. Moreover, the odds are that those who do have jobs consider themselves underemployed, for the artistically significant positions are only a small percentage of those available. Thus, the director who yearns to create a cinematic masterpiece may work for years, or even for an entire career, shooting insurance commercials or daytime soap operas. But this well-known fact does not discourage ever-increasing numbers of students from enrolling in directing classes at universities. The desperation and fear that are the background of the typical Hollywood novel reflect this fact that the industry does not conform to rational economic models of how labor markets work, but is in permanent disequilibrium.

The financial and emotional atmosphere of the industry is only made worse by the collaborative nature of the work performed in Hollywood. Artists are consumed by the need to realize their inner visions. For most artists—poets, sculptors, composers—the urge to create can be satisfied in solitude. A poet whose work goes completely unnoticed by anyone else has at least experienced the joy of invention.

But screen artists cannot create alone. Even in the unlikely circumstance that they are financing their own picture and therefore have no need to placate investors (and this possibility, rare in the movies, is entirely lacking in television), they are forced to rely on dozens of other artists and craftspersons. No auteur in the history of motion pictures—not Sergei Eisenstein, not Charlie Chaplin, not Jean Luc Godard—has been actor, director, writer, camera operator, set designer, sound technician, film editor, and all the less celebrated contributors whose competence is nevertheless vital to the film as a whole. Most artists, even those who are successful and pursued by the studios or networks, never approach this level of self-realization. The result is an industry based on the work of frequently temperamental, often antisocial participants who are forced to cooperate and who, by doing so, compromise their deepest principles.

Working in Hollywood is therefore a series of battles in an unending guerrilla war in which the artists constantly struggle for greater control over the product against the executives who have authority over them and against the other artists with whom they are forced to cooperate. To the group insecurity caused by the vicious competition for jobs is thus added a perennial resentment grounded in artistic frustration.

Compounding the psychological impact of risk is the unusual pattern of work within the industry. This pattern mandates that its labor force operates within an environment characterized, above all, by a crushing burden of stress. Among the common causes of emotional strain are the following:

Uncertain support from above. When new studio executives move into their suites, their first thought is how to make themselves look good by making their predecessors look bad. One of the ways they customarily do this is by sabotaging the projects that were in development when they arrived. The people working on those projects therefore live in a constant state of apprehension that the fruits of their labors are about to be poisoned by new bosses brought to the top by a management shuffle.

Impossible working conditions. People involved in the shooting of feature films and television programs often have to be on the set more than fourteen hours a day for weeks on end. Once a film or videotape is shot, those laboring to turn it into something marketable frequently must operate under extreme time pressure, which makes their workdays unending. If a motion picture is shot on location, the cast and crew are often forced to live and perform under primitive (if not dangerous) conditions and are frequently subject to the authority of an egomaniacal director whose main concern is cutting costs. The unions try to protect cast and crew from too much abuse under these circumstances, but companies often move a shoot to a foreign country or a nonunion state precisely to escape such oversight. Recent accounts of location shooting, such as Steven Bach's tale of woe surrounding the creation of *Heaven's Gate,* Stephen Farber and Marc Green's report on the murderous atmosphere on the set of one segment of *The Twilight Zone— The Movie,* or Julia Phillips's narrative of the troubles that had to be overcome to complete *Close Encounters of the Third Kind,* all depict a location movie set as a sort of temporary hell.[16] In other words, in Hollywood, having a job is often nearly as stressful as not having one.

Lack of privacy. Actors, who make up a large proportion of the artists in Hollywood, are vulnerable to a particularly acute form of stress: When they become successful, they lose their privacy. Writers for supermarket tabloids and "personality" magazines and gossip columnists lurk everywhere, ready to print any evidence of actors' love lives, sexual tastes, personality quirks, dieting habits, political views, health, or personal finances. It is commonly believed in Hollywood, for example, that there are agents of the tabloids in every hospital in the Los Angeles area, ready to notify the world if a star checks in and eager to sell information about the clinical details of his or her illness. Actors therefore live with the knowledge that the more successful they become, the more likely it is that they will be forced to live their lives under the microscope of publicity. Constantly harassed by the media, actors frequently respond by behaving in rude or bizarre ways, which draws more attention to themselves and only worsens their problems.

Put all this together and it does not form a pretty picture. Whether they are working or not, most Hollywoodites live in an emotional world characterized by paranoia, suspicion, resentment, and dread. It is thus a risky business not only in the financial but also in the psychological sense. Economic uncertainty coexists with emotional instability. Executives whose tenures are precarious are forced to cooperate with artists whose neuroses are permanent. It is amazing that this unhealthy collaboration often produces wonderful entertainment—and sometimes even great art.

POLITICS AND THE HOLLYWOOD PSYCHE

Hollywood's existential situation has both sociological and political consequences. In their struggle to live and prosper in the harsh economic and emotional environment of the industry, its residents create a distinctive community with its own folkways, vocabulary, and psychological tone. Further, the group psychology forged in that community carries an intense, coherent political outlook that then expresses itself when Hollywoodites participate in national public policy debates. Unlike the situation in nearly every other community in the country, the lifestyles of even the rich and famous in Hollywood include an allegiance to political liberalism.

Paradoxically, this near-unanimity on political ideology does not mean that the industry is without internal disputes—quite the contrary. As we will see, the town is riven with quarrels: management versus labor, artists versus business people, and producers versus distributors, to name three perennial sources of civil war. The distinctive emotional tone of the industry saturates its interior struggles and makes politics in Hollywood, like everything else about the place, different.

Before exploring these conflicts, however, we must recognize one more oddity about Hollywood: the importance of symbols.

Unlike traditional American industries, which produce tangible products such as cars, appliances, computers, and diapers, Hollywood's product is intangible. Films and television programs consist of ideas, symbols, images, dreams, and fantasies. Most people in the industry spend their working lives creating and selling make-believe.

People who work with tangible products tend to participate in politics that are relevant to their livelihoods. Farmers become involved with questions of agricultural price supports; auto workers pay attention to the level of import quotas for foreign cars; everyone worries about taxes. Occasionally, people can become exercised by issues that do not touch them directly (such as Alaskan oil spills or airline hijacking), but their focus is normally on issues that directly bear on their careers.

At times, those who work in Hollywood become embroiled in relevant issues of who-gets-what, such as the fight over the FCC's financial interest and syndication rules. But it seems that when Hollywood workers involve themselves in political issues, they often give a far greater portion of their attention and energy to issues that do not concern their professional careers than do workers in other industries. Observers of the entertainment industry must be struck by the very high level of concern with subjects that seem to have only a peripheral relationship to Hollywood. This observation seems to be most true of the artists, but it also applies to the executives and technicians.

The struggle against apartheid in South Africa is just one example of an issue that has no direct bearing on the lives of the vast majority of Hollywood's residents, yet elicits a great deal of attention there. It is one of the *symbolic* issues to which people in the entertainment industry consistently give time and money. Hollywood's odd preoccupation with symbolic politics adds to its unusual economic situation and bizarre sociology to create a community whose attitudes, values, and behavior are in marked contrast to those in the rest of the country.

The peculiar economics of the screen entertainment industry is thus the basis for an eccentric group psychology that in turn creates anomalous patterns of political behavior. The remainder of this book will explore the implications of these connections.

PART TWO

PART TWO

Economic Anxieties

2

The Industry

*I*F HOLLYWOOD ENTERTAINMENT is such a risky business, how do so many firms manage to prosper for so long? Universal has been functioning, in one corporate form or another, since 1909; Paramount, since 1912; and Warner Brothers, since 1918. The survival of these companies is proof that long-term success can be achieved in the screen entertainment industry despite its uncertainties. What is their secret?

The short answer to this crucial question is that these companies have never depended on a single product to keep themselves in business. They do not produce just one film or television series. They deal in bulk. Although any *particular* entertainment offering is liable to fail, in any *group* of productions by a competently run company, there will be enough hits to make up for the losses of the rest. The long-term gamblers in the industry thus hedge their bets by spreading the action.

THE STRUCTURE OF THE SCREEN ENTERTAINMENT INDUSTRY

A capital-intensive industry that delivers products to a mass market will organize itself to serve five major functions: It will gain access to a stable means of finance; It will produce something to sell; It will distribute the product; It will create a means of selling that product at retail; And it will advertise the product to insure that there will be people who want to buy it. The public, however, finds the production function by far the most interesting part of the motion picture and television industry, and it is this part of the business that goes by the catch-all name "Hollywood." But it is impossible to understand production without having a basic grasp of distribution, retail sales (called "exhibition" in the entertainment industry), and, to a lesser extent, financing and advertising, as well as an awareness of the way they all interrelate.

Motion pictures are produced by one of the seven major studios ("majors") in the Los Angeles area or by one of the hundreds of independent production companies ("indies") that survive for relatively short periods, some of them allied with the majors, some of them on their own. The majors finance their own films, usually employing their own money, sometimes using revolving accounts that they maintain at friendly banks. If an independent company can convince a major studio that its project has commercial potential, it may obtain financing from that studio. Most independents, however, must raise their own capital.[1]

The major studios maintain distribution networks across the country and in many foreign cities to insure that their films get to theaters. Independents must either induce one of the studios to handle their film, have it picked up by one of the handful of distributors that are not affiliated with a studio, or, in rare cases, attempt to distribute it themselves.[2]

Prior to the 1950s, many theaters—and all the important ones—were owned by the major studios. Today, only about 10 percent are part of a studio system, although the trend is toward more theater-studio affiliations. The remaining 90 percent (the nonaffiliated exhibitors) must bargain with both the major and independent distributors for access to the products of each. A theater, especially one that is part of a chain, will sometimes have access to the films of a particular studio; but theaters usually operate on a freelance basis.[3]

A theatrical film thus passes through a chain of supply from the producer to the distributor to the exhibitor. Distribution is even more complicated when a motion picture is to be shown on television. Most films first go to theaters, then to television, although the "made-for-TV" variety skip the first step. In either case, the films must be delivered to video receivers in homes, bars, hotels, and so on. Most commonly, one of the three major networks acts as the middleman, distributing the film at an announced time to all of its hundreds of affiliated broadcasting stations. Since about 1980, however, cable companies have more and more frequently taken over the job of distribution.[4]

The basic pattern is reproduced in the videocassette industry, with a complex of businesses functioning to deliver cassettes to the by-now familiar neighborhood stores where they are rented or sold at retail.

Screen entertainment made specifically for television follows a similar path from production to exhibition, but the system is differently organized because television programs are not physically delivered, as are cans of film, to the screening rooms where they are viewed by the public. Instead, the image itself is furnished electronically to video receivers. The most common practice is for one of the three dominant networks to buy the rights to exhibit programs from the Hollywood producers. The network then delivers the programs over wires, according to a known schedule, to its affiliated stations who, in turn, broadcast them in their locality.

The independent stations, that is, those not affiliated with a network, must either produce their own programming or, more commonly, buy the rights to broadcast various shows from the syndication market. A large part of this market consists of series that were previously run on the networks and were cancelled, but some of it, especially daytime fare, is original programming made up of shows created especially for syndication ("Wheel of Fortune," for example). Independent stations also rely heavily on motion pictures obtained through the syndication market. Thus, although the producers of programs broadcast by independents are usually the same Hollywood companies that produce programs for the networks, and although the exhibition (home viewing on video receivers) is the same, the distribution system is separate and is organized differently.[5]

The same is true for cable television. Hollywood producers create the programs, and people watch them on their home sets, but the distribution system is different. Instead of being broadcast, programs are delivered to the sets via a coaxial cable owned by one of the many cable companies.[6]

A relatively concentrated, simple Hollywood industry producing screen entertainment therefore attempts to get its output viewed by the public on either theater or television screens. To reach the audience, however, it must work through a vastly complicated, dispersed system of distribution that includes many different kinds of firms employing a profusion of technologies.

The key to understanding this system is the fact that power lies largely in distribution. Producers of motion pictures cannot make money unless their films are delivered to theaters; television programs are useless unless they find their way to millions of video receivers. Exhibitors are also dependent upon distributors to keep them supplied with a product. Where power exists, it is likely to be misused—or at least the people over whom the power is exercised are likely to believe that it is being misused. The history of screen entertainment is consequently at least partly the story of the complaints of producers and exhibitors that distributors are abusing them as well as tales of their efforts to avoid being abused.

The motion picture industry rings eternally with the complaints of independent producers against the major studios who, after all, are major because they contain distribution arms. Independents accuse the majors of being too lacking in vision to recognize the merit in their films (and therefore refusing to distribute them); or having distributed them, of marketing them incompetently so that they do not make money; or having distributed and marketed them well so that they generate a great deal of revenue, of cheating them out of their just share of the profits.

Meanwhile, the major studios join the independents in being endlessly resentful of the television networks and cable companies on whom they rely for distribution of their programs. The studios charge that the networks use their power (by refusing, for example, to buy a program) to bully the producers into permitting incessant interference with the creative process. Studios further charge that the networks schedule programs stupidly and advertise them clumsily. Finally, studios feel that the networks are too impatient, cancelling programs that are not instant hits before they have a chance to build an audience. In addition to feeling at the mercy of the networks (which, being three, at least afford some measure of competition), producers are antagonistic to the cable companies, each of which is a monopoly within its own delivery area.

Along with braving the risks of an unpredictable market, therefore, firms in the entertainment field always feel vulnerable to predatory practices by the distribution wing of the industry. Their continuing problem is the constant need to invent strategies that allow them to cope with ubiquitous threats—so that they can get on with the business of selling amusement to the public.

STRATEGIES OF RISK REDUCTION

Within this financially dangerous and conflict-ridden industry have evolved various strategies for reducing risk and gaining some measure of control over, or protection from, a treacherous market. Some of these strategies have been used since the infancy of the motion picture industry around 1910, and some have been developed relatively recently. As a general rule, they are more readily available to the major studios than to the independents, and that is a principal reason for the short life span of the typical independent. But some of these strategies are within reach of the little guys as well. None of them works all the time, but taken together, they almost guarantee the prosperity of a firm that is able to take advantage of the protections they offer.

Probably the most important risk-reducing strategy in the industry is *vertical integration*. This term refers to the combination of production, distribution, and exhibition into one corporate whole. In its infancy, the motion picture business was fragmented, with separate firms in the three segments of the industry. But shortly after World War I, some leading entertainment entrepreneurs saw that they could be even more successful if they controlled every aspect of the business. In 1916 Adolph Zukor, an important producer, merged his Famous Players company with Paramount, a distribution firm. In 1919 he began to acquire theaters, and thereby was the first to achieve integration.[7] Meanwhile, a few exhibitors were integrating in the opposite direction, beginning with theater chains—exhibition—and then acquiring both distribution and production. By the late 1920s, the movie industry was dominated by five vertically integrated corporations: Paramount, Warner Brothers, Fox, Loew's (parent company of Metro-Goldwyn Mayer), and RKO.[8]

From the point of view of the firm, vertical integration was protective for several reasons. A company could produce many films (later this would also apply to television programs), betting that while most might flop, the others would produce enough revenue to make the whole enterprise profitable. A movie that came from a studio with an exhibition arm was guaranteed access to many theaters, insuring the possibility, if not the certainty, of a large audience. Integrated companies could freeze out potential competitors, while defending themselves against being frozen out. And since the various parts of the business were controlled by a single company, they had no incentive to cheat one another.[9]

The very collection of functions that gave a vertically integrated company commercial protection, however, aroused the suspicion that Hollywood was attempting to concentrate the marketplace of ideas. Hollywood was, therefore, the target of a federal antitrust suit that culminated in the Paramount decree of 1948, which, in essence, forced the studios to sell their theater chains. In the 1970s, similar concern with the vertical power of the television networks inspired the Federal Communications Commission (FCC) to issue rules forbidding the networks to have a financial stake in most prime- time programs.

But the urge to expand vertically is a natural force in the industry, and all of its segments are constantly maneuvering to reestablish integration. Under the Reagan administration, the Justice Department relaxed its enforcement of the 1948 decree. Soon Universal had bought half of the Cineplex Odeon exhibition chain, Paramount had purchased the Mann theaters, and Columbia, through its affiliation with Tri-Star, had acquired the Loew's chain (divorced from MGM after 1948). Slightly more than 10 percent of America's twenty-three thousand movie screens are now integrated into the majors' new studio system.[10] They are also moving to buy into cable companies.[11]

Meanwhile, the networks have been pushing the FCC to rescind its rules barring them from program ownership. And most importantly, in 1985 Rupert Murdoch created the first integrated movie-television company when he bought 20th Century Fox and combined it with his chain of six independent television stations, each located in a large city. Subsequently, Fox has been attempting to create a fourth network by inducing other independent stations to subscribe to its products.

More recently, the studios have been expanding up instead of out, by becoming parts of larger corporate entities. In 1989, Warner Brothers merged with Time, Inc., and Sony purchased Columbia; and in 1990 MCA, parent of Universal, merged with Matsushita, while MGM was purchased by the Italian firm Pathé Communications. All of these mega-studios hope to provide insurance against the inevitable failures by simply being too big to be fazed by them.

Again, if the market for screen entertainment is so capricious, it seems a logical activity for studios to diversify into other industries in less whimsical markets. Disney began this trend in 1955 when it opened an amusement park in Anaheim, California. Universal and Warner Brothers have since followed suit. Paramount owns Madison Square Garden, the New York Knicks and Rangers, and Simon and Schuster, a publishing house; several studios own music companies; and all, of necessity, are managers of real estate.[12]

Screen entertainment companies have also evolved a plethora of business practices to make their market more manageable. Most of these are available only to the majors, but a few aid the independents as well. They range from the perfectly respectable to the marginally sleazy to the outright illegal. A major distributor poised to supply a film everyone expects to be a hit will offer it only to those exhibitors who agree to also take a group of less desirable movies; this practice is called *block booking*. Usually, exhibitors must choose these films without having seen them, which is called *blind bidding*. In the heyday of the old studio system before 1948, these were the major means by which the studios forced the independent theaters to exhibit all of their products. More than twenty states have outlawed both practices, but they continue. There is too much incentive for distributors to try to exercise control over the future market and too much pressure on exhibitors to insure themselves full theaters on at least some occasions by taking a chance on unexamined products.[13]

Nevertheless, exhibitors deeply resent these practices, which are among the chief causes of the constant friction between distributors and theater owners. Exhibitors have attempted to exert counterpressure by organizing various market-rationing schemes, but most of these have either not worked or been quashed in the courts; these actions have succeeded only in antagonizing distributors without altering their behavior. The result is a more-or-less perpetual state of warfare between the two industry segments. As Paul Lazarus, a motion picture executive with more than four decades in the industry, has written, "All exhibitors hate all distributors and vice versa."[14]

Audience research is another means of attempting to control the market. Since the 1930s the studios have habitually offered groups of citizens the opportunity to view new motion pictures in small, relatively obscure theaters before the films go into general release. If the sneak preview goes poorly, the movie will often be reedited or even partially reshot before the public sees it. With the decline of the old integrated system, this practice is less often used; but it still exists.[15]

In television, it is not the studio but the network that attempts to divine how the public will react to a new program by observing the reaction it provokes in a small audience. All three networks operate elaborate research facilities in which volunteers are exposed to everything from the basic, written summary of a show to its completed pilot. Although the results of this research are consistently poor (otherwise, why do three-quarters of new programs fail?), TV executives cling to them because they provide the illusion of predictability in a chaotic world.[16]

In addition, both industries have come up with many different institutions that enable companies to share, avoid, or postpone financial risk. In motion pictures, there are *completion guarantors,* rather like insurance companies, who will, for a fee, guarantee the money necessary to finish production if other sources of financing turn out to be inadequate. Sometimes they will also guarantee that the film be completed within budget and on time. This is a particularly useful institution to independent producers, who often have no backup capital.[17]

Also helpful to independents is the *negative pickup*—a major studio agrees to pay part of the cost of the motion picture upon delivery of the negative. The studio is exposed to less risk because if the film is not completed it does not pay. The independent producer has the advantage of being able to take the studio promise to a bank and use it as collateral for a loan.[18]

In television, the networks reduce their own risks, while increasing the producers', by forcing them to employ *deficit financing.* The network pays a "license fee" to the producer for the right to distribute a program, usually for two runs. But this fee never covers the producer's actual cost. For a typical hour show in 1990 costing $1.2 million an episode, the network would normally not pay more than about $900,000 per episode. Over the course of even a successful season of twenty-two episodes, this arrangement would force the producer to go into the hole to the tune of a little over $6.5 million. For a half-hour show, the average loss is smaller, but it still adds up to a strain on a company's budget. It costs Warner Brothers about $600,000 to make one episode of the sitcom "Murphy Brown," for example. Since CBS reimburses the studio $425,000 a show, the studio goes into the red $3,850,000 over the course of a season.

In the 1970s and early 1980s, producers could count on recouping their costs by selling foreign rights and then making a big profit when (and if) the program went into syndication after its first run was completed. Thus the average producer was compelled to wait about eight years before seeing a serious return on the investment. If the program succeeded in syndication, however, the ultimate payoff could be a bonanza. But in the past few years, the syndication market has been very soft. In the late 1980s, fewer than 10 percent of programs survived into syndication. This means that producers have been looking at major deficits for the usual eight years, but now with a steadily shrinking probability of hitting the jackpot at the end of the wait. Producers therefore are growing increasingly pessimistic about the odds against them, and even major studio heads are darkly warning that they will be unable to finance television programs of the quality U.S. viewers have grown accustomed to watching.[19]

One financial strategy used systematically by the major studios is referred to informally as *creative accounting*. This is not, as the phrase implies, the practice of out-and-out embezzlement. Rather, it is wielding the power of distribution to forcibly extract payments from the revenue stream that would otherwise be used to calculate the return to various profit participants: an independent production company, a leading actor, or someone who has negotiated a percentage of the take.

Paramount's response to Art Buchwald's 1990 lawsuit for a portion of the profits of the movie *Coming to America* is a good illustration of creative accounting. Buchwald, having established in court that the idea for the film was suggested by his own script *King For A Day* and having shown that he possessed a contract stating that a film based on that script would pay him $250,000 plus 19 percent of the "net profit" of the film, asked for an accounting. Paramount replied that although the film had grossed more than $250 million at the box office, it had lost money and that, therefore, there was no net profit to divide. Television talk-show hosts had a great deal of fun with the notion that a movie that had garnered more than a quarter billion at the box office had lost money. According to the customary method of studio accounting, however, the claim was valid. Here is Paramount's breakdown of the revenue and costs of *Coming to America*.[20]

Although this accounting insults common sense, it has an esoteric logic of its own. The key to understanding the arithmetic is to remember that studios are not only producers; they are also distributors. The producing segment can go blithely along losing money on every film as long as the distributing segment is making enough to balance its paper losses. In this example, Paramount's production arm has "paid" a $42 million fee to its distribution arm. The film lost money, but the studio made a fortune.

Most people, reading about this case in the newspapers, are likely to agree with Pierce O'Donnell, Buchwald's attorney, that "the net-profit system in Hollywood is a scam."[21] An understanding of the industry, however, can create more sympathy for Paramount. To the net-profit participants, what counts is the one film in which they have a share. But to the studio, attempting to spread its risk, what counts is the entire stream of films it produces. To the individuals, their film either made or lost money; but to the studio, revenue from the few successful films must balance losses from the many flops. This is known as "cross-collateralization." Thus the customary 35 percent distribution fee from the occasional *Coming to America* must not only support the studio's distribution network but also pay its overhead in its corporate arm, function as a revenue pool from which future films can be financed, and contribute to an annual profit statement that will satisfy stockholders.

Paramount's error was not in taking a distribution fee, but in setting that fee so high that the studio could then make the preposterous claim that it

TABLE 2.1   Breakdown of Revenue and Costs of *Coming to America*

Worldwide box-office receipts: $250 million

Costs

Retained by theaters	$125 million
Distribution fee	42 million
Distribution and marketing costs	36 million
Film production costs	57 million
Interest on financing	5 million
Total Costs	265 million

Net loss: $15 million

owed Buchwald nothing. Buchwald won the suit, but was awarded only $150,000 by the court. Whether this sum will encourage or discourage further legal attacks on the studio system is too early to say.

Similar practices are used in television. Many stars of successful series have a contractual right to share in studio profits. But the studio (corporation) pays itself for the use of its studio (building), pays itself a commission for "selling" the program to the network, pays itself a distribution fee when the series goes into syndication, and deducts a variety of other charges as the series passes through its life on the screen. Always bleeding from these financial wounds, the program is eternally in the red and never generates any profit to share.[22]

A classic example of this accounting method is observable in the financial history of the Universal series "The Rockford Files," starring James Garner, which ran on NBC from 1974 to 1980 and then moved into off-network sales, where it is still going strong. After determining that the show had taken in more than $120 million from syndication, foreign, and other markets, the studio's accountants informed the actor that it had earned less than $1 million in profits and that his share of the pie fell a little short of $250,000. Garner sued and nearly a decade later settled out of court for a reported $5 million.[23] Although this court action satisfied one star, however, it did nothing to alter studio accounting practices, which will endure until they are forbidden by the courts.

The "Rockford Files" episode also calls attention to a practice that has become very important in recent decades in both the motion picture and television industries, that is, searching for *ancillary markets*. Filmmakers have sold their products to the television networks for decades, and now they also peddle them to cable companies, to the syndication market, to airlines for in-flight showings, and to the armed forces. Most important, they sell videocassettes both to neighborhood video stores (which rent them) and to the general public through these stores and others. These markets can be extremely profitable. During the 1987 holiday season, for example, Disney sold three million cassettes of the 32-year-old animated classic *Lady and the Tramp,* bringing the studio $60 million of almost pure profit.[24]

Producers also sell television programs into the syndication market (and also into cable) where such channels as USA Network get by with showing quarter-century-old black-and-white sitcoms, such as "Mr. Ed."

Hollywood seers believe that the true potential of the ancillary market will not be tapped until they can solve the technical problems that have so far hindered the development of pay-per-view (PPV), a cable technology that allows home consumers to select individually paid-for programs, the charges being added to their monthly bills. The boxing match in March 1991 between Mike Tyson and Razor Ruddock brought in $35 million, as 6 percent of the sixteen million households wired for cable PPV ordered the event.[25] If PPV technology were available to most American households, an event such as the Tyson-Ruddock match might produce a stupendous fortune in a single night. The talk at cable industry conventions is about new technology that will allow each consumer to have access to more than 100 PPV channels, so that all of the most popular movies in a given month would be available at the flick of a dial. This, enthuses one cable marketing executive, "would make impulse buying of movies on pay-per-view a reality."[26]

Until that glorious day arrives, Hollywood is concentrating on the most rapidly expanding type of ancillary market: *foreign sales.* From 1985 to 1990, overseas purchases of American motion pictures doubled, and a film may now earn up to 90 percent of its gross abroad. In 1980, Hollywood collected 80 percent of its income from the domestic market; a decade later that figure was down to 30 percent. Indeed, the 1990s look to be a decade of extraordinary growth. In 1990 alone, income from foreign theaters grew by 16 percent over the previous year, television revenues increased by about 29 percent, and home video shot up 39 percent. The overseas market is so vital that studios make strenuous efforts to eliminate foreign "piracy," the unauthorized duplication and sale of movies without a payment of royalty. In 1990 the Motion Picture Association of America, the majors' trade organization, spent between $40 million and $50 million to combat piracy and millions more to lobby foreign governments to loosen their import restrictions.[27]

With the expansion of ancillary markets, the risk involved in the failure of any one production shrinks steadily, for the market not only expands for the mediocre efforts but grows huge for the big successes. Don Simpson, a very successful producer, asserted in the mid-1980s that "the truth is that with ancillary sales ... very few pictures lose money. ... The studio can't lose. I've been with Paramount for eleven years, and I can only remember two pictures losing money."[28] Simpson was speaking of a major studio, whose size and diversity permitted it to take advantage of the expanding supply of outlets. The small independent producer has far fewer opportunities. Moreover, Paramount itself experienced less success after the period Simpson describes, leading to a shakeup in its top management. But there is no doubt that, for the big guys, the odds are improving.

Meanwhile, with the increase in private television broadcast stations in Europe, producers are looking at that continent as a potential cornucopia of cash. A 1991 study by Frost and Sullivan predicts that the global market for programming will hit $5 billion in 1995, up from less than $1.5 billion in 1987.[29] Articles in the Hollywood trade papers confirm that producers expect the market overseas to open up and take some of the pressure off the stagnant domestic syndication industry.[30] While the overseas market is not yet as important for television as for film, the potential is there.

STRATEGIES FOR DUPLICATING THE UNIQUE

Although works of screen art cannot be duplicated, that fact does not stop producers from trying. Their desire to repeat their successes is encouraged by the mass audience, the members of which often value familiar plots, characters, and morals over more artistically innovative fare. The industry and the public thus collaborate in creating stories that are "the same but different," and Hollywood prospers by replicating the unreplicable.

Since about 1910, the major means of creating the-same-but-different motion pictures has been the *star system*. A recognizable face and voice and, just as important, a familiar persona can move from film to film, infusing each with comfortable recognition. Actors who become stars discover that the public wants to see them continue to play a certain type of character in a similar setting and is unwilling to see them stretch their skills into different roles. The first major star, Mary Pickford, was the darling of the nation for the two decades during which she appeared in role after role as a spunky teenager, and a failure, soon retired, when advancing age forced her to play other types of heroines. Since then, Cary Grant, Sylvester Stallone, Clint Eastwood, and many others have discovered that their personal magic, so lucrative in one kind of role, fizzles in others.

When the vertically integrated Hollywood system was in its heyday from the late 1920s to the mid-1940s, studios kept flocks of actors under seven-year contracts, casting them in roles expressly tailored to their star images. With the decline of that system in the 1950s and increasingly sporadic movie-going by the public, the star system became less important. Today, only a handful of leading actors—Eddie Murphy, Arnold Schwarzenegger, and Julia Roberts, for example—are box-office powers of the old type, players whose mere names are enough to guarantee at least a big opening weekend.

The public still uses stars as one criterion in deciding whether to attend a film—but not necessarily a decisive one. Films featuring very well known and respected performers frequently fail to attract an audience. For example, the following figures are estimates by Rod Granger and Doris Toumarkine of the total amount of money lost in the domestic box office between 1981 and 1988 by the films of four stars:[31]

Star	Number of Films	Approximate Total Lost
Meryl Streep	9	$16 million
Robert De Niro	9	$89 million
Richard Gere	8	$27 million
Burt Reynolds	17	$49 million

Stars, it is clear, cannot guarantee a film's popularity. They must nevertheless serve some function for the industry. The Hollywood saying "You're only as good as your last film" obviously misses an important business dynamic; otherwise the four actors listed above would have been less frequently employed.

The most likely reason that stars continue to be hired, even when their previous pictures have lost money, is that a well-known name in the cast makes it easier to sell the film to everyone from banker to exhibitor. It is unreasonable to expect potential financiers to lend or invest millions of dollars on a dream. But a dream starring Robert De Niro—that seems sensible and safe. Later, when the film is in post-production and distributors are attempting to convince theater owners to "blind bid" on it, the presence of a known talent such as De Niro is persuasive and reassuring. This reassurance is even more important for producers who are attempting to pre-sell foreign distribution rights. Therefore, regardless of whether the public demands movie stars, the business needs them as risk-reducers.

In television, the situation is quite different. The presence of a big name from the movies has never assured the success of a television series, perhaps because such programs customarily revolve around a work group or family rather than a single character. Moreover, once a series becomes a long-running hit, its leading actors become so identified with their roles that the public usually refuses to accept them as other personalities in other programs. (Actors often go from starring roles in daytime soap operas to a prime-time series, but only rarely from one prime-time program to another.) As a consequence, potential series are usually not sold on the basis of their leading actors. In television, the producer functions as the well-known "star" in whom the business people invest.

Whereas stars serve as risk-reducers for the movies but not television, *genres* function in that capacity in both media. A genre is a familiar type of story, written to the requirements of a formula, offering stereotypical characters facing standard problems in a recognizable setting. In the movies, westerns, musicals, horror stories, action films, family melodramas, and other cliched products historically have composed a large majority of Holly-wood's offerings. On television, the dominant genre has always been the sit-uation comedy, but cop/detective stories, soaps, game shows, and talk shows have also been well represented.

Genre stories, of course, institutionalize the notion of "the-same-but-dif-ferent" entertainment. Within a genre, audiences can be assured that the story elements that thrilled them in the past are present in the current offer-ing. Motion picture exhibitors need not be given a detailed description of the plot, for naming a movie's generic category conveys more information than a long prospectus. Furthermore, genre combines powerfully with star recogni-tion to lower uncertainty about the content and quality of a picture. To de-scribe a film as a "western" supplies a good deal of information about it; to describe it as a "John Wayne western" reduces the ambiguity almost to the vanishing point.

Genre stories feature settings and characters that are similar, but not iden-tical, to one another. *Sequels* further eliminate variation by casting the same actor in the same role and setting as in a previous success. In modern Holly-wood, a sequel is probably the easiest property to finance and the easiest to sell to exhibitors. *New York Times* reporter Aljean Harmetz quotes Samuel Z. Arkoff, founder of American International Pictures, as saying, "Sequels are ... the path of least resistance. Exhibitors can be sold with them. In a business that has no signposts, exhibitors can only recognize what they just did well with."[32] Producer Leonard Goldberg, emerging from an industry luncheon in the 1980s, reported that several studio heads had agreed that "the only thing the audience is interested in seeing is sequels."[33] These state-ments exaggerate the situation, but there is no doubt that recombinant prop-erties have a better chance in Hollywood than original material.

If a sequel is successful at the box office, it is sure to spawn another sequel, and at some point the films become a *series*. Series can consist of true se-quels, in which each successive story builds on events in the previous offer-ings (the *Rocky* movies, for example), or simply a string of films about the same character in a formulaic setting, with little or no connection between the stories (the "James Bond" films are examples). If a series is enduringly popular, it becomes virtually a genre unto itself. Dozens of films present story variations built around the characters of Sherlock Holmes and Dracula, and the Bond movies are beginning to achieve the same status.

In television, the series is the backbone of the medium, especially in prime time. But TV has also given birth to a special type of series, rare in the mov-ies, called the *spinoff*. In a spinoff, a supporting character who proves popu-lar in a hit show is moved to the lead in a new program. Thus "The Mary Ty-ler Moore Show," which ran on CBS from 1970 to 1977, begat "Rhoda" (1974–1978), "Paul Sand in Friends and Lovers" (1974–1975), "Phyllis" (1975–1977), and "Lou Grant" (1977–1982). There are also variations on the spinoff theme. The series "Star Trek," for example, which ran on NBC from 1966 to 1969, proved so popular in syndication that it inspired a spinoff that began to run wholly in the syndication market in 1987. Since the original cast was by that time unavailable for television, the new series was set eighty-seven years farther into the future than the original program and stocked with entirely different characters. Only the spaceship "Enterprise," arguably a "character" in this science-fantasy series, returned. "Star Trek—The Next Generation" has proved to be an even bigger hit than the original series and has generated more episodes.

CAPITALIZING ON A HIT

Because hits are unpredictable, producers naturally wish to squeeze every possible dollar from the successes they do create. But the number of times any one fan will pay to watch a movie is limited (usually, only once), and the potential audience for a television program is similarly finite. Hollywood has therefore evolved alternative marketing strategies that tap into the emotional satisfaction induced by the original entertainment. Since there is a potentially infinite number of these, the possible ways that a hit can generate income is beginning to seem unlimited.

The most obvious way to produce more income from a story originally told on the screen is to retell it in a new medium. As soon as the American film industry began to produce longer films than the 15-minute nickelodeon fare that occupied it in its first decade, it learned to adapt novels for the screen. Almost immediately thereafter, about 1912, some genius got the idea of reversing the process and turning movies into books. Thus the *novelization* was born. By the mid-1970s, there were sometimes two novelizations of films on national best-seller lists simultaneously. David Seltzer's adaptation of *The Omen* in 1976 went through twenty-five printings in four months, for a total of 3,375,000 copies.[34] Such income, in addition to that generated by a successful film's theater run, can obviously compensate for many other movies that never recoup their investment.

Even more lucrative than novelizations are *tie-ins*, merchandise such as tee shirts and toys that are associated with a film or television series. Disney pioneered the tie-in in the 1950s when it began to sell items at its California amusement park that were inspired by its films and its "Mickey Mouse Club" television program. Disney's success inspired other producers to sell similar merchandise. Today, the auxiliary income from a hit movie or television program can be equal to the gross income of a major theatrical success. Merchandising for the *Star Wars* trilogy, for example, has earned a reported $2.6 billion. Because the studio normally collects a royalty of between 6 and 10 percent of the wholesale price (which is roughly half retail) on such products, 2oth Century Fox earned an additional income of up to $130 million on *Star Wars* merchandise.[35] *Batman* products have garnered close to $500 million, which puts Warner Brothers' return at about $25 million, enough to finance another film.[36]

On television, the tail of merchandising long ago began to wag the dog of entertainment, especially in regard to children's programming. In the late 1970s toy manufacturers began to create "kidvid" shows specifically designed around characters that could be turned into toys. Mattel's "He-Man" toys, for example, based on a half-hour animated television series, were estimated to have earned $250 million in merchandise sales by 1988.[37]

But even this pales in comparison with the phenomenon of the "Teenage Mutant Ninja Turtles." By Spring 1991, the "turtles" had starred in comic books, a television series, videocassettes, and two motion pictures, the first of which grossed over $133 million domestically through January 1991, making it the most successful independently distributed film in history.[38] By Spring 1991, 650 Ninja Turtle consumer products had collectively brought in $1.5 billion.[39] A typical consumer, six-year-old Matthew Prindle of Austin, Texas, watches the television series every Saturday morning. He has watched the videotapes so often that he has memorized most of the dialogue. He saw the first film in the theater and later watched it on his family's VCR; he attended the Austin premiere of the second movie with his friend Jake Patoski; and he has acquired so many plastic turtle figures, either through purchase or gifts, that they overflow all the bookshelves in his bedroom.

The potential income from tie-ins is so great that a major studio (or, in the case of the Turtles, an independent producer) can earn enough with one hit, properly exploited with merchandise, to finance its whole operation for a considerable period. The great number of flops, then, become irrelevant.

This is not to say that all risk in Hollywood has been eliminated. None of the strategies discussed here—not vertical integration, not ancillary markets, not tie-ins, not sequels—guarantees overall success. If they did, then MGM-Pathé would not, as I write this, be threatened with bankruptcy and Paramount Communications, Inc., would not have fired the head of its motion picture studio. But in the long run, for most big companies, these risk-reducing strategies permit not merely survival, but prosperity.

Although the big companies have found ways to adapt to the dangerous environment of Hollywood, however, the small companies continue to have a high mortality.

INDEPENDENTS: THE LITTLE GUYS

Pity the poor independent producers. Exploited by the majors, abused by the networks, unable to take advantage of most of the available strategies for reducing risk, they are an endangered species, and they know it. One of the most popular topics of discussion within the industry is that things are terrible for the indies and are only going to get worse. Consider some headings from articles in *Daily Variety:*

High Price of Successful TV Puts Squeeze on Little Guys (April 24, 1989)

Indie Film Future Bleak, Pessimistic IFP Panel Says
(September 14, 1989)

Noose Tightens Around Indies (May 16, 1990)

Striking Out: Numbers Don't Add Up for Indies (June 27, 1990)

In the motion picture industry, the vulnerable position of the independent producers derives from their defining characteristic: They do not possess a distribution arm. (There are a few large "independents" who do distribute, but they are not typical.) Since power resides in the ability to move films to theaters, the independents are, in fact, *dependent* on the major studios for their survival.

This places them at a disadvantage in several ways. Independents automatically lose a large slice of the potential revenue from their films because of the studios' standard 35 percent distribution fee. If the major has no financial stake in an indie's film, it has little incentive to advertise it vigorously or place it advantageously in theaters. It may, in effect, shunt the independent movie aside in favor of its own offerings. If the studio has participated in the financing of the film, it has an incentive to handle it well; but it takes a large portion of the revenues as its cut. In either situation, the independent is at the mercy of the major's accounting department. Furthermore, in order to raise the money to make the film in the first place, indie producers often pre-sell foreign rights, which prevents them from benefiting from that market if the film proves popular.

There are independent distributors who pick up indie productions and sometimes make startling successes out of them. New Line distributed the film with the third highest gross revenue of 1990 (*Teenage Mutant Ninja Turtles*) and also made money with *House Party, Pump Up The Volume, Heart Condition,* and others, so that its total market share for the year was 4.8 percent, an enormous portion for an indie. Miramax scored well with two foreign imports, *My Left Foot* and *Cinema Paradiso,* among others, and the Samuel Goldwyn Company profited from *Wild At Heart, Henry V,* and *Longtime Companion.*[40] So indies can be profitable.

But just as the life of an independent producer is more harrowing than the life of a major producer, so also is the life of an independent distributor more fraught with danger than the life of a major distributor. The big studios supply a steady stream of products to their distributing arms, whereas the indies must hustle to find films to carry. Because exhibitors expect majors to be able to supply them with products indefinitely, they are receptive to their sales pitches, a situation that is intensified by block-booking practices. However, because they doubt the independents' staying power, exhibitors will often slight indie movies to the benefit of the majors. Thus deprived of well-situated theaters, the independents cannot become wealthy enough to acquire good films, so they cannot attract enough customers to insure truly useful revenues. This vicious circle keeps them small.

Even the biggest independent distributors are therefore always teetering on the brink, when they are not actually falling into the abyss. In the mid-1980s, three ambitious independents—Cannon, De Laurentiis, and New World—went belly up. Orion, one of the oldest, most successful, and most respected independent distributors, succumbed to bankruptcy in 1992. The majors grab at least 85 percent of the box-office sales every year, and there is no reason to expect their share to diminish.[41] As a consequence, the independent producers seem to be faced with the choice of becoming vassals of the majors or running the risk of having no one see their films by joining with an independent distributor.

So the bleak headlines in the trade papers appear to afford an accurate assessment of indie prospects. But the situation is not always what it seems. Life itself is a struggle against unfavorable probabilities, and although many fail, some succeed. Dozens of independent producers manage to beat the odds and prosper for a few years or several decades. No formula or single business strategy explains their success. About all that can be said is that like all entrepreneurs, they combine imagination, nerve, and energy with a ferocious determination to survive.

Some of these successful independents are filmmakers who have come up through the ranks, proved their worth to the studios by crafting movies that made money, and so have earned not only an association with a major that affords them financial support and a distribution system, but also, just as important, a relative degree of freedom from interference. One such successful independent is Ron Howard (familiar from the "Andy Griffith Show" and "Happy Days" television programs), whose Imagine Entertainment Company had a friendly and favorable relationship for several years with Universal.[42]

Roger Corman followed a different path to success. He has turned New World Entertainment into a Hollywood legend by ruthlessly suppressing costs (no union crews), shooting with unrivaled efficiency (making *The Little Shop of Horrors* in 1960 in two-and-a-half days), picking schlocky, teen-oriented subjects that were bound to draw at least a small audience, and distributing his films himself.[43]

A different means of survival has been discovered by Propaganda Films, which earns a steady $15 million to $20 million a year by producing rock videos for music companies. So accomplished at this form of entertainment is Propaganda that it manufactures one-third of the videos seen on American television. This reliable source of income allows Joni Sighavatsson and Steve Golin, Propaganda's founders, to invest in motion picture ideas that catch their fancy, such as David Lynch's *Wild at Heart*.[44] So much for headlines.

When it comes to television, an independent producer is in a fundamentally different relationship to the major studios than is one who is attempting to make films. Networks and cable companies—not studios—control the distribution of video. As a result, the major studios are, like the indies, dependent on outsiders to distribute their products. The situation is complicated, but not basically changed, by the fact that some studios own parts of some cable systems. With similar vulnerability come similar interests. Whereas indies making films usually view the majors as their natural enemies, those manufacturing television programs think of the majors as allies against the power of networks and cable. Since all majors and some independents produce for both media, this means that their relationship is not constant, but changes on the basis of who is trying to market what product to what outlet at what time. An independent operating in both media must think of the majors within the context of both conflict and cooperation simultaneously. This makes for uneasy and unstable politics between the two.

The most serious problem faced by an independent producer in television is lack of capital. Because networks do not pay all the costs of making a television series, producers must have the financial flexibility to wait for years until a program produces revenue from syndication. While the major studios are able to endure this deficit financing, most indies do not have the resources to hang on until the eventual profit.

As in the case of film production, however, a few independents manage not only to survive but to prevail. Such is the case with Carsey-Werner, which has managed to dominate two of the top ratings spots during the late 1980s and early 1990s with "The Cosby Show" and "Roseanne." Moreover, cable companies have been increasing their orders for original programming. More than fifty two-hour original films were produced for basic cable channels in 1990, up from only one in 1988. Most of this programming has been coming from the independents. Cable license fees being generally higher than those of the networks, they do not put the indies under such pressure to carry deficits.[45] And as the foreign market for American programming increases, independents hope that they can slice enough of that pie to keep themselves afloat. In 1989, eight independent television producers formed Alliance Communications, Inc., with the intention of distributing their programs to foreign countries.[46] Despite the changes taking place in Hollywood, if the past is any guide, the future will see plenty of independents, although which ones will survive is impossible to predict.

A reasonable question to ask at this point is, Who cares? Besides the independent producers themselves, would anyone mourn their loss? Put more analytically, do the independents do anything that the majors could not do just as well? Yes.

Some of the independents, for example, are ahead of the majors in progressive employment practices. Leaders of the women's movement inside the industry point to the "glass ceiling" that seems to stop females from rising to top positions in the networks and major studios. This gender barrier is less frequently encountered in the independents. Marcy Carsey, of Carsey-Werner, is a woman who had to leave network employment to achieve fame and fortune as an independent producer. Motion-picture producer Gale Anne Hurd, who learned her trade working for Roger Corman, reports, "I never even realized sexism [existed] in Hollywood until I got outside New World. ... Initially, when I went to studios after Roger, I got a lot of 'How can a girl like you expect to do a big movie like this?'"[47] Because of the fluid, free-lance nature of employment in Hollywood, it is very difficult to prove discrimination, and because of the pervasive fear of being labeled a trouble-maker, women are reluctant to bring court cases against the networks and studios. This leaves the independents as proving grounds for female talent.

The labor unions also prefer to have independent producers around. On the one hand, independents cause them more trouble than the studios; the smaller ones often work with nonunion crews, are notorious for cutting corners on safety and working conditions, and sometimes cheat on compensation. On the other hand, although labor leaders dislike individual indies for these misdemeanors, they love them as a group because they provide work. In a town where most people are unemployed most of the time, there is a comfort in knowing that a horde of avaricious hustlers is dreaming up schemes that have the potential to create thousands of jobs. Barry Gordon, president of the Screen Actors Guild, says simply that "the more independent production ... the better off we are."[48]

But the main reason for cherishing the independents is that they serve the public interest by taking chances. In many industries, small, non-mainstream producers take risks shunned by the dominant firms and are thereby responsible for much of the industry's innovation and vitality.[49] So it is in the entertainment business.

The majors, large corporations responsible to impatient stockholders, tend to be very cautious in their artistic decisions. They like stars, sequels, and series. When a new project is pitched to them, they respond best if it is a "high-concept" idea. This term refers to a description that can be encapsulated in a sentence or two and whose commercial potential is immediately discernible. Because the audience for both films and television is assumed to be immature and unsophisticated, high-concept ideas tend to involve card-board characters, melodramatic plots, flashy special effects, and as much vi-olence as possible. High-concept entertainment, in other words, is a cartoon with live actors. It is natural, then, that the movie studios would produce *Batman* and television would produce "The Flash"—if you are going to serve cartoonish fare to the audience, you might as well go all the way.

In motion pictures, the majors' emphasis on high-concept fantasy leads them to turn down many ideas that an independent is then willing to em-brace. The first two Academy Awards for best picture in the 1990s, for ex-ample, went to low-concept films (*Driving Miss Daisy* and *Dances with Wolves*) that suffered multiple rejections from the big studios and finally had to be produced independently.

In television, also, many innovative ideas come from independents. In the mid-1970s, for example, producer Bernie Brillstein approached CBS with an idea for a puppet show featuring various animal characters. The network re-ported that its market research division had established that there was no de-mand for a program hosted by a frog. Brillstein then took "The Muppet Show," hosted by Kermit, into syndication. There it became "probably the most widely viewed television program in the world during the late 1970s ... it has been seen in more than 100 countries by upward of 235 million peo-ple."[50]

It is not that the big guys never do anything daring. In 1989 Universal pro-duced *Field of Dreams, Do The Right Thing,* and *Born on the Fourth of July,* all nonformula, low-concept art. (All of them, incidentally, were successful at the box office.) But in general, the public relies on the independents to provide something other than violent cartoons and childish fluff. In the high-risk, high-concept world of Hollywood, the big guys, with the most to lose, play it closest to the vest. The little guys, therefore, are useful to the rest of us, and their fates should be of concern to everyone who cares about good entertainment. Consequently, it is in the public interest to insure that no one acquires the power to strangle the indies by achieving monopoly control over distribution.

3

Distribution Blues

I N THE RISKY BUSINESS OF SCREEN ENTERTAINMENT, producers are most vulnerable to those who control distribution. The history of American television provides the best illustration of the distributors' dominance.

In the days when radio was the main form of broadcast entertainment, production costs were low. Radio stations could supply their own programming by filling the broadcast day with local talk, local music, and local news. But even from the beginning, television was expensive. Viewers preferred polished shows featuring top national talent to the low-budget fare that broadcasters could provide themselves. A station that tried to lure viewers with inexpensive local programming soon discovered itself outperformed by competitors that imported costly dramas and comedies from Hollywood. As a result, most owners of video broadcasting stations chose to affiliate with one of the three national companies whose business was providing Hollywood entertainment to the rest of the country. While fewer than one third of radio stations were affiliated with a network, by the mid-1960s over 90 percent of television stations received their programming from the American Broadcasting Company (ABC), the National Broadcasting Company (NBC), or the Columbia Broadcasting System (CBS).[1]

The stations were thus dependent upon the networks and so also were the production companies. When the enormous financial potential of television had become clear in the late 1940s, the Hollywood studios tried to get into the business of distributing programs. This would have, in effect, substituted a vertical integration in video for the integration that they were losing in film because of the Paramount decree. But their efforts never got off the ground. Economic problems, along with the political opposition of the networks, blocked them, and they had to remain as suppliers only. The studios, once masters of entertainment because of their control over distribution, now found themselves serving new masters: the networks.[2]

For their part, the networks, or "webs," quickly began to obey the primal urge to integrate into all phases of the business. In the early 1950s, CBS had declined ownership of the situation comedy "I Love Lucy" because it had feared that WASP America would not be interested in a family program that featured a Cuban husband. When the show was not only a smash in its first run but also went on to perpetual success in syndication, the networks learned an important lesson: To milk the cash cow of television, they needed at least partial ownership of its programs.[3]

The networks therefore ruthlessly used their control of distribution to extort (the word is not too strong) a part-ownership in any program they put on the air. It was not that the webs produced everything in-house, although many of their shows did come from their own facilities. But if an outside producer, either a major studio or an independent, approached one of them with an idea for a pilot, the web would simply refuse to consider placing the show on its schedule unless the producer not only gave up some ownership percentage but also ceded the right to syndicate the program after its first run. Thus faced with a choice between relinquishing control over their own product or going out of business, the producers always made the obvious decision. Without actually owning and operating the television production facilities in Hollywood, therefore, the networks had, by the 1960s, established what one historian referred to as "vertical integration by contract."[4] Studios might create the shows and stations might broadcast them, but networks determined what went on the air.

AIR POWER

Because it is the responsibility of the Federal Communications Commission (under the Communications Act of 1934) to regulate broadcasting in the "public interest" and because Congress oversees the FCC, the networks found it necessary to defend their broadcasting power with political influence.[5] In doing this, they were aided by their affiliated stations.

There are broadcasting stations in almost every congressional district. Representatives want to stay on the good side of the owners of these stations, partly because they wish to receive good publicity in local news programs and partly because the stations are organized into a forceful and wealthy lobbying group, the National Association of Broadcasters. Because the affiliated station owners were happy with the big profits they were making as part of the network system, they made it clear to their congressional representatives that they wished to leave that system alone. And because Congress controls the purse strings of the FCC, its opinion that the agency should refrain from meddling with the networks was heeded.[6]

As a consequence, through the 1950s and 1960s the FCC tamely gave the network/affiliate coalition anything it wanted. The commission pretended that networks did not exist, confining its regulation to the stations. Even that was mostly theoretical, for it regularly granted renewal of their broadcast licenses. Meanwhile, the FCC fashioned a host of regulations that stifled competition to the existing system. One way it did this was by hampering the expansion of the broadcast spectrum, making it difficult for UHF to compete with the established VHF stations. Even more important, it suppressed the growth of cable television by ensnaring it in a tangle of restrictive rules. All through the 1950s and 1960s, therefore, the networks and affiliated stations made millions of dollars, network programming was almost the only entertainment on television, and the system seemed immortal.[7]

But powerful institutions attract powerful enemies, and by the end of the 1960s, the networks had offended so many sectors of American society that they had become a major national bogeyman.

The first of these enemies were the Hollywood producers. They naturally resented their vulnerability to the networks and the webs' expropriation of the big profits available in syndication. Norman Horowitz, a long-time executive for Columbia Pictures Television, recalled in the late 1970s that "they made you *give* them the syndication rights to the programs that went on the air, and it really was an example of the naked exercise of power. ... I have a lot of hostility in me for the way they exercised that power."[8] His attitude was typical.

The last straw fell when the networks began to produce their own motion pictures in the late 1960s. In 1970, the studios filed a lawsuit against the webs, contending that they were profiting from activity that had been specifically forbidden to the producers by the Paramount decree. The networks won this case because the studios could not prove that the networks had favored their own allegedly inferior films over the studios' films in programming.[9] It was only the first skirmish in a war, however, and the studios were already planning other campaigns.

They had found many allies. On their side were the independent stations, who languished in the backwaters of prosperity while the affiliated stations made big profits every year. Tired of being strangled by FCC rules, cable companies joined the team. Even some of the affiliated stations, frustrated by network rules preventing them from controlling any of prime time, supported the anti-web coalition. Most importantly, in 1969 the Nixon administration arrived in Washington. Nixon, a politician who believed in getting even with his enemies, resented the networks for what he believed was the bias of their news departments against him. The commissioners he appointed to the FCC were thus sympathetic to the producers' arguments about overwhelming network power.[10] Finally, the American educated elite was, by the end of the 1960s, so thoroughly disgusted with television that it was brewing a major revolt.

Network programmers in this period attempted to secure the largest possible audience for their shows. They believed that the way to accomplish this was to aim their programs at the least educated and excise anything from the programs that might require thought or emotional effort.[11] Under network guidance, nitwit comedy and lowbrow melodrama filled the airwaves. It was, as screenwriter Paddy Chayevsky once observed, "democracy at its ugliest."[12]

But the elite within the American democracy was also watching, and it was not happy with what it saw. The ugliness of television may have been acceptable to the masses, but it offended people who believed that the public interest—an interest that the medium was sworn to uphold—demanded more than network profits. In the late 1960s, a variety of critics of commercial television began to coalesce into a chorus of complaint. They deplored television's violence, its blandness, its lack of intelligence, its disregard of social problems, its monotonously white faces, its lack of constructive programs for children, its absence of interaction with its viewers, and its failure to provide alternative visions for a just society.

In the late 1960s, therefore, the networks had enemies on both the right and left of the political spectrum as well as purely business antagonists. By 1970, this group of disparate critics had come tacitly to an agreement on the overall problem: lack of diversity. It also agreed on the solution: cable television.[13] Cable had to be encouraged, and in order for this to happen, the networks had to be reined in.

In 1970, advances in the technology of opinion surveys induced the networks to adopt a new method of targetting their audience. Instead of attempting to maximize viewers, they would pursue superior "demographics," that is, they would try to attract the educated, middle-class viewers valued by their advertisers. Thus a schedule dominated by "Gilligan's Island" and "Marcus Welby, M.D." gave way to one featuring "All in the Family" and "The Mary Tyler Moore Show." Almost everyone agrees that this represented an increase in quality and relevance.[14]

But it was too late for the networks. Having made several corporate interests, millions of good citizens, and the president of the United States mad at them, they were going to have to live with the consequences.

DESIGNING A NEW SYSTEM

When the political pendulum swung against the networks, it swung hard. During the 1970s, the FCC, sometimes on its own and sometimes prodded by the courts, adopted a series of policies aimed at hindering the power of the networks and liberating the cable television industry. From the point of view of Hollywood, the most important of these were the "prime-time access" rule and the "financial interest and syndication" (fin-syn) rules.

The prime-time access rule limited the amount of programming any network could supply to its affiliates to three hours a night. This opened up a half hour of formerly network time to the discretion of the affiliates. The result was a boom in the syndication market, which of course was very good for Hollywood.

Even more important, the fin-syn rules prevented the networks from having a financial interest in most of their programs and consequently from sharing in the syndication rights. In essence, the webs were forced out of their "vertical integration by contract," and the producers were freed to profit from their programs in perpetuity. Hollywood rejoiced.[15]

The liberation of cable had even more important long-run consequences. By 1975, 12 percent of the television households in the country were cable subscribers. That year RCA launched a commercial communications satellite, and a small entertainment company, Home Box Office (HBO), rented its services. Already freed of most government regulation (and with further loosening to come), cable now had a means by which to distribute its product nationally. By creating a nationwide audience for entertainment, HBO was able to generate the large revenues needed to bid on first-run motion pictures. With HBO's movies as a lure, millions of consumers signed up with local cable services. The result was that cable, with better picture quality and more channels than broadcast TV, suddenly became the American entertainment of choice. Between 1975 and 1981 the number of subscribers doubled, then jumped another 50 percent by 1985. By 1990, almost 60 percent of the American homes with television sets subscribed to a cable service, and industry revenue had reached $19 billion.[16] The networks still reached more homes and attracted more viewers, but the trend was clear.

In 1984 the FCC loosened its rules on who could own television stations and on the number any one firm could own. Immediately the number of independent stations more than doubled, from 120 to nearly 300. Some of these stations concentrated on broadcasting the traditional indie fare of old movies, local sports, and syndicated reruns, which by the late 1980s reached an annual value of $3 billion. Others supplemented their schedules by signing up with the new Fox mini-network for its two nights of programming. In either case, the independent stations represented one more challenge to web dominance. Competition, once nearly absent from American television, was now the order of the day.[17]

While the Hollywood producers profited from all these changes and while the cable industry mushroomed, the networks foundered. Every year more viewers drifted away to one of the increasing number of cable channels or independent stations, until by 1991 the three networks' combined portion of the video audience was less than 63 percent and declining steadily. Until the 1980s, an individual prime-time program had to achieve a rating (that is, a percentage of the total sets turned on at any given moment) of more than 30, or it would be cancelled. By 1991, the highest rated program on the airwaves ("Cheers") was garnering a rating of only 18.8, and some shows won their time slot with scores of under 10. The slide was so steep that NBC took first place in the 1990-1991 season with an overall rating of 12.7, a score that would have placed it last during any season prior to 1989.[18]

Because cable stations receive most of their revenue from subscriptions, relatively low ratings are acceptable to them. Such a station can make a comfortable profit with a rating of 2.[19] But to the networks, who sell advertising based on the number of people tuned in to a show, this long-term slide in viewership was a slow-motion disaster. By cutting compensation to their affiliate stations, laying off hundreds of employees, scaling back their news operations, reducing the number of new pilots they ordered, and cutting back in other ways, they managed to keep their profits high.[20] Such belt-tightening could only go so far, however, and it was clear to the network executives that some structural changes had to be made if they were to survive.

HOLLYWOOD VERSUS THE NETWORKS

To the networks, the solution to their problem was evident. The FCC should repeal the financial interest and syndication rules. Thus freed once more to own programs, the webs could not only produce their own but again take a slice of the ancillary market for those shows they ordered from the outside.

Although President Nixon departed in 1974, the election of Democrat Jimmy Carter in 1976 meant that the networks still had little hope of relief. In 1981, however, Ronald Reagan came into office, bringing with him a philosophy hostile to government meddling in business concerns. In this new deregulation atmosphere of the 1980s, the webs hoped that an appeal to the FCC would be answered, and they unlimbered their lobbyists. In 1983 they appeared to have convinced the agency to jettison the fin-syn rules. But the studios, with nightmares of returning to the bad old days, launched their own lobbying blitz of Congress and the White House. Among other tactics, they persuaded President Reagan, who spent much of his young manhood under contract to Warner Brothers, to intervene on their behalf. Opposed by both the president and Congress, the FCC put off reconsideration of the rules until 1990.[21]

In the ensuing six years, the networks slid farther away from a position of preeminence. Republicans captured the presidency twice more and persevered in their habit of appointing members of their party to the FCC. Foreign investors bought several Hollywood studios, and the American economy became more intertwined with those of other nations. Warner Brothers merged with Time, Inc., in what seemed to be a harbinger of things to come.

Meanwhile, Hollywood producers and the networks had six years to hone their arguments, perfect their lobbying ability, and cultivate relationships with members of Congress. As the end of the decade approached, they engaged in a titanic struggle to win the hearts and minds of the FCC commissioners, Congress, and, if all else failed, the public.

Shorn of hyperbole, irrelevance, and rhetoric, the network position boiled down to five arguments. First, the webs asserted that their oligopolistic control over television programming was a thing of the past. Producers could now take their shows to cable companies or directly to the syndication market. With the introduction of this competition, their grip on distribution was broken, and they were no longer in a position to extort favors from producers (not that they admitted having done so in the first place).

Second, the networks highlighted their shrinking market share and earnings and argued that they needed the revenue from ancillary markets to stay in business. Unless they received cash infusions from syndication, they claimed, they would not be able to bid competitively for programs in the first place. Cable networks would then be the ones with the wealth to purchase series, and the webs would become first superfluous and then extinct. Similarly, they had to have ownership of programs in order to compete in the international market.

Third, the fin-syn rules were, in the words of NBC President Robert Wright, "reverse protectionism" for Hollywood. Other industries—airlines, for example—had benefited from deregulation, and it was time to eliminate the insulation from competition enjoyed by the producers.

Fourth, the studios themselves had apparently been freed from the restraints of the Paramount decree and were now busily reintegrating themselves. If vertical integration was so terrible, asked the webs, why was it permitted to the studios? Or if it was so good, why was it denied to the networks?

Fifth, the networks derided the idea that they would discriminate, in programming, between those shows in which they owned a percentage and those shows in which they didn't. They argued that it would be irrational of them to schedule any show but the best (the one most likely to attract an audience), regardless of whether they owned a piece of it.[22]

It did not hurt the network case that the Bush administration was vocally in favor of eliminating the fin-syn rules.[23]

Hollywood producers reacted to these arguments like a flock of chickens who had been asked to allow a family of foxes to come back into the henhouse. But in all of their own disputation, there was an air of unreality, for they never brought forth their own best reasoning. It was not that they were stupid: far from it. But the politics of the situation demanded that their strongest case go unmade.

The power of the distributor has long been recognized as a good reason for government regulation. In the oil industry, to take one well-documented case, John D. Rockefeller was able to monopolize the nation's petroleum supply in the nineteenth century with his Standard Oil Trust because he

dominated transportation. Controlling pipelines and having made arrangements with railroads, Rockefeller could prevent competing producers from
marketing their product and thus eliminated them. As soon as Rockefeller's
methods were understood in the rest of the country, oil operators moved to
insure that government protected them from Standard Oil's tactics. In 1917,
for example, the state oil and gas agency in Texas was given the power to
regulate pipelines. With governmental power protecting them from suffoca-
tion at the hands of the distribution companies, independent producers
thrived and Texas became the home of the wildcatter.[24] The historical record, at least in oil, is absolutely clear: If left to their own devices, vertically
integrated companies will use their control of pipelines to strangle their
small competitors. If it is in the public interest for many firms to compete in
oil production, therefore, it is necessary that government regulate transportation of the product.

Just so, the original fin-syn rules were based on the realization that the
networks, as the "pipelines" of the television industry, possessed the power
(which they were using) to choke off competition and monopolize production for themselves. If it is in the public interest not to have three firms dominate the airwaves, then government regulation is not only justified, but man-
dated. The major studios, large entities that benefit from vertical integration
in motion pictures, are only partially vulnerable to domination by networks.
Anyway, studios generate little sympathy among any group except their
stockholders. The real beneficiaries of regulation, as in the oil industry, are
the independents. The fin-syn rules, in 1990 as much as in 1970, were valuable because they protected small producers from some of the risks to which
they are particularly vulnerable, thereby preserving diversity in the entertainment marketplace.

Neither the major studios nor the independent producers were ignorant of
this truth. Early in the battle, the studios joined with virtually every independent in Hollywood, as well as with all the labor unions, to form the Coalition to Preserve the Financial Interest and Syndication Rules. This coalition shattered precedent by presenting an almost unbrokenly united front to
the FCC for years. Given the importance of the question of distribution, this
issue might be expected to have been the cornerstone of the coalition's rebut-
tals to the network position. Yet because of the peculiar structure of the industry and the coalition, that argument was forbidden to them.

The coalition could not discuss distribution because the studios were
themselves motion picture distributors. By arguing that the power of the
pipeline is one that always contains potential for abuse and that therefore
government regulation is necessary, the coalition would have raised questions about the possibility of regulating the majors. Still more, this argument
would have constituted a tacit admission that reversing the Paramount decree and reintegrating the studios was a mistaken policy. As the networks ar-

gued, what was good for the studios must also be good for the webs; if one
vertical integration was contrary to the public interest, then so was the other.
The studios could not make their own most persuasive argument regarding
television without destroying the rationale of their expansion in motion pictures.

The result was a strange debating style. The coalition spokespeople denied
that the networks no longer dominated the video market, asserting that over
60 percent of anything is a dominant chunk, especially considering that
there are only three networks whereas there are dozens of cable stations. The
coalition scoffed at the networks' promise to resist the temptation to favor
their own productions over the offerings of outsiders and rejected their contention that they would refrain from using control over entry to the market
as a club to coerce profit participation agreements from the producers.
Pointing out that American television programs dominated the world market during the period of fin-syn, they wondered how the networks could
claim that repeal was necessary to insure global competitiveness. And they
dismissed the webs' discussion of mergers and acquisitions in Hollywood as
irrelevant, having nothing to do with network power. Jack Valenti, president
of the major studios' trade association, summed up the producers' argument
when he claimed that the "terrorizing truth" was that "if networks are ever
unshackled, competition is stone cold dead" in television.[25]

But the word "distribution" never passed the lips of anyone in the coalition. It was there implicitly, of course, underlying their alarums about the
dangers to competition. Unwilling to open a can of regulation worms in the
film industry, however, they refrained from discussing basic principles at all,
leaving the debate to consist largely of rhetoric and implication. The chief
coalition tactic was to focus on the danger to indie producers. Whenever
Jack Valenti testified at a congressional or FCC hearing, he was sure to be accompanied by a phalanx of independents who bashed the webs enthusiasti-
cally. There was no lack of volunteers for this task, because indies as a group
have an intense hostility to the networks, based on their memories of their
treatment prior to 1970 and the webs' insistent interference with the creative
process ever since. Still, the act of publicly standing by the side of the majors,
within the context of the general suspicion they feel for them, privately generated a good deal of cognitive dissonance among the independents.

Occasionally, the basic instability of the coalition threatened to shatter its
composure. The MPAA, for example, has refused to recognize the Producers
Guild of America (PGA), making producers the only artists' group without a
functioning union. At one point in the battle, the PGA threatened to withdraw its support from the majors in the fin-syn fight unless they agreed to
recognition. This incipient rebellion was smoothed over, most likely because
the members of the PGA fear the networks even more than they resent the
studios. Still, the rebellion illustrates the unnatural cooperation within the

coalition and the conflicting interests that mutual hatred of the networks brought together.[26]

Twentieth Century Fox muddied the coalitional waters still further. As both a studio and a mini-network, it remained noncommittal about the basic question of the fin-syn rules, but requested that whatever the FCC decided, Fox be exempted from restrictions.[27]

These divisions inside Hollywood, however, were of relatively little importance. The main struggle was not within the production community in Hollywood but between the coalition and the three major networks in Washington.

The lobbying machines of both sides shifted into high gear. All the network heads and many members of the production community courted members of Congress over lunch, dinner, and movies. Jack Valenti hosted fundraisers at the homes of studio heads to fill the coffers of Democratic members of the Senate and House. Under his guidance, the coalition employed lobbyists Peter Teeley, President Bush's former press secretary, and Diane Killory, the former general counsel to the FCC. To make their own case, the networks hired Richard Wiley, a former FCC chairman, as well as sundry former congressional staffers and Justice Department officials. When Pathé Communications, an Italian firm, bought MGM, NBC sent pizza to about seventy members of Congress with the message that if foreigners could get a piece of the syndication pie, networks ought to be able to, as well.[28]

It didn't work. With powerful forces urging them in both directions, it was a no-win situation as far as members of Congress were concerned. Moreover, there was no very compelling moral issue. "We're not talking about lunch programs for children here," said one discouraged lobbyist. "We're talking about who gets what." Additionally, this was not an issue that could galvanize the public and make a representative look like the people's champion. Representative Michael Oxley, a Republican from Ohio, summarized the general experience when he reported that he did not have "one constituent who gives two hoots in hell" about the fin-syn issue. It was, as one observer suggested, like the war between Iraq and Iran: It was hard to root for either side.[29]

So Congress ducked. The House sent an institutional letter to the FCC urging that agency to make a decision in "the public interest" and then washed its hands of the affair.[30]

Thus left free to follow its policy inclinations, the FCC might have been expected to produce a clear-cut decision in favor of the networks. The five members of the panel were all Republicans; the chairman, Alfred Sikes, was a strong proponent of fin-syn repeal, as was Commissioner James Quello; the administration was urging deregulation. Everything combined to make it look hopeless for Hollywood's position.

But it did not turn out that way. One commissioner, Sherrie Marshall, had once aspired to be a screenwriter. This may have caused her to identify with the producers, for she showed great sympathy, throughout the proceedings, for the Hollywood position. Two others, Ervin Duggan and Andrew Barrett, seemed worried about the survival of the independents if fin-syn were repealed. As the two contending sides turned their lobbying force on the commission, the result seemed surprisingly in doubt.[31]

Commissioner Quello claimed that in his fifteen and a half years on the panel, fin-syn was the most heavily lobbied issue he had seen. Duggan, only half-jokingly, publicly referred to the struggle as the "proceeding from hell." As the commissioners attempted to make up their minds, hints dropped to the outside world showed a genuine wavering. In the summer of 1990, the network position seemed to dominate, but the commission postponed a vote to allow more time for argument and in the hopes the two sides would come to an accommodation. They didn't. In the winter of 1991, it looked like the studio position would prevail. Desperate, the networks hired former Illinois governor James Thompson, Commissioner Barrett's political mentor, to remonstrate with his protege.[32] Given this intense application of force and the uncertainty of the commission, it was probably inevitable that what would emerge would be a compromise.

On April 9, 1991, by a vote of three to two, the FCC promulgated an even more complex and confusing set of rules to govern network participation in production. The webs were granted full rights to nonprime-time programs and, more importantly, were allowed to acquire foreign syndication rights to programs they did not produce. However, they were restricted to having syndication rights to 40 percent of prime-time programs, and made to go through a two-step acquisition procedure for outside shows, in order to prevent them from coercing financial agreements in return for placing a show on their schedule. Fox, exempted from the rules, was encouraged to go on developing its alternative network. The rules were to last for four years and then be reviewed.[33]

As with most compromises, this one pleased almost nobody. "The game is over for independent producers," grimly prophesied Jack Valenti. If so, the networks were not gloating. "What we received was a myriad of new hoops and hurdles that can only complicate our business dealings," fumed Capital Cities/ABC Chairman Thomas Murphy. One journalist wrote that "Hollywood television deals have always involved a ritual of personal contacts accompanied by a series of winks and nods conveying mutual distrust and self-interest. It is now likely that these deals will take on even more of the form of twitchy signals passed from a third-base coach to a batter." Only Fox seemed a clear winner.[34]

Neither side accepted the decision. Both the networks and studios filed suit. The webs drew first blood in this legal battle when a three-judge federal panel overturned the new rules in November 1992. In writing the decision, Judge Richard Posner declared that "the commission's articulation of its gounds is not adequately reasoned. Key concepts are left unexplained, key evidence is overlooked, arguments that formerly persuaded the commission, and that time has only strengthened, are ignored, contradictions within and among commission decisions are passed over in silence." The court, in other words, declared the FCC's political compromise illegal.[35]

This decision will of course be appealed. The FCC will go on struggling with the issue of fin-syn. The studios and networks will go on grappling with one another in the halls of Congress. The new president, Bill Clinton, will appoint commissioners and judges with a different set of biases. But the issue will never be resolved as long as there are distributors who want a free hand to order their business as they see fit, and suppliers who implore government to save them from distributors.[36]

CABLE VERSUS EVERYBODY

While Hollywood was attempting to prevent the return of one set of distributors to power, it was also trying to suppress the rise of a new set.

After its emancipation in the mid-1970s, the cable industry partially fulfilled the hopes of its proponents. It provided reception superior to that offered by over-the-air stations, and it serviced many rural areas that broadcasting did not reach. Required by law to offer several kinds of public-access channels, many systems also voluntarily subsidized quasi-public service channels such as Black Entertainment Television and Cable News Network. Because cable did not rely upon attracting a mass audience to each program, it could offer "narrowcasting" channels appealing to elite audiences, such as Bravo and the Arts and Entertainment channels. Similarly, it provided the venue for an entirely new sort of entertainment, music videos, which, if they were not to everyone's taste, at least provided some of the "diversity" that commercial television's critics had requested.[37] But as a powerful delivery service with its eye primarily on the bottom line, the cable industry managed, over the course of the 1980s, to acquire even more enemies than the networks.

In 1984, still in the early stages of its growth, the cable industry had convinced Congress to deregulate it by law. Among other liberations, city governments, formerly able to set cable rates, found themselves helpless once a franchise was awarded.[38] Because every cable company was a monopoly within its area of service, this meant that cable became the only government-sanctioned but unregulated monopoly in the country.

By the end of the decade, every other interest that impinged on cable was accusing it of abusing its power and freedom and was demanding reregulation. Moreover, unlike the fin-syn fracas, which was ignored by ordinary people, the cable controversy involved consumers directly. With voters loudly accusing their cable companies of multiple misdemeanors, members of Congress were eager to become involved. Whereas the fin-syn battle was mostly a private showdown between two industries, therefore, the cable fight was a media circus involving everyone from the president to the general population.

City governments were apoplectic. It was bad enough that many cable companies had behaved very badly during the franchise application process, making glittering promises, then reneging and demanding renegotiation once the franchise was awarded. But really unendurable were the subscription fees that had been shooting up out of control while service had been declining. In Tennessee, for example, increases between 1986 and 1989 were 115 percent in Chattanooga, 99 percent in Crossville, 116 percent in Knoxville, and 113 percent in Nashville. Delegations of mayors descended on Washington, imploring the legislators to pass a new law.[39]

Consumer representatives fretted about fee increases too. They also worried about the companies' practice of "tiering," which is a way of raising rates without seeming to. Companies establish tiers of programs, charging the consumer extra for the higher tier. Then, while keeping the price of the "basic" service stable, they continually raise the price of the more expensive tiers, meanwhile putting more and more of the formerly basic channels into the higher tiers. In addition, cable's ever-growing appetite for sports programming raised concerns that free sports would someday disappear from the airwaves. Consumer advocates also charged that most cable companies failed to provide adequate public-access channelling.[40]

Broadcasters, once the beneficiaries of networks, now found themselves at the mercy of this new distribution technology. The FCC required cable systems to carry the over-the-airwaves channels—but it didn't say where. Broadcasters believed that consumers preferred to watch programs in the lower reaches of the spectrum, for example, channels 2, 3, and 4 in preference to channels 22, 23, and 24, which in turn are preferred to channels 32, 33, and 34, and so on. Cable companies sometimes repositioned a broadcast station from its customary single-digit channel to one farther up the list. The broadcasters believed that this was part of a cable company conspiracy to starve them of viewers and give advantages to those channels in which cable has an investment. Broadcasters also reported a more subtle ploy in which the cable company threatens to reposition the broadcast station unless it pays compensation.[41] In either case, broadcasters cried foul and demanded Congress do something to save them.

Meanwhile, cable companies were obeying the natural media law of vertical integration and acquiring interest in production companies. Here is where they ran afoul of Hollywood. By acquiring production capabilities, cable companies were putting themselves in the same position to mistreat suppliers that the networks enjoyed before 1970. Hollywood feared that if this new distribution system were allowed to expand into production, it would act no more responsibly than had the networks: It would favor its own productions over everyone else's, and the Hollywood companies would once again be forced to give up control of their products in return for access to consumers.

The early evidence on this point was not encouraging to Hollywood. In 1988, Jones Cable of Denver dropped the USA Network, in which it had no financial interest, and added Turner Network Television, of which it was part owner.[42] In 1990, independent television producer Marcy Carsey testi-fied before the FCC that on three occasions, cable networks had refused to purchase her company's products because she had declined to give them an-cillary rights.[43] These and similar incidents convinced the producers that they were facing another tyrannical distribution system. As a result, they participated in the anti-cable coalition at the same time that they were at-tempting to forge a broader anti-network front. Their goal was, in essence, to see a set of financial interest and syndication rules imposed on cable companies.[44]

In the cable quarrel (as in the anti-network crusade), companies' political opinions are shaped by their corporate interests. Warner Brothers, for exam-ple, is not at all enthusiastic about cable-bashing. This is probably related to the fact that Warners itself is a major investor in cable systems.[45]

Whatever the divisions in Hollywood, the anti-cable movement had so many participants that Congress could not ignore it. In the late 1980s and early 1990s, numerous reregulation bills were proposed in every session. Committees and subcommittees held hearings at which various interests would recount horror stories of cable abuse and then representatives of the indicted industry would try to defend the record. Legions of Democrats, and even a few Republicans, would excoriate the wicked industry for its trans-gressions and promise legislative relief. Sponsors of the particular bill with the most support would predict quick passage. Then the Republican presi-dent would announce that he would veto any reregulation bill, and the hub-bub would subside until the next session.

By 1992, however, the national frustration with cable had become uncon-tainable, and the influence of Republican President Bush had declined in the partisan atmosphere of an electoral campaign. The Democratic-controlled Congress passed a cable regulation bill, and for the first time since he took office, overrode Bush's veto. The era of the unrestricted cable industry was over.

Hollywood might have been expected to celebrate this new law as a great victory over a long-time foe, but instead its attitude was ambivalent at best. The MPAA had lobbied Congress to include in the bill a repeal of the "compulsory license" that permitted cable operators to carry programming from local television stations at a nominal fee. Producers had reasoned that with the removal of this provision, they would be able to negotiate much higher payments for the use of their programs from cable companies. When Congress refused to add the repeal of the compulsory license to the bill, Hollywood, in an unexpected alliance with the cable industry, opposed it. When it succeeded anyway they found themselves in the odd position of lamenting the passage of legislation that they had recommended for years.[46]

Meanwhile, competition—the most economically consistent response to the cable monopoly—does not draw much support, except in Hollywood. Producers generally endorse the creation of as many delivery systems as possible, although some of the studios follow their own interests in being lukewarm about this. At the beginning of the 1990s, the most promising new contenders in the distribution wars are the telephone companies.

The "Baby Bells" are eager to enter the video business. Using fiber-optic wires, phone companies could provide an almost limitless number of television channels, with fewer technical problems, probably at less expense, than current distributors. Federal law now forbids the telephone companies from participation in video supply, a restriction they resent and constantly ask Congress to overturn.[47] But the cable companies, ardent anti-regulationists in their own case, cry that the public must be protected from the potential power of this new delivery system. Without a trace of irony, James Mooney, president of the National Cable Television Association, warned, "The telcos could wipe everybody out. ... They would have a virtual monopoly on TV within their regional areas. That's dangerous to the interests of society. You could end up with Big Brother."[48]

Because the cable industry has such a bad reputation in Washington, one might expect the city's politicians to welcome the prospect of more competition in video distribution. In fact, the National League of Cities backs entry of telephone companies into the business.[49] But the outcome is in considerable doubt. The Baby Bells, with their vast financial resources, research capabilities, and already-existing lines into almost every home in the country, frighten more than just the cable companies. Newspapers, for one, are concerned that once telephone lines begin to carry video information, the printing press could be rendered obsolete.[50] Furthermore, many politicians have no love for phone companies, claiming they have a history of misusing their monopoly power. Congress displays no sense of urgency to allow a completely unregulated video marketplace.

In the summer of 1992, the FCC voted to allow telephone companies to begin to transmit video into homes over their fiber-optic phone lines and also to take a 5 percent equity stake in programs. This decision instantly drew the wrath of broadcasters, consumer groups, and House Telecommunication Subcommittee Chairman Ed Markey. The turmoil growing out of this issue promises to rival the conflicts over cable and fin-syn, and keep the problem of the power of the distributor on the public agenda for the forseeable future.[51]

THE FUTURE

Business and technology continue to create new delivery systems. In direct-broadcast systems (DBS), for example, a satellite beams programs directly to home dishes that are now as small as three feet in diameter. A variety of commercial enterprises have attempted to set up DBS networks, so far without much success. The FCC is encouraging DBS technology, however, and a cable-like breakthrough may be just around the corner.[52] In a variation of this scheme, some entrepreneurs have set up receiving dishes on the roofs of apartments and condominiums and then wired the building in their own cable mini-system. The local cable companies, ever alert to the intrusion of competition into their bailiwicks, have launched political and legal offensives against the interlopers, and distribution brush wars are consequently being waged in some American cities.[53]

The history of the video industry thus falls into a pattern, well illustrated by network television, the cable industry, and the emerging technologies briefly discussed here. Every time a new delivery system arrives on the scene, it threatens to disrupt old patterns of domination and sets off political warfare between the old system, which attempts to enlist the power of the state to suppress the threat, and the new system, which appeals to the public in its struggle to survive. Because the public interest lies on the side of diversity and the benefits of competition, economists, journalists, and others who attempt to transcend self-interest begin a campaign of argument on behalf of the new technology. In this conflict, independent producers, who resent the way they have been victimized under the old system, side with the public. If they have no interests in the old system, the major studios generally support the new technology as well; if they do, however, their loyalties are divided. But once the new system has survived and prospered, it both abuses its power and seeks to expand vertically into production, which affords it many new opportunities for misbehavior. Taking enthusiastic advantage of these, it thereby creates a host of enemies for itself that ally themselves with any newly emerging technologies. This pattern goes on and on in an endless cycle.

This analysis suggests a plan for liberation from the ongoing tyranny of the distributor: Regulate all delivery systems as common carriers and forbid them to have any interest in production. The television networks should be shorn of all interests in any programming—daytime, prime time, anytime. The major studios should be forced to divorce themselves not only from their theater chains and their interests in cable companies and broadcast satellites but also from their motion picture distribution systems. Cable companies should be forbidden to have a penny invested in production. Telephone companies should be permitted to bring entertainment into homes, but prevented from owning any part of that entertainment. Everyone would have one interest only, either production, distribution, or exhibition.

Thus reformed, the entertainment marketplace would consist of a few large (and hundreds of small) production firms doing business with scores of distribution companies using many different kinds of technology, all independent. Although the distribution wing of the industry would still dominate, the large number of distribution companies would provide competition for product, thereby reducing the power of any one firm. Production companies with many competing distributors to choose from would not have to please such a narrow range of opinion in order to get their wares to market. Economic risk would still exist, but there would be more opportunities for taking artistic risks. The result would be far more diversity in the product, offered more cheaply to the public through more delivery systems. Moreover, this atomized system would result in a greater quantity of entertainment, which would also add to its diversity. It would not produce the milleneum in entertainment—as long as millions of people want to watch trash, then trash will be served. But a reformed system of production, distribution, and exhibition would create many additional opportunities to buy, sell, and view non-trash, which is good enough.

PART THREE

Sociological Nightmares

4

Coping with Paranoia

WHILE THE INDUSTRY AS A WHOLE fights its battles over cable television, the financial interest and syndication rules, and other broad issues, most people in Hollywood have more narrow concerns. Their attention is focused on their careers. Just as firms face a threatening economic environment in Hollywood, individuals—especially artists—face careers fraught with psychological risk. The astronomically high unemployment rate, the stressful work environment, and the constant artistic frustration make for an emotional tone in Hollywood that is always converging on the pathological. And like businesses that must attempt to reduce their economic risks, individual people must develop strategies to cope with the nightmare of everyday life in the industry.

It is important for individuals to adapt some sort of defense against stress, for otherwise Hollywood would be one large asylum. The psychological tone of life there consists of paranoia leavened with anxiety and envy. It is not only that the odds against becoming a success are impossibly steep; but even worse, nobody knows how to go about beating them. In a community full of talented people, it is not clear to the ambitious arrivals why one person becomes an overnight sensation and another tries for years to break into the business, to universal indifference.

The experience of those artists who have been successful is not much help. Hollywood is full of testimonies to the decisive intervention of sheer luck. Looking back on his career in 1960, Henry Fonda mused, "Practically everything that has ever happened to me has been the result of coincidence. It's been a matter of getting the lucky break."[1] Many Hollywood biographies make similar assertions.

To the aspiring actor, writer, director, or producer, this sort of recollection is profoundly demoralizing. These artists are willing to pay any personal price or bear any burden to become a success, but nobody can tell them how to begin paying or where to find a burden that wants to be borne. It is little wonder that Hollywood has a reputation for providing recruits to oddball religious cults and customers for astrology. If hopefuls in the business cannot see a rational means of ascent in front of them, then they are bound to explore the irrational.

Actors set the emotional and intellectual tone for the artistic community. There are simply more of them. The membership of the Hollywood branch of the Screen Actors Guild is more than 35,000—twice the number in the Writers, Directors, and Producers put together. Although it is impossible to measure the size of the amorphous mass of not-quite-professional artists who hang around on the fringes of the industry, observation suggests that it, too, is composed mostly of would-be actors. The "public opinion" of the industry tends to be strongly influenced, therefore, by the way performers see their lives and the world. And of all of Hollywood's denizens, actors seem most vulnerable to the paranoid mindset.

This is partly because the odds are stacked even more against actors than against others due to their large number. More competition means fewer jobs for each. But it is also because actors in general are peculiarly unfitted to handle the sort of emotional stress that the industry imposes on them. A reader of the biographies and autobiographies of performers must be struck by the very large percentage of them who come from broken homes. Divorce, desertion, and death are common themes in the early chapters of these books. Even those who did not experience an actual separation from one or both of their parents record an astounding number of fathers who were alcoholic wastrels, of mothers who were mentally ill, and of parents or guardians who were emotionally withdrawn or abusive.

Psychologists suggest that the personality type that emerges from such a childhood tends to have a low sense of self-worth and seeks to escape from his or her feelings of inadequacy into other, imaginary characters; thus the choice of profession. Through the adoration of the audience, such a person may be seeking the love that was denied by his or her parents.[2] By outwardly drawing attention to themselves, performers may be attempting to compensate for personal insecurity and fear.

Aspiring actors undergo a training process that emphasizes the very aspects of their character that are liable to make them dysfunctional in the off-camera or off-stage world. The American tradition of training performers, which derives from various Russian theories of the art, emphasizes the casting off of inhibitions and the primacy of emotional expression. Actors are taught not to be analytical and suspicious of intuition but instead are encouraged to be truthful conveyers of passion. Simplifying somewhat, it would seem that the ideal performer is all "id."

In the high-stress, continuous-rejection world of Hollywood, even strong, mature individuals would be expected to show some signs of neurosis. With their vulnerable personalities, it is little wonder that one of the most commonly repeated bits of folk wisdom in the business is that "all actors are crazy." This assertion is an exaggeration, but it nevertheless partially explains the sometimes peculiar behavior observable in Hollywood.

Paranoids, not accepting the fact that chance and necessity may impersonally produce results unsatisfactory to themselves, look for personal malice. They believe that people in positions of power are somehow prejudiced against them. When the phone doesn't ring, many Hollywood artists are certain that they have offended someone, or failed to cultivate the right person, or ruined their career through some thoughtless blunder. (In the midst of an otherwise candid interview, a famous director suddenly blurted out, "Has everyone else been this frank?" I was surprised, because he had been making general and common observations about difficulties he had been having in his work and had named no specific person or institution. I saw nothing provocative in anything he had said to me. I told him truthfully that some had been as frank and some had not. He was unsatisfied. "If the producer wants to employ me but the network guy doesn't like something that I said to you that you published, he'll say no," he asserted. I promised to show him any page on which his name appeared, and he rather nervously continued.)

Although it is a personal affliction, paranoia has social consequences. When artists are members of some group that has suffered discrimination in the larger society, they often believe that their personal lack of success constitutes further evidence of this discrimination. It frequently does no good to suggest to a black actor that a white one is also unemployed; that actor may believe that racism underlies his failure to achieve stardom. A Latino or an Asian may feel the same way. Despite considerable evidence that homosexuals have risen to every level of achievement in Hollywood, those who remain behind are certain that they detect prejudice against themselves. Women charge that their gender has been used as an excuse to smother their talent. In many cases, these suspicions may be founded on truth. But the impossibility of confirming the suspicion adds to the general atmosphere of desperation, and personal hysteria worsens social conflict.

And so, when an identifiable villain comes along, a person or thing that is genuinely trying to deprive them of employment, Hollywoodites react almost with relief. This is the most likely explanation for the industry's preoccupation with the blacklist.

The Hollywood blacklist began in 1947, when ten members or former members of the Communist party refused to cooperate with the Committee on Un-American Activities of the U.S. House of Representatives (usually called HUAC, "House Un-American Activities Committee"). Leaders of the film industry, worried lest groups boycott their movies, adopted a policy of not employing the ten "unfriendly witnesses," or any future noncooperators. In the ensuing years, as McCarthyism spread over the country and the hunt for Communists and Communist sympathizers became ever more reckless, the original tightly focused blacklist expanded to include former Communist party members (who had never been asked to testify about anything), their friends and relatives, people who had once attended a meeting at which Communists were present, citizens whose opinions made someone in power suspicious, anyone who made any blacklister angry for any reason, and random victims who were accidentally caught up in the net. Several hundred Hollywood artists and craftspeople working in both films and television became unemployable, sometimes for reasons they well understood, occasionally for no cause they could identify. Blacklisting petered out in the early 1960s, when changing national attitudes and court decisions reaffirming the rights of potential blacklist victims removed its motivation and legal basis. The decline of the studio system further dismantled the organizational structure upon which the blacklist depended.[3]

Blacklisting affected many institutions of American society other than film and television, including, for example, the military and the universities. In these institutions, however, blacklisting is a dim memory, bearing only indirect relevance to the problems of the 1990s. But in Hollywood, the blacklist still lives, at least in the minds of its citizens. It is part of common conversation, as though McCarthy were still stalking the halls of the Senate and HUAC hearings were scheduled for next week.

Artists still honor each other with prizes for having stood up to the blacklist. (In 1988, the Hollywood/Beverly Hills chapter of the American Civil Liberties Union gave Kirk Douglas its annual Bill of Rights Award for having employed blacklisted screenwriter Dalton Trumbo on *Spartacus* in 1960. Press reports indicate that the largest crowd in its twenty-two-year history attended the ceremony.)[4] They still get into personal fights over the issues involved. (At a panel on the McCarthy era in 1988 in Barcelona, screenwriter Walter Bernstein and director Jules Dassin repeatedly insulted director Edward Dmytryk for having cooperated with HUAC almost four decades earlier. Dassin stated, "They made a mistake by inviting Dmytryk. There are no two sides to the question, only one side." Bernstein said, "It's not a debatable subject. I'm not interested if he [Dmytryk] is free or not.")[5] Attempts are still being made to besmirch or erase the memory of dead artists who participated in the hunt for Communists. (In 1990, for example, Lorimar, on what used to be the MGM lot, renamed the "Robert Taylor Building" the "George Cukor Building" because of a petition circulated by screenwriter Stan Zimmerman. Taylor had cooperated with HUAC in 1947 and according to those who signed the petition, was so morally repugnant that he did not deserve to be memorialized.)[6]

There are legitimate issues involving the blacklist, and it is understandable that those who lived through it would still be holding grudges. But Hollywood's preoccupation with its effects is far out of proportion to the importance of the issues it raises in contemporary society. The town's fixation on the blacklist extends to much of its population, not just to the relatively few remaining survivors of the era. The neurotic preoccupation of the industry has to be explained, not with reference to the importance of the blacklist in its history, but by the function it fulfills for the Hollywood psyche. It objectifies the paranoia; it provides a tangible enemy. At last, proof that they have real enemies! Someone is conspiring to deprive them of work! And so, as long as the phone doesn't ring and the artist doesn't know why, the memory of the blacklist will be kept alive in the entertainment industry. Sometimes it is better to fight against imaginary enemies than to struggle against an undefinable reality.

INTERPERSONAL RELATIONS

In the fluid business structure of Hollywood, no one knows what will work, executives come and go quickly, every project is put together from scratch, and trust is in short supply. To survive, members of the Hollywood community must evolve some methods of protecting themselves from the vicissitudes of working in this environment. One such method of self-protection is their insistence on having very detailed contracts with the studios and networks that employ them. Because the person with whom they are dealing may be fired tomorrow and replaced, Hollywood artists try to foresee every possible area of contention and eliminate all ambiguity. A contract thereby becomes, in the words of studio executive Dan Melnick, a document that "lays out the terms by which the parties get a divorce," and such agreements are liable to be excruciatingly detailed.[7]

Consequently, Hollywood contracts are known for their length and complexity. For example, when Paramount signed producers Don Simpson and Jerry Bruckheimer to a five-year, five-picture deal in 1990, the contract ran over two hundred pages.[8] As it turned out, the agreement soured within ten months, and the studio and the producers parted company.[9]

More than they rely on contracts, however, Hollywoodites depend upon interpersonal relations. A search for powerful friends is probably the primary psychological strategy they use for dealing with the industry's emotional risks.

A word heard frequently in industry conversation is "shmooze." According to Leo Rosten's *The Joys of Yiddish*, it means "to have a friendly, gossipy, heart-to-heart talk."[10] If so, the meaning has evolved to meet the needs of Hollywood. In that community, it is used to convey a different meaning: to have a friendly heart-to-heart talk with the purpose of advancing your career. Actors are said to shmooze producers with the hope of landing a part; writers shmooze agents in an attempt to get representation; executives shmooze higher executives to remain in their good graces. In the absence of the routinized path to success found in a corporate or government bureaucracy, success depends on establishing agreeable personal relations with people who can help you. Hollywood is an endless round of parties, lunches, and meetings at which the arts of flattery and charm are put to practical uses.

English as much as Yiddish illustrates the importance of interpersonal relations. Studio heads are often said to have established "relationships" with many of the prominent artists in town. Producers are said to be successful because they have many "contacts" in the business. These words reflect the utilitarian, manipulative nature of many of the interpersonal connections on which the industry depends. The word "friendship," which implies that humans value one another intrinsically, is less often heard. People in Hollywood have friends, but they understand the difference between an acquaintance based on mutual affection and one based on business usefulness. In an industry in which very little is to be trusted, decisionmakers tend to do business with the people they know. Those who are unknown must therefore be good shmoozers so that they can become known. "My agent yelled at me for not going to parties," reports one aspiring writer. "It wasn't friendly advice. She told me that if I didn't get out and meet people, I was wasting my time and hers."[11]

The result is that the people who make films and television programs are the ones who have somehow established contacts within the coterie that controls financing and distribution. These executives and agents return again and again to the artists they know. Consequently, an industry that attracts thousands of men and women to Hollywood every year ends up admitting only a few hundred, total, to the charmed circle. Within the industry, a person who has access to serious deal-making is called a "player" and is the object of frenetic shmoozing by everyone else in town.

Sociologists Robert Faulkner and Andy Anderson studied the phenomenon of deals and jobs based on personal contacts in the motion picture industry. They discovered that older, more eminent producers tended to make films with directors who had achieved a similar level of success, whereas newer or less successful filmmakers also tended to work together. The more successful artists working with other more successful artists tended, not surprisingly, to produce the more successful movies; and in doing so, they became even more likely to get a chance to work next time, and so on. Meanwhile, the less successful artists, working together, tended to generate a higher proportion of flops, so that they lost their chance for a second opportunity. As a result, between 1965 and 1980, 7 percent of the producers made five or more films and accounted for almost one-third of all the pictures made. Meanwhile, 64 percent of producers made one film and were never heard from again. The pattern was similar for directors.[12]

Todd Gitlin discovered the same dynamic at work in the field of television production. "Because the buyers' calculations of marketability are necessarily crude and clumsy," he asserted, "they resort to sellers they've worked with before, sellers they're comfortable with," with the result that "the same names keep showing up in the credits."[13]

For similar reasons, Hollywood has always been known for practicing nepotism. Relatives don't have to shmooze you; you already know them. Under the old studio system, children, nephews, and brothers-in-law filled the middle ranks of authority in the organization. In the new Hollywood, people make deals with their relatives or use a connection with a family member as a means of introduction to someone with clout.

The importance of personal connections within a fluid system of employment only increases the difficulties of aspirants who are members of groups not historically a part of the chain of relationships. White producers may feel more personally comfortable with white directors; Jews may feel more comfortable with Jews; men may feel more comfortable making deals with men. In choosing to deal with individuals who are agreeable to them, they are not consciously discriminating against members of certain groups. But the system nevertheless produces a set of players who are markedly homogeneous. It is difficult for blacks, Latinos, Asians, and women to sue for equality of shmooze time.

Minority groups and women sometimes do better confronting the studios, which have a stable group of employees and can enforce hiring policies over a set of productions. As a result of steady pressure from a variety of sources, for example, the proportion of black actors cast in motion picture and television parts by the majors has been rising.[14] But as long as the system of advancement in the industry as a whole is based on personal contacts, progress in creating a Hollywood population more representative of the larger society will be slow.

THE AWARDS INDUSTRY

When Kevin Costner walked down the aisle of the Shrine Auditorium at the Academy Awards ceremony on March 25, 1991, to accept his Oscar for producing the best picture (*Dances with Wolves*), he was not unfamiliar with the process. For one thing, he had already made the same trip to receive the award for best director. For another, however, he was used to picking up statues honoring that film. *Dances with Wolves* had already won the top prizes from the Directors Guild of America, the American Cinema Editors, the National Board of Review, and the Hollywood Foreign Press Association. The film won so many best picture awards that observers could be forgiven for believing that it had swept all competitions.

But this was not the case. *Dances with Wolves* was far from being the only picture that won a "best" award that year. At the People's Choice Awards, *Pretty Woman* was anointed the cream of 1990's crop. The New York Film

Critics judged *Goodfellas* to be the best that Hollywood had to offer. The members of the Writers Guild of America thought that Barry Levinson's *Avalon* was based on the best screenplay. The Motion Picture Sound Editors judged the sound of *Total Recall* better than the sound in Costner's film. Given the number of awards ceremonies in Hollywood in 1991, there was a good chance that any well-done motion picture could be proclaimed the best at something.

The town is in fact awash in awards. At the Margaret Herrick Library of the Motion Picture Academy, the card file labeled "awards" (excluding theater and television prizes) contains 116 entries under the first letter of the alphabet alone. In one year, from June 1, 1989, to May 31, 1990, there were 191 awards ceremonies, either in Hollywood or dealing with Hollywood products, that were important enough to be listed in *Daily Variety*. This is an average of 3.67 ceremonies per week.[15] And since most of these events bestow multiple awards (in 1991 the Daytime Emmys alone dispensed 212), there must be well over a thousand individual prizes that can be won in any given year.

Table 4.1 shows the variety of prizes in the screen entertainment industry by listing the awards received by just three individuals in the eighteen months from January 1989 to June 1990.[16]

Not only is there already a plethora of ceremonies, but new ones constantly arise. In April 1991 Laurence Austin and Dorothy Hampton, operator and owner of Silent Movie, a Fairfax Boulevard theater devoted to showing pre-1927 films, received the first Max Laemmle Award from the American Film Institute/L.A. Film Fest honoring exhibitors "for recognizing and promoting film as an art form."[17] The Environmental Media Association launched its first annual awards show in September 1991 to "recognize members of the industry who have used their talents to advance environmental concerns."[18] The Screen Actors Guild is planning to join its fellow artists' unions soon in presenting yearly awards for best performances.[19]

The rate at which awards multiply, however, is not rapid enough for many Hollywoodites. Indeed, to read the trade papers, one would think that there is an awards shortage, so frequently is someone lobbying to either institute a new prize or carve out another category within an existing ceremony. This pressure is most often applied to the Motion Picture Academy, the originator of the most prestigious awards show. In March 1991, Stunts Unlimited, a fraternal organization of stuntmen and stuntwomen, called on the Academy to create awards for its profession.[20] The next month, Budd Friedman and Mark Lonow, owners of the Improvisation Comedy Club, asked the organization to create new categories especially for comic films and performances.[21] If the trend continues, Hollywood award ceremonies will come to resemble kindergarten athletic competitions, where everyone goes home with at least one ribbon.

TABLE 4.1 Awards Received by Three Hollywood Artists, January 1989 Through June 1990

STEVEN SPIELBERG

January 1989	American Cinematique Award
July 1989	Man of the Decade Award/Video Software Dealers Association
July 1989	Distinguished Eagle/Boy Scouts
November 1989	Mass Media Award/American Jewish Committee
February 1990	Filmmaker of the Decade/American Cinema Editors

SHERRY LANSING

January 1989	Motion Picture Showmanship Award/Publicists Guild of America
November 1989	Woman of Achievement/L.A. Hadassah
January 1990	American Cinema Award/ACA Foundation (operates Motion Picture Country Home and Hospital)
April 1990	Raquela Woman of Valor Award/American Associates of Ben Gurion University

BOB HOPE

September 1989	Lifetime Achievement/Institute for the Study of American Wars
September 1989	Spirit of America Patriot Award
November 1989	Life Achievement/Friars' Club
November 1989	Man of the Century/Palm Springs Rotary Club
June 1990	Humanitarian Award/Nosotros

The ceremonies continue all year, except for a slack period in late August and early September. At almost any other time, at least one industry gathering can be anticipated. After the New Year's holiday, the tempo of prize-giving gradually increases, with a veritable orgy of awards in March, culminating in the Oscars. After the Oscars, it resumes a steady pace until late summer.

Awards are given for a multitude of accomplishments. The best known, including the Oscars (from the Academy of Motion Picture Arts and Sciences) and the Emmys (given by the Academy of Television Arts and Sciences), are for artistic achievement on a specific entertainment project. Several press associations also present prizes each year, as do most trade associations and the producers', writers', and directors' guilds. Other prizes presented by these organizations, however, are unconnected to any particular undertaking (for example, the many "Life Achievement" awards). Still others are connected with an industry or quasi-industry charity and are presented for service outside the recipient's professional capacity. Most of the major industry charities, including the Motion Picture Pioneers, the Will Rogers Memorial Fund, Variety Clubs International, and the Motion Picture and Television Fund, host annual awards banquets. Local charities with no direct connection to Hollywood (but whose membership may include many film and television industry members) frequently tap a celebrity to help draw a crowd to the annual fund-raiser. Love Is Feeding Everyone (which distributes surplus food to the needy), the Santa Monica Hospital Foundation, the ERAS Center for Learning Disabled Children, the Starlight Foundation, and many others give one or several awards to industry members who have volunteered their time.

A panoply of ceremonies is staged by ethnic, gender, or religious groups to thank artists or executives who have done something to improve the image or the employment opportunities of people in the group. In 1991, Women in Film presented its Crystal Awards to Ruby Dee, Penny Marshall, and Jessica Tandy; its International Award went to Liv Ullmann; and its Norma Zarsky Humanitarian Awards were presented to Billy Crystal, Whoopi Goldberg, and Robin Williams.[22] Likewise, the Association of Asian Pacific American Artists bestows the Jimmies (after the late cinematographer James Wong Howe); Nosotros presents the Golden Eagles; the National Association for the Advancement of Colored People (NAACP) dispenses the Image Awards; and a variety of Jewish organizations contribute their share to the sum of annual festivities.

To this total are added the prizes political organizations use to encourage people with compatible ideologies to support them. The Gay and Lesbian Alliance Against Defamation (GLAAD) staged its second awards banquet in 1991, honoring the films *Longtime Companion* and *The Handmaid's Tale* and television programs "Designing Women" and "L.A. Law" among others.[23] The Hollywood/Beverly Hills chapter of the American Civil Liberties Union has presented its Bill of Rights Awards for a quarter of a century. In 1991 the Liberty Hill Foundation, founded in 1976 to help finance social justice organizations "that promote long-term change but often lack access to traditional or government funding sources," presented its Upton Sinclair Award to Jane Fonda.[24]

Some awards come from organizations normally unconnected with Hollywood whose members find it useful to honor a star that none of them would otherwise meet. The March of Dimes, the National Association of Social Workers, the American Humane Association, the Winston Churchill Foundation, Mothers Against Drunk Driving, the Eastman Kodak Corporation, the International Wilderness Leadership Foundation, the Fund for Animals, and many others have staged a single event honoring an entertainment celebrity. Whether famous or obscure, central to the business or irrelevant, no organization desiring to bestow an award ever seems to have trouble finding a prominent person willing to accept it.

An indication of the important role that awards ceremonies play in the culture of Hollywood is their capacity to generate struggles over control. For example, there used to be a continent-wide National Academy of Television Arts and Sciences. Arguments between its eastern and western factions about how the Emmy Awards show should be structured split the organization in 1976. For more than a decade thereafter, the Academy of Television Arts and

Sciences, based in Hollywood, handed out awards for prime-time television, and the National Academy, headquartered in New York, dispensed the prizes for daytime television, sports, and documentaries. The organizations remain separate but now cooperate on both ceremonies. To cite another example, in the late 1980s, the NAACP was displeased with the way its Hollywood branch was administering its annual Image Awards. The conflict finally resulted in the president of the Hollywood branch resigning his office and the national leadership taking over control of the ceremonies.

There are, of course, good reasons that awards ceremonies occupy such an important place in the Hollywood psyche. They are a tangible means of coping with a stressful environment and lowering the general paranoia level. As a result, the process of giving and accepting prizes is institutionalized to the point where it has become an industry in itself, one that assists the purposes of the larger one to which it is attached.

There are several reasons that organizations want to give awards. A celebrity in attendance at a ceremony or banquet draws publicity, which has a legitimizing effect and may increase the organization's membership. Many awards ceremonies are also fund-raisers, in which the honoree is asked to provide the names of friends and colleagues who are then sent invitations. The tickets to these occasions are never cheap.

For an organization that exists not just to accomplish a specific goal but to affect the image of some group in a general way, celebrity awards provide a means of ensuring an audience for the group's message. Nosotros, for example, is dedicated to improving the image of Latinos in the media. Its televised 1990 Golden Eagle Awards ceremony was hosted by performers Rita Moreno and Jimmy Smits and featured entertainment by Susan Anton, Alaina Reed Hall, Raul Martinez, and Fred Travelena, among others. Included in the fifteen award winners for the evening were actor Raul Julia, singer Gloria Estefan, and producer Moctesuma Esparza.[25] The purpose of the show was quite consciously to do more than just hand out prizes. It was, says Nosotros President Marc Allen Trujillo, to "enhance and promote the positive image of Hispanics in the media by basically highlighting their participation, both old and new." Trujillo wants Hispanic viewers to "walk away with a feeling of pride," saying perhaps, "'Hey, they're doing some good things,' or 'I didn't know so-and-so was Hispanic.'. . . It's a celebration of Hispanic achievement."[26]

Ceremonies have another, more subterranean purpose as well. In the paranoid, high-unemployment environment of Hollywood, awards banquets and shows provide an opportunity for the less successful and the temporarily out-of-work to flatter the powerful elite. To an actor between jobs, the most terrifying thought is that he or she will be forgotten. If out of sight is out of mind, then presenting an executive or a producer with a plaque, a speech, and a meal is a good way to remind that person that you exist. Award-giving, in other words, is a kind of institutionalized shmoozing. It artificially stimulates the social interaction that forms the basis of the industry's all-important "relationships."

But the recipients also have good reasons for participating in the ritual. Because the successful are generally just as anxious and insecure as the unsuccessful, they lose no opportunity to validate their popularity and publicize themselves. Winning an award is an unusually good way to advertise one's self. Sometimes the benefits are clearly measurable. In the 1980s, the winners of the Academy Award for best picture garnered an additional $30 million at the box office (adjusted for inflation) after the ceremonies, whereas those films that were nominated but did not win averaged only an additional $6 million. Jodie Foster had been paid less than $200,000 for acting in *The Accused,* but when she won the Oscar for best actress for that movie in 1989, her asking price immediately leapt to $1.5 million and in fact she received more than $1 million for her next film, *The Silence of the Lambs,* for which she again received the Oscar.[27] An Emmy also unquestionably helps a career. Although it is unlikely that any other award would help nearly as much as an Emmy or an Oscar, it can't hurt, so artists are inclined to participate. In their insecurity, they believe that they need all the help they can get.

The shmooze factor also operates from the perspective of the recipient. Nobody feels so strongly embedded in the industry that he or she can afford to pass up the opportunity to make a few more contacts or strengthen a few existing relationships. The beneficiaries need the awards ceremonies as much as the organizations that hold them. Prizes and testimonials will therefore continue to be dispensed at an increasing rate in Hollywood, while organizations and recipients will go on helping one another manufacture publicity and money.

THE CELEBRITY INDUSTRY

For performers, the greatest anxiety is that they will be forgotten. Believing that the world is somehow conspiring to shove them back into obscurity, they pursue publicity with compulsive fervor. Because the public seems to have an unquenchable desire to see "celebrities" in the flesh, a mutually agreeable solution is evident. The celebrity industry has arisen to serve the needs of both performers and the public for personal contact.

In 1938, Earl Blackwell, a contract player at MGM, was asked for Ginger Rogers' unlisted phone number. He had the number, but more important, he realized that he was in a position to supply information—at a price. With publicist Ted Strong, whom he later bought out, he founded Celebrity Service. Blackwell and Strong began to market a daily bulletin on the comings and goings of the Hollywood elite. Their first subscriber was CBS. In 1939, the New York World's Fair became the first client to pay Celebrity Service to furnish personal appearances by actors. By the late 1980s, Celebrity Service International, Inc., offered services including a telephone hotline ($1,250 a year for answers to as many as five questions per day about the doings of more than 35,000 people); a biweekly theater newsletter ($100 per year); an annual entertainment industry contact book ($15); and the *Celebrity Register* ($80), a "who's who" compendium published once every ten years. Blackwell also furnishes celebrities to help businesses publicize one of their products or services.[28] He is probably most famous, however, for putting out an annual "worst dressed" list on which entertainers invariably dominate.

By now, of course, Blackwell is not alone in the celebrity business. Celebrity Connection charges charities $1,000 per celebrity for local fund-raisers, $2,000 per celebrity for national fund-raisers, and $6,000 for recruiting a spokesperson who agrees to represent a charity for one year. Celebrity Outreach, a nonprofit corporation that does not charge for its services, recruits entertainment and sports notables to make television and radio public service announcements and attend fund-raisers. For example, Celebrity Outreach arranged for actor Gregory Harrison, a recovering cocaine user, to be spokesperson for The Entertainment Industry Referral and Assistance Center, which supports substance-abuse treatment.[29] Cook International Productions, Inc., lines up celebrity contestants for charity sporting events; former actor and evangelist Marjoe Gortner and former publicist David Mirisch are also in this business.[30] In general, with either a good cause (for a charity) or enough money (for a commercial endorsement), it is now possible to recruit almost any performer in Hollywood to appear at a fund-raiser or give a sales pitch on a client's behalf.

No one keeps track of how much money has been raised for charities, overall, by celebrity appearances, but it is clear that society's unfortunates would be very much worse off without them. David Mirisch's figures show that from the mid-1970s to the late 1980s, he raised more than $5 million in three hundred sports events. Bob Hope's Desert Classic golf tournament, the oldest celebrity-oriented charity event, raised $17 million for the Eisenhower Medical Center and ninety other charities from 1959 to 1988.[31] Given the number of fund-raisers that either take place within Hollywood or employ members of its community, the total must be much higher.

All this would not be possible, of course, without the enthusiastic participation of actual, quasi, and would-be celebrities. There are a few genuine superstars who are "celebritied-out" and who lead semireclusive lives when they are not working. The most extreme case of the reluctant celebrity was the late Greta Garbo, who refused any sort of public appearance or statement for the last half-century of her life. For most performers, however, there is no such thing as too much publicity. They are of course paid for product endorsements, and the charities, although not actually giving them a stipend, normally supply them with first-class air fare, lodge them at the best hotels, and give them a generous expense account while they are appearing. But the greater benefit to the performer is the confirmation of their celebrity status.

Not only do performers cooperate with the celebrity-supplying businesses but they also invent their own ways of keeping their names before the public. Actors between roles, for example, may participate in the Hollywood All-Stars, a softball team that plays benefits in Southern California.[32] They may also write their autobiographies, despite the fact that their lives are far from over. It is not uncommon for performers in their thirties and forties to present their personal stories to the public. The record for early recitation, however, is probably Drew Barrymore's account of her drug and alcohol abuse as a nine-year-old, which was published when she was fourteen.[33] Of course, many performers pay personal publicists to insure their frequent appearance in the media.

However, many of the efforts made by performers on behalf of good causes stem from genuinely altruistic impulses, and it would be unjust to be entirely cynical about them. In charity work, for example, celebrities often contribute far more time and energy than would strictly be necessary if they were only in it for the publicity. Some retired actors and actresses spend the rest of their lives assisting organizations that are working to improve the lot of the sick, the poor, and the disadvantaged—an activity that cannot be interpreted as an attempt to bolster a career that no longer exists.

Yet there is no doubt that a large part of Hollywood's frantic search for visibility is motivated by fear. The industry's ever-present paranoia acts as an inner spur to the many who need the extra publicity and the few who do not. Even under normal circumstances, anxiety over unemployment and artistic frustration molds the behavior of the members of the community. But in extraordinary circumstances, when there is an added threat, the anxiety rises to a pitch of hysteria. Such was the case during the era of the blacklist. And such is the case today, in the age of AIDS.

5

The AIDS Epidemic

*H*OLLYWOOD HAS ALWAYS BEEN an economically and emotionally high-risk industry. With the advent of the AIDS epidemic in the 1980s, it became physically high-risk as well. The increase in physical risk also intensified the emotional pressure on an important segment of the entertainment community. Always an arena of paranoia, Hollywood is now more anxious and suspicious than at any time since the era of the blacklist a generation ago.

The motion picture and television industries are particularly vulnerable to AIDS because artistic communities traditionally include a high percentage of homosexuals.[1] This is, however, a topic seldom discussed publicly because a great many Americans consider homosexuality to be either sinful or sleazy. Evidence of the pervasive hostility toward gays is easy to come by. Public opinion surveys regularly uncover large numbers of people who are ready to express contempt for gays and only a few who are willing to admit a favorable attitude toward them. Voters frequently defeat gay rights referenda in both states and cities, and there have even been attempts to impose discrimination on homosexuals through the ballot box. In 1992, for example, Colorado voters approved an amendment to the state constitution that took away restrictions on job discrimination against gays (a somewhat similar Oregon initiative was defeated). Despite some relaxation of the laws in recent years, twenty-three states continue to outlaw homosexual acts. Violent attacks on gay men are a regular occurrence in many American cities.[2] It is no wonder that most gays have, until quite recently, preferred to stay "in the closet," attempting to pass for straight in an aggressively straight society.

For these reasons, it is impossible to arrive at an accurate estimate of how many homosexuals there are in the screen entertainment industry. In the most thorough and scientific survey of American sexual practices, Alfred Kinsey reported in the 1940s that 4 percent of his male respondents were exclusively homosexual as adults and about 12 percent had been predominantly homosexual for at least a three-year period.[3] Perhaps, then, it would not be entirely fantastic to suggest that among males, one-quarter of Hollywood's artists and a somewhat smaller percentage of its executives and other non-artists might be gay or bisexual. There are fewer lesbian women than gay men in the industry, but again, accurate figures are not attainable. Whatever their exact number, homosexuals are clearly a significant force in motion picture and television production, and whatever affects them has an impact on the rest of the industry.

This is not to say that Hollywood has been hospitable to a gay sensibility. Because the industry's public image has historically been one of moral turpitude, its leaders have attempted to counter that reputation by stifling any expressions of deviant sexuality that may be under their control. The taboo against portraying "sex perversion," for instance, was the last part of the Motion Picture Production Code abandoned in the 1960s.[4]

Moreover, as an industry that caters to the desires of the majority, Hollywood has always been careful to present an image of robust heterosexuality. As Vito Russo points out in his study of homosexuality in American movies, The Celluloid Closet, nothing is more imbedded in industry culture than a belief that the public would never accept a gay hero.[5] For most of its history, therefore, the screen entertainment industry pretended homosexuals did not exist; when they did appear, they were portrayed as harmless buffoons or as murderers, murder victims, or suicides.[6] Public antipathy to departures from this stereotype is quickly felt. ABC lost $500, 000 in ad revenue in December 1990, for example, when advertisers pulled out of an episode of its prime-time series "thirtysomething" that featured two occasionally recurring gay characters.[7]

Such swift retribution reinforces the tendency to demean homosexuals. In the 1985 film Teen Wolf, the character played by Michael J. Fox announces to his best friend that he has something to confide. "You're not gonna tell me you're a faggot, are you?" asks the friend suspiciously. "No," replies Fox. "I'm a werewolf." The friend is visibly relieved. Here, suggests Russo, is a synecdoche of the attitude Hollywood has traditionally projected in its entertainment: Better a werewolf than a faggot.[8] Although many homosexuals have cordial personal relationships with many heterosexuals and vice versa, in an official, public sense, the industry has usually been at best indifferent and at worst antagonistic to gay aspirations.

The result has been that the industry's large gay population has for most of its history hidden deeply in the closet. To the ordinary paranoia, frustration, envy, and anxiety that permeate Hollywood's psychological atmosphere, homosexuals added a layer of resentment about their oppression, targeted both at American society in general and at the industry in particular.

The stress of living with this victim psychology was relieved somewhat by informal networks of homosexuals who helped each other's careers. Becoming acquainted with one another at parties or through mutual friends and lovers, gay men offered one another assistance and support. In an industry in

which shmoozing is vital to personal advancement, a homosexual orientation could be an advantage that might, if the artist remained firmly in the
closet, outweigh the disadvantages he would otherwise face. "Oh, sure, there
is an underground," says Geoffrey Barr, a personal manager of many actors
and actresses. "All the guys in the business who are homosexual know all the
other guys in the business who are homosexual, and they do each other favors. Why not?"[9]

This underground is known to the heterosexual artists, and they resent it.
Although gays believe themselves to be the oppressed minority, the vicious
competition of the Hollywood labor market gives everyone a persecution
complex, and straight actors grumble to each other about the disadvantages
they endure by being ineligible for membership in this particular mutual help
association. In the 1950s, with communism on everyone's mind, straight actors sometimes referred to the homosexual network as "The Homintern."
Later, it would come to be known as "The Gay Mafia."[10] With this support
network, homosexuals have thus succeeded in improving their employment
chances from microscopic to slim; but at the same time, they increase the an-
tagonism they generate in the straight world.

In the 1970s, with the rise of the gay liberation movement, homosexuals'
perceptions of themselves as victims were beginning to change. A few gays
were emerging from the closet, and both films and television programs were
becoming marginally more accepting of positive gay themes. Some homosexuals looked forward to the day when their sexual orientation would be
considered irrelevant by the public as well as by Hollywood. Then came
AIDS.

THE COSTS OF AIDS

Since the epidemic began in about 1981, more than 100,000 people have
died from AIDS in the United States. Approximately one million Americans
are thought to carry HIV, usually believed (the medical community is not
unanimous about this) to cause the disease. Forty thousand new cases of
AIDS were reported to the Centers for Disease Control in 1990. Although
AIDS is now considered a chronic rather than an invariably fatal disease, it is
still extremely dangerous, and the death toll continues to rise.[11]

For reasons that are not completely clear, homosexuals have been the primary carriers of AIDS in the United States and Western Europe. Although
the proportion of cases caused by the use of contaminated needles to inject
illegal drugs is rising, about three-quarters of the disease's victims have been
male homosexuals.[12] In cities with large gay populations, such as New York,
San Francisco, and Los Angeles, and in industries with a large number of homosexuals, such as entertainment, the infection rates are much higher than

for the population as a whole. So although it is technically not correct to refer to AIDS as "The Gay Plague," the fact remains that the disease has had a
devastating effect wherever there is a high proportion of homosexuals.

The official statistics from Hollywood are bad enough: A survey conducted by the Entertainment Industry Workplace AIDS Committee found
that the larger entertainment industry companies had experienced an average of seventeen AIDS cases each compared to an average of six cases for
large companies nationwide. [13] In 1991, Hollywood's talent guilds reported
that their health insurance costs had risen between 300 and 400 percent in
the previous decade, forcing many of them to raise their eligibility requirements. Although the guilds did not publicly blame the out-of-control health
care costs on any one factor, an informed observer could surmise that it was
the expense of caring for those stricken by AIDS that had placed such a
strain on the system.[14]

But the unofficial story is worse. Because a diagnosis of AIDS automatically creates the stigma of "homosexual," victims frequently deny the nature
of their illness and enlist friends, relatives, and doctors to conceal the truth.
Evasion continued even after the much-publicized deaths of Rock Hudson in
1985 and Liberace in 1987 destroyed the illusion of Hollywood's immunity
to the epidemic. As a consequence, obituaries of AIDS victims are still often
quasi-fictional, and much of the ongoing tragedy in Hollywood is not evident from the official statistics. A study of AIDS in the industry must therefore be creative in measuring its extent.

In an effort to acquire some objective understanding of the impact of the
epidemic on Hollywood, I kept track of all the obituaries in *Daily Variety*
from September 1, 1989, through August 31, 1991. During those two years
there were a total of 1,929 deaths listed from every cause, of both sexes, in
every relevant entertainment profession, everywhere in the country and occasionally the world. I did not try to separate out the "Hollywood" deaths
from this number because people in the industry travel and an AIDS case in
New York can be quite significant in Hollywood. In the period under consideration, there were 286 *confirmed, probable,* and *possible* AIDS deaths in
Hollywood, or 14.8 percent of the total listed. (These terms are defined in
the appendix at the end of this chapter.) One hundred seventy-two of these,
60 percent of all AIDS obits and 9 percent of all reported deaths, fall into the
"confirmed" category. About one-fifth of the total deaths were female,
whereas there were only two female AIDS deaths. I concluded from these figures that somewhere between 10 and 18 percent of all male deaths in the entertainment industry during those two years were due to AIDS.

About two-thirds of the reported AIDS deaths were among artists, with
actors and dancers being the two groups hardest hit. But every profession
and every level of success suffered losses. The list of those dying before their
time included costume designers, network television executives, film histori-

ans, union leaders, story editors, choreographers, producers, personal managers, art directors, talent agents, writers, prop makers, video engineers, producers, publicists, graphic designers, studio executives, film distributors, makeup artists, and casting directors. The numbers represent a tragedy of wasted talent and blighted hope, of millions of dollars spent on ultimately futile medical care, of friendships and love affairs cut short, of private suffering and corporate disruption. They suggest, in other words, a catastrophe with which the industry has only recently begun to come to terms.

THE IMPACT OF AIDS ON INDIVIDUALS

The most immediate problem of someone ill with AIDS, of course, is the inability to work. In the highly competitive world of Hollywood, a drop in energy level or a sudden string of absences spells the end of a career. Stephen Kolzak, former vice president of Columbia Pictures Television, explained it succinctly: "That's because in Hollywood they kill the runt of the litter."[15] (An intelligent, energetic man with many friends, Kolzak died of AIDS in September 1990.)[16] Although those who actually acquire the disease pay the greatest price, however, those who escape physically are not spared its psychological ravages.

Many diseases have symbolic resonances beyond their meaning as personal and social dangers. Historically, for instance, bubonic plague was interpreted by many people as a divine punishment for sin, theirs or someone else's. Tuberculosis (in the nineteenth century) and cancer (in the twentieth) were often laden with metaphorical meaning that went far beyond their status as a physical threat. For centuries, leprosy turned its victims into hated outcasts, a reaction hardly justified by its relative lack of virulence and its difficulty of transmission. Of all diseases, however, the ones that are sexually transmitted seem to carry the heaviest burden of symbolic weight. Such diseases seem to bring out people's anxieties about spiritual and physical pollution, their dread of being exposed as hypocritical sinners, their yearning to condemn those less righteous than themselves, and their fear of the power of the unconscious. Syphilis, gonorrhea, and herpes have always been dramatic, shameful afflictions that attacked the victims' self-esteem and social standing almost as much as their bodies.[17]

As an infection that is not only sexually transmitted but also brought about by activities that are considered depraved by much of the population, AIDS may be the most symbolically charged disease in history. But even though most homosexuals do not carry the sickness, they have found themselves, as members of a "high-risk" group, associated with AIDS in the public mind. Having just begun to make some progress in the 1970s toward social acceptance, in the 1980s homosexuals began not only to lose whatever ground they had gained but also to become identified as the carriers of both a physical and moral contagion. Personal attacks against homosexuals rose sharply during the 1980s.[18] Many conservative clerics used the epidemic to illustrate the sinfulness of homosexuality, and many conservative politicians employed it to assert the consequences of a degenerate (liberal) lifestyle.[19]

Meanwhile, male homosexuals needed no taunts from outside to intensify their personal insecurities. They were simultaneously grief-stricken and terrified. A grim saying commonly heard in gay circles as the decade progressed was, "We used to go to parties, bars, and bathhouses for a social life. Now we go to funerals." Like the bubonic plague of the fourteenth century that created, in historian Barbara Tuchman's words, "a dementia of despair" in Western Europe, AIDS has knocked the emotional underpinnings from under a generation of homosexual men.[20] "The psychological impact of AIDS on the gay community is tremendous," commented Richard Failla, an openly gay judge in New York. "It has done more to undermine the feelings of self-esteem than anything Anita Bryant could have ever done. Some people are saying, 'Maybe we *are* wrong—maybe this is a punishment.'"[21] In Hollywood, the epidemic has piled more suspicion and dread on top of a population already wrung out with paranoia. Artists still wonder if they have offended some powerful person who will insure that they never work again; now some of them realize that such people might actually be afraid of them. All rational, informed people know that AIDS is not spread by casual contact, but who expects a Hollywood player to be rational and informed? Perhaps he or she believes that a gay writer or director is no threat—but why take the chance? After all, there are plenty of safely straight artists eager for work. When the phone doesn't ring, there could be a thousand reasons; AIDS is one more. As Marvin Kaplan, president of the Los Angeles local of the American Federation of Television and Radio Artists (AFTRA), puts it, "AIDS is the new blacklist."[22]

As usual, actors are in the most vulnerable position. Unlike executives and most other artists, performers' careers depend upon their public images. For this reason, male actors have traditionally been reluctant to accept homosexual roles. The well-known tendency of fans to confuse performers with the characters they play has made the risk of portraying a homosexual greater than most actors are prepared to run. When Perry King was offered a gay part in the motion picture *A Different Story* in 1978, he reports that Sylvester Stallone warned him, "Don't play no faggots."[23] King took the part anyway and came to regret disregarding his friend's advice. "Playing a homosexual really hurt my career," he said later. "Because of that part, producers and casting directors in the motion picture industry didn't cast me in a lot of roles. I had a reasonable film career, and it began to stumble."[24]

Despite the concern forthrightly expressed by King, there is no good evidence that playing a gay role damages an actor's career. Many well-known performers have played homosexual characters without becoming typecast. Marlon Brando (*Reflections in a Golden Eye*, 1967), Richard Burton (*Staircase*, 1969), Martin Sheen (*That Certain Summer*, 1972), Al Pacino (*Dog Day Afternoon*, 1975), Harry Hamlin (*Making Love*, 1982), and William Hurt (*Kiss of the Spider Woman*, 1985) are among the actors who continued to receive offers to play masculine leading men after they had appeared on the screen as homosexuals. Robert Preston's moribund career was actually revived by his appearance as Julie Andrews's flamboyantly homosexual mentor in 1982's *Victor/Victoria*. And despite his lamentations about not being able to find work, Perry King later co-starred in the hit television series "Riptide." As with so much else in Hollywood, however, the inhibition for actors comes not from the definite knowledge that accepting a gay part will besmirch their careers but from the uncertainty. Maybe it will, and maybe it won't—why take the chance?

Even more damaging to "image," however, is the revelation that an actor is homosexual in real life. A generous proportion of macho leading men are gay, but as with Rock Hudson, their sexual orientation is irrelevant to their work as long as their private lives are not publicized. Even before AIDS, anxiety about being identified in the public mind as not fully masculine haunted gay actors' actions. When Vito Russo sought to set up interviews for *The Celluloid Closet* in the late 1970s, he reports that "screenwriters and directors were almost always willing to talk. Actors were terrified and remained silent. Only two or three, all heterosexual, were willing to discuss their work."[25] Again, there is no definite evidence that the exposure of the private life of a gay actor ever prevented him from landing work. Several leading men have been identified in print as homosexual, yet they continue to find good parts. But actors *believe* that exposure will destroy them, and so they stay in the closet if they can.

With homophobia sweeping the nation after 1980, anxiety became hysteria. Gay actors now live in terror that some journalist with nothing else to do will "out" them and in the process destroy their careers. To all the other fears, then, "tabloidaphobia" must be added.

Even gossip is to be feared. In 1985, Burt Reynolds lost some weight because of an entirely non-AIDS-related illness. Rumors circulated in the gay community that Reynolds had the dread disease, and the speculation began to leak out into the more disreputable segments of the mainstream press. Fighting not only for his health but also for his career, Reynolds felt obliged to go on talk shows to scotch the rumors before they became accepted as fact.[26] As a big star, he was able to command the publicity necessary to meet the gossip head-on. Lesser actors, however, believe that if they were the object of similar rumors, they would never work again. Thus the Hollywood saying that "all publicity is good publicity" no longer applies. In an attempt to forestall speculation about their sexual inclinations, several famous gay or bisexual actors got married in the late 1980s. The motivations of their brides in cooperating with this subterfuge will probably be the subject of several trashy novels and at least one movie-of-the-week.

As with any other plague, the impact of the AIDS epidemic extends beyond the arena of direct danger. In Hollywood, even those who do not feel personally threatened are pummeled with grief by the constant news of dying friends. Performer Bette Midler was not untypical when she reported in 1991, "Nearly everyone I started with in the business in 1965 is dead."[27] George Kirgo, president of the Writers Guild of America West, acknowledges that the epidemic has affected the scripts of even heterosexual writers. He explains, "You cannot easily do gay jokes anymore. We've all lost dozens of friends, so it's no joke."[28] With every new case of AIDS, ripples of distress spread out through the industry. Today the community is in an almost continuous state of mourning.

THE IMPACT OF AIDS ON THE INDUSTRY

Like the rest of the nation, Hollywood attempted to ignore AIDS in its early years. But as the death toll mounted and individual tragedy multiplied into social scourge, the industry slowly began to evolve collective responses to the epidemic. Some adjusting mechanisms were already in place. In the 1970s, gay rights groups, like other minority-rights organizations, established institutionalized access to the television networks. Both the webs and the producers consulted with members of the Gay Media Task Force whenever scripts dealt with homosexual themes. Often scripts were changed considerably during the negotiation process, although the inevitable compromises were not always agreeable to every homosexual who viewed the shows. Nevertheless, movie and television themes evolved into messages for tolerance, with the general focus of the plot becoming the acceptance of gay characters by the regular heterosexual characters. This process of mutual adjustment was so successful that one critic labeled television's 1976 season "The Year of the Gay."[29] The advent of AIDS, however, strained this friendly relationship between the industry and the organized gay community. As a deadly threat, the disease was made to order for melodrama; as potential sexual assassins, HIV carriers could easily be portrayed as demons. Hollywood was therefore more tempted than it had been to turn homosexuals into villains. At the same time, the gay rights movement was becoming radicalized, at least partly because of the desperation homosexuals felt as the epidemic continued to spread. Less willing to compromise on the way they were portrayed on screen, homosexuals were more willing to disrupt the filming of motion pictures and television programs they found objectionable. The result has been a series of clashes between the industry and gay rights activists.

One of the most intense conflicts involved a 1988 episode of the television series "Midnight Caller" in which a bisexual man who is an HIV carrier intentionally infects women. Homosexual activists found the premise of the show bad enough; they believed that it fed the stereotype that gays were somehow responsible for the disease. Even more disturbing to many gays, however, was the original script in which the man is murdered by one of his former lovers. Gays believed some viewers would see this story as encouragement to direct violence against real people with AIDS.[30]

"Midnight Caller," produced by Lorimar Telepictures, is shot in San Francisco, a city with a large, militant gay community. After several negotiation sessions failed to convince Lorimar to cancel the episode, protestors from the San Francisco AIDS Foundation (SFAF) and the AIDS Coalition to Unleash Power (ACT-UP) decided to take matters into their own hands. Assembling a crowd at the sight of outdoor shooting, they made so much noise that continuing to film the scene was impossible. Because the disruption was obviously going to continue, Lorimar went to court and obtained a temporary restraining order that required protestors to remain at least 100 feet from the set and imposed noise limitations.

Lorimar also had second thoughts, however, and rewrote the ending of the script to eliminate the killing of the villain. In the final version, the hero (Gary Cole, playing an ex-cop turned radio talk-show host) merely confronts the villain, verbally abuses him, roughs him up a little, and vows to seek legal means to stop him from spreading the virus.

As journalists noted, this left the program with less action than the political conflict surrounding it. SFAF and ACT-UP were not satisfied, however. "The show is still exploiting the disease and promoting irrational fears," asserted Rene Durazzo, spokesman for the AIDS Foundation. "We will continue to speak out and take action."[31]

On the night the program was broadcast, a crowd of gay activists gathered outside station KRON-TV, the NBC affiliate in San Francisco. At first they picketed peacefully, shouting protests and carrying signs with such messages as "Nazi Broadcast Company" and "Disconnect Midnight Caller." Eventually, about thirty of the group rushed the front door, overwhelmed security guards, and staged a sit-in in the lobby in an unsuccessful effort to prevent KRON from airing the episode. Even if they had succeeded, of course, the program would still have been broadcast in other cities.

Despite the evident failure of this particular protest, it has most likely made production companies and the networks more careful in their depictions of the AIDS problem. As long as the industry needs villains, however, it will be tempted to cast homosexuals in the role. Consultants such as the Gay Media Task Force are therefore likely to get a good workout in the coming years.

Other conflicts have proved more difficult to handle. Hollywood productions, needless to say, involve a great deal of intimate personal contact. A leading actress can expect that a role she is offered will include kissing. And suppose her leading man is gay? And suppose he is HIV positive? In the mid-1980s, these questions threatened to cause major problems on sets. A successful actress summarized the concern when she said, "If Rock Hudson were cast as your leading man today, what would an actress do? She'd have him fired. ... If you are offered a role on TV, one of the first things you say is, 'Who is the leading man and is he straight [?]' "[32]

The consensus among medical researchers is that AIDS cannot be contracted by kissing or casual contact, but this consensus was not at first accepted by the public. The Screen Actors Guild, attempting to prevent any panic that would make gay performers' lives even harder, passed a resolution in 1985 requiring producers to notify the cast in advance if "open-mouth kissing" would be required in a scene.[33] As it turned out, however, the medical consensus rapidly filtered down to the ordinary performer, actresses stopped worrying about this particular threat, and the requirement to notify the cast about types of kissing fell by the wayside.

Other effects of the epidemic are even harder to deal with because their very existence is arguable. Fifteen years ago, almost all of Hollywood's independent casting directors were male. Today most are female. Some say this change is at least partly due to the fact that many of the male casting directors have died. But other observers claim that there has also been a subtle discrimination at work. Male casting directors had the reputation, in some circles, of being associated with "The Gay Mafia" and supplying homosexual actors at every opportunity. Female casting directors, rightly or wrongly, have the reputation of being more likely to supply a straight actor. As a result, the studios have tended to patronize female-run agencies. Thus the male casting directors who survive physically have languished professionally.

Not everyone endorses the theory that AIDS is responsible for the shift away from male casting directors. Some observers ascribe the increasing numbers of female casting directors to the laudatory advance of women in general within the industry. As with so much else dealing with AIDS and Hollywood, there is no way to confirm or disprove this explanation.

Even more difficult to prove or disprove is the allegation some gay activists propound about another threat to the careers of homosexual artists. According to these people, if there are rumors about the sexual orientation or HIV status of a leading actor or director being considered for a project, insurance companies threaten to deny coverage to the project unless that particular artist is replaced. A scene in the motion picture Longtime Companion dramatizes the way this alleged practice ends the career of a gay (but healthy) actor. Every executive and producer I interviewed denied knowledge of such practices, and all proclaimed that they would fight if they ever discovered them. This belief may be merely a product of the paranoid gossip mill. Yet as a charge impossible to refute or confirm, it adds to the burden of suspicion that gay artists must carry along with their more tangible fears about their health.

HOW NOT TO FIGHT AN EPIDEMIC

Hollywood began to make an organized response to the AIDS epidemic in the late 1980s. As with any other human enterprise, efforts to deal with the disease were hampered by inefficiency, stupidity, and bad faith. The best example of the sorts of difficulties that can obstruct progress in helping those who are stricken is the short but troubled history of the Actors Fund and Hollywood Helps.[34]

The Actors Fund, founded in 1882, is an important charity that provides assistance to any professionals (not just actors) who have worked in the entertainment industry. The Fund offers financial assistance to people in times of need—regardless of the reason. Some are supported by monthly stipends, some by one-time grants, some once a year, and so on, depending on their personal history in the industry and their need.

As befitting the geographic bifurcation of the industry, the Actors Fund's headquarters is in New York but it also has a branch in Los Angeles. The Fund has a variety of institutionalized connections with entertainment industry businesses. For example, Actors Equity (the stage performers' union) has a standard clause in its contract that stipulates that when a show has run for fifteen weeks, the cast must give an extra performance, the proceeds of which must go to the Fund. The Fund has similar close relationships with the other entertainment industry labor unions. It also runs various fund-raising benefits and solicits contributions from individuals.

In 1987, the Fund hired Marcia Smith as its West Coast representative. A former actress, counselor, personal manager, and administrator of volunteer programs, Smith had a background ideally suited to raising money for a Hollywood charity. It soon became obvious to her, however, that AIDS was rendering the old patterns of giving and receiving obsolete. So many people were sick from the new disease that their needs were threatening to overwhelm the organization; there would soon be no money left over for anyone with any other problem, let alone enough to cover those with AIDS.

When she discovered that the union assistance funds were facing the same problem, Smith proposed a cooperative solution. Together, fifteen unions and the Actors Fund set up a separate organization in 1988 called Hollywood Helps. Its purpose was to raise money to assist AIDS victims. (The West Coast benefit premiere of the motion picture *Torch Song Trilogy* officially launched the charity on December 7 of that year.) Smith and the West

Coast staff of the Fund volunteered their time to run the new organization. A separate bank account was opened, and all the money Hollywood Helps raised went into it. When the Actors Fund decided to support someone diagnosed with AIDS, Hollywood Helps would reimburse the Fund for its costs. That left the ordinary Fund accounts unencumbered and thus free to help people with non-AIDS-related problems. Because Smith was in charge of both Hollywood Helps and the western branch of the Actors Fund, she could easily coordinate the financial transactions of the two organizations.

The new charity was immediately successful. "The reason it's been easy to raise money at the grass-roots level for Hollywood Helps is that everybody has worked with someone who has died," explained Smith. At first the studios gave little, but individual contributors were so generous that Hollywood Helps raised $137,000 in 1989, the fourth largest source of support for the Actors Fund. Although Smith found that she could not persuade any male performers to chair benefits, Cher and Madonna volunteered, and several celebrity couples also gave their time.

As a mere appendage of a charity centered in New York, however, this independent activity by the western branch of the Actors Fund created resentment back east. Vincent Vitelli, the Fund's general manager, ordered Smith to turn over control of the Hollywood Helps finances to him. Because she believed that Hollywood Helps, being partly a union organization, was not subject to Actors Fund authority and because she harbored suspicions about Vitelli's accounting practices, Smith refused. On September 20, 1989, Vitelli fired Smith from the Actors Fund, claiming that she had maintained "too high a profile" in her fund-raising efforts for Hollywood Helps, which, he asserted, had damaged the Fund's ability to raise money for non-AIDS causes.

Because he lived on the East Coast, Vitelli evidently did not understand the web of personal obligations that Smith had created in Hollywood through her charity work. She was a living example of the way skill at interpersonal relations produces clout within the industry. Her removal caused a fire storm. The Los Angeles presidents of the Screen Actors Guild, AFTRA, and Actors Equity immediately flew to New York to remonstrate with Vitelli, to no avail. The Theater Authority, a union charity organization that had contributed to Hollywood Helps, announced that it was suspending future donations. The Western Council of the Actors Fund passed a resolution demanding Vitelli's resignation. In January 1990, Smith brought suit, charging defamation of character and illegal dismissal. The trade papers covered the controversy in detail, generating widespread sympathy for Smith and indignation at her dismissal.

Vitelli soon compounded his first mistake. He reacted to the Western Council's insubordination by disbanding it. Ed Asner, Carroll O'Connor, Jean Stapleton, William Shatner, and other well-known performers were booted out. With them went any remaining confidence that Hollywood had in the Actors Fund, and contributions dwindled. At the end of the 1990 fiscal year, the Fund showed a deficit of $1.9 million; plans were made to reduce its financial assistance to needy members of the industry by 23 percent, cut back its staff and benefits, cancel its plans for capital expenditures, and negotiate a restructuring of its bank loans.

That spring, with their West Coast fund-raising in shambles, bad publicity appearing regularly in the trade papers, and Smith's lawsuit hovering, the board of trustees of the Actors Fund ran up the white flag. They fired Vitelli and recruited three dissident former members of the Western Council to join them on the board. They also settled out of court with Marcia Smith. In a few months she found another job as administrator of the Wellness Community, a support group for people with cancer, while continuing voluntarily to run Hollywood Helps from the basement of her home.

In September 1991 the Actors Fund and Hollywood Helps formally reconciled. Representatives from the two organizations now meet regularly, in an atmosphere of good will, to coordinate their charity work. There has as yet been no public announcement about whether this end to the feuding has resulted in a better financial situation for the two organizations.[35]

BETTER RESPONSES

Although the events involving the Actors Fund illustrate one way that incompetence can make dealing with an epidemic harder, there are also examples of the means by which intelligence can combine with compassion to result in progress.

One hopeful sign is the manner in which members of the industry have applied one of the talents at which they excel—fund-raising—to the problem of AIDS. Hollywood Helps is not the only charity that has arisen since the mid-1980s to raise money for AIDS victims. The town has bloomed with generosity, spending an enormous amount of time, money, and effort in fighting the disease. The odds are very good that during any given week there is at least one benefit scheduled to raise money for the epidemic's victims in general or for some specific cause associated with them. Many of these events support organizations that are not specifically connected to the entertainment industry, such as AIDS Project/Los Angeles (APLA), the Pediatric AIDS Foundation, the AIDS Hospice Foundation, the AIDS Healthcare Foundation, and Project Angelfood. The entertainment industry is so willing to help that Stephen Bennett, CEO of APLA, estimates that between 20 and 25 percent of his organization's $12 million annual budget is donated by studios and networks—and this figure does not include individual contributions from industry professionals.[36]

Indeed, there are now so many charities dealing with the disease that a common complaint is that the system of raising money is too scattered and that it would benefit from some centralized coordination.[37] This seems a fairly minor problem, however, and will probably be resolved soon.

Another hopeful approach originated on the fringes of the industry and gradually spread to its core. In early 1987, few companies in Hollywood had coherent policies or programs regarding what to do about sick employees, what sorts of information to make available to their workers, how to prevent panicky discrimination against homosexuals, and other related problems. In April of that year, however, the Entertainment Industries Council (EIC), a nonprofit organization devoted to using the power of the industry to fight substance abuse and related social problems, sponsored a conference at the Directors Guild on ways in which Hollywood could help the nation deal with the AIDS threat. More than 100 television, radio, and film professionals attended.[38]

Speaking at the conference was Dr. Thomas Backer, a psychologist from UCLA's medical school with long-term interests in the psychology of creativity and in helping creative people reduce stress in their lives. Backer spoke about the policies adopted by some American companies (such as Wells Fargo Bank and Levi Strauss) to assist their employees in dealing with AIDS. At the conclusion of his presentation, Backer asked for the business cards of anyone interested in forming a volunteer committee to look into ways that the entertainment industry could adopt a similar strategy. The half-dozen volunteers from that meeting evolved, over the course of the next two months, into the Entertainment Industry Workplace AIDS Committee (EIWAC), with Backer as chair and more than thirty corporate and union executives as members.[39]

The committee members agreed that they would not become another fund-raising organization, or an advocacy group, or an institution that attempted to influence the depiction of AIDS in the media. Other organizations, they decided, were already fulfilling those functions. Their purpose would be to supply information to companies and unions about how to deal with the epidemic.[40]

In that capacity, EIWAC has sponsored a variety of useful projects that have helped to calm the atmosphere in Hollywood's workplaces. Their first event, in April 1988, was a conference that brought together labor leaders and industry executives to hear discussions of practical ways of developing AIDS policies and programs. Later in the year they conducted a study on the incidence and impact of the epidemic on the entertainment industry.[41] In 1989 they produced a 150-page book and information kit for the smaller employer (distributed free of charge) that included instructions on how to educate employees about the disease. At the same time they launched a consultation service, offering volunteer speakers from the committee to assist companies trying to develop an AIDS policy.[42] In the ensuing years they have become a well-known and well-used resource for companies and unions that are trying to prevent the spread of AIDS, deal with those who are ill, and forestall uninformed and hysterical reactions to the disease among workers.

So the news is both bad and good. As an international problem, the AIDS epidemic will not be solved in Hollywood. And given the high-stress nature of the entertainment community and its large population of high-risk people, there is not much that can be done about the intensification of anxiety that accompanies the advance of the disease. But Hollywoodites are tough. Accustomed to working in an atmosphere of anxiety, they are capable of functioning despite the burden of stress they carry. And so although AIDS has made a bad emotional situation worse, it has not paralyzed the industry. Paranoid or not, Hollywoodites have begun to work together to deal with the disease. In fact, the irony of the epidemic is that the Hollywood community seems to be considerably ahead of the rest of the country in acknowledging the existence of the epidemic and in mobilizing to meet its challenges.

APPENDIX:
CATEGORIZING AIDS DEATHS IN OBITUARIES

To adjust for the tendency of people to evade the stigma of an AIDS death, I kept track of the following categories of obits:

1. *Confirmed.* A death was listed under this heading if AIDS was listed as the cause or if there was a statement that contributions were to be sent to an AIDS research foundation or a gay or lesbian organization.

2. *Probable.* A death was listed in this category if the victim was a male American, the cause of death was given as cancer or pneumonia, there was no wife named as a survivor, and the victim was 50 years of age or younger.

3. *Possible.* A death was listed in this category if the victim was a male American, 50 years of age or younger, the cause of death was unlisted, or the obit contained the phrase "after a long illness." This category also includes persons, irrespective of their obituaries, for whom there was good reason to suspect an AIDS death (if I knew the victim, for example).

Some people in the industry have argued with me that this method will still undercount the total number of AIDS deaths because many of the sick have been extremely creative about concealing the true nature of their illness. Perhaps so. Nevertheless, I feel that to loosen the "possible" category still further would make the whole enterprise merely speculative, which is what I am trying to avoid.

PART FOUR

Political Paradoxes

6

Political Ideology

*A*LTHOUGH IT MAY SOMETIMES SEEM as if Hollywood is a self-contained world, its inhabitants are of course members of a larger society. But just as the economics and psychology of Hollywood are unusual, so are the political views of its residents. This is no accident. In fact, the economic and sociological environment of the screen entertainment industry is the major force causing the political ideology of Hollywood to be eccentric. Before we pursue that theme, however, it may be helpful first to define ideology.

People's political ideas tend to hang together in recognizable patterns. When those patterns are coherent, they form a system of beliefs and values called an ideology. Since the 1930s Americans have classified the two dominant ideological tendencies in their politics as either liberal or conservative.

Conflicts in societies tend to bring out different ideologies. One important conflict in modern society is between economic classes, that is, between those people who have more of what there is to get and those who have less. In general, economic liberals favor the lower classes in this fight by supporting government activity that equalizes wealth and power or access to them. Economic conservatives favor the upper classes by opposing government interference with the workings of the market. Economic liberals typically favor (and economic conservatives typically oppose) graduated income taxes, regulation of business, affirmative action programs, and increased government spending on welfare, education, and health. Consistent with their support of society's less wealthy people, liberals tend to favor workers in general, and labor unions in particular, in their eternal conflict with management. As a rule, conservatives regard unions as a corrupt interference with market forces.

Another conflict that takes place more on the social than the economic plane is the conflict between those who value personal expression and those who emphasize social responsibility. Social liberals oppose government intrusion into personal life; social conservatives endorse it. Thus, liberals typically favor legalized abortion and gay rights legislation while opposing prayer in public schools. Conservatives take the opposite position on all three issues. One of the reasons that discussion of American ideology is so confusing is that liberals usually *endorse* government activity in the economic sphere but *oppose* it in the social sphere, while conservatives endorse it in the social sphere but oppose it in the economic sphere. Partisans of each ideology can thus be found both recommending and resisting government vigor in the same argument, which does not make for lucidity of discussion.

Another factor leading to confusion is that both liberals and conservatives seem to be inconsistent on some issues. It might be assumed, for example, that conservatives would endorse gun control and liberals oppose it, because gun control would mean government intervention in the individuals' freedom to handle firearms according to their personal desires. In fact, the opposite is true: Conservatives generally think government should not regulate ownership of guns, while liberals are eager to regulate it.

When it comes to foreign policy, the two sides seem to revert to a sort of global class loyalty. Liberals think that most of the problems in the world are caused by injustice and poverty, and therefore they try to deal with international trouble by offering sympathy and economic aid. Conservatives think that most of the problems in the world are the result of people trying to take what is not theirs, and therefore they try to deal with international trouble by using (or threatening to use) armed force. Conservatives usually support large defense budgets and the use of the military in foreign relations, while liberals generally argue for lower budgets and a reliance on diplomacy.

Underlying these differences of principle and further muddying the conceptual waters, there frequently seems to be a difference of temperament. Conservatives often seem to identify with society's winners and insiders, and consequently, being generally content, they tend to endorse institutions and regimes that support the status quo. Liberals seem to identify with society's losers and outsiders; being generally disgruntled, they seek change in institutions and regimes. People who are subjectively satisfied with the world will therefore tend to express conservative allegiances and vote for conservative parties, however wretched those people's objective conditions might seem to outside observers. Conversely, people who are subjectively discontented will tend to express liberal sentiments and vote for liberal parties, however delightful their lives might seem to others. It is useful to keep these tendencies in mind when discussing Hollywood's political ideology.

In the normal use of language, a liberal is on the left and a conservative on the right. Sometimes leftists prefer to call themselves progressives. Occasionally, a conservative will prefer to be referred to as a traditionalist. At the extremes, both may be radical.

In the United States, the Democrats have generally been the more liberal party. The typical Democrat thus endorses government intervention in the economy but not in personal life and would rather have the administration favor human rights over national power in foreign policy.

HISTORICAL IMPRESSIONS OF
HOLLYWOOD IDEOLOGY

For two generations, observers of the Hollywood scene have claimed that it is a left-wing town. During the old studio era, the most powerful studio head, Louis B. Mayer, was an enthusiastic conservative Republican; but to judge by the rather spotty records available on campaign contributions, the other moguls tended to support Democrats, at least at the presidential level.[1] Their employees had the reputation of being anything from liberal to leftist radical. A nonscientific poll taken by a trade paper during the 1936 presidential campaign concluded that the motion picture community was intending to vote for Roosevelt by a ratio of six to one.[2] At about the same time, writer Philip Dunne estimated that "probably 70 percent of the writers, directors, actors, and so on were liberally inclined."[3] Campaign contribution records from the 1940s suggest that the trend continued at least through World War II.[4] Although it is impossible to obtain accurate figures about the comparative level of Communist activity in Hollywood in the 1930s and 1940s, historians suggest that the Party raised a substantial percentage of its funds among movie folk in that era.[5]

The federal anti-Communist crusade and the blacklist that began in 1947 not only obliterated the Party, but also suppressed left-wing politics generally in Hollywood. As recently as the early 1960s, the industry was close to being apolitical, and there was little comment from outside about its leanings. With the decline of the power of the studios, however, the "normal" liberalism of people in Hollywood began to reassert itself. A few celebrities worked for Eugene McCarthy in 1968 and George McGovern in 1972, but their numbers were not large enough to inspire much comment.[6] In a popular book called *The View from Sunset Boulevard* (published in 1979), however, Ben Stein attracted a good deal of attention when he alleged the overwhelming liberalism of the people who create television programs. Although it did not include the words "liberal," "radical," or "leftist," Stein's discussion of the supposed values and opinions of the television elite clearly placed that group on the progressive side of the spectrum.[7]

As the nation swung to the right in the 1980s, Hollywood seemed to emerge as not only one of the few remaining liberal communities but also as a place of remarkably unanimous views. When journalist Ronald Brownstein asked actor Rob Lowe (whose extracurricular frolicking at the 1988 Democratic convention overshadowed the fact that he was a bona fide delegate) if he personally knew any conservatives in Hollywood, Lowe answered, "I can't think of one example."[8] There were some, but they seemed to be either outnumbered or outshouted.

As its liberal reputation has grown, the town has become a principal conservative bogeyman. Right-wing commentators often refer to the motion
picture and television industries as being on "the left coast." The Media Research Center publishes *TV etc.,* a bimonthly "review of the entertainment
industry and the Hollywood left," a perspective that, it has no doubt, dominates the industry.[9] Writing in the conservative magazine *National Review,*
journalist David Brooks contends that "for many people in Hollywood, progressive politics are a professional and psychological necessity."[10]

POLITICAL OPINION IN HOLLYWOOD

Amidst all the confident assertion about Hollywood's liberalism, however, it
is not possible to find systematic evidence. No one has ever taken a survey of
the beliefs, values, and opinions of important people in the screen entertainment industry and then compared the answers to the ones given on the same
survey by the American public as a whole. If such a poll were taken, however, it would at last be possible to confirm or deny Hollywood liberalism
with something better than anecdotes and polemics.

I culled forty-seven questions from a national Times Mirror/Gallup survey
and administered them to a group of thirty-five Hollywood opinion leaders,
mostly during the summer of 1990. The opinion leaders consisted of studio
heads, presidents of artists' unions, trade association leaders, editors and
publishers of trade papers, leaders of interest groups, and various industry
people who were active in social and political organizations. The questions
were chosen to draw forth the political opinions of the respondents in relation to general ideology and specific issues. Because statistics about the
American public's distribution of opinion on these questions were available
from the Times Mirror/Gallup surveys, I was thus able to compare "American opinion" to "Hollywood opinion" in a systematic, quantitative manner.
Readers interested in some of the procedures I used can read the Methodological Appendix at the end of this chapter.

The expressed views of these thirty-five opinion leaders do nothing to dis-
pel the notion that Hollywood is a liberal bastion. As Table 6.1 shows, when
Americans are asked to place themselves on the ideological spectrum, fewer
than one-third admit to being liberal, while between one-third and two-
fifths claim to be conservative. In Hollywood, however, 60 percent of those
questioned describe themselves as liberal, while only 14 percent consider
themselves conservative. In addition, a fair number of Hollywood respondents chose (left-wing) "radical" or some comparable designation to describe
their belief system.

The party identification question reinforces the ideology question. Republicans are a rare breed in Hollywood: Fewer than 10 percent of the survey re-

TABLE 6.1 General Ideological Positioning: The American Public and Hollywood Opinion Leaders, 1990

	American Public (percent)	Hollywood Opinion Leaders (percent)
When it comes to politics, do you usually think of yourself as a liberal, a conservative, or what? (Times/Mirror, 1987)		
Liberal	30	60[a]
Conservative	43	14
Other	3	23
Neither/DK	24	3
Self-placement on seven-point scale (here collapsed) (NORC, 1990)		
Liberal	26[a]	
Conservative	35	
Moderate, middle/road	35	
DK/no answer	4	
In politics as of today, do you consider yourself a *Republican, Democrat*, an *Independent*, or what?		
Republican	28	9[b]
Democrat	33	49
Independent	28	40
None/DK/NA	11	2

Statistical significance (based on chi-square):
[a] significant at .001 level
[b] significant at .05 level

spondents claimed allegiance to the more conservative party, while almost half proclaimed loyalty to the Democrats. ("I'm a Democrat. I've always been a Democrat. I always want to be a Democrat," stated one head of a major studio during an interview.) Forty percent of this sample, a significantly larger proportion than in the general population, claim to be independent, and several made comments to the effect that they did not identify with either party because neither was left-wing enough.

Mere self-placement on an ideological questionnaire is not conclusive, however. Many scholarly studies have established the difficulty of deducing people's issue positions from either their professed ideology or their party identification.[11] It is always necessary to ask about specific public policy issues and then see if the answers are consistent with ideological loyalty.

The industry leaders' answers to specific issue questions do nothing to shake Hollywood from its position on the left side of the spectrum. As Table 6.2 shows, on a variety of issues, industry opinion leaders are at least as eco-

TABLE 6.2   Economic Liberalism: The American Public and Hollywood Opinion
Leaders, 1990

	American Public (percent)	Hollywood Opinion Leaders (percent)
If you had a say in making up the federal budget this year, for which of the following programs would you like to see spending increased?		
The homeless	69	86[a]
The environment	72	94[b]
Health care	81	86
Public schools	77	94[a]
Defense	19	3[a]
Favor income tax increase to reduce federal deficit (Times/Mirror, 1987)	30	65[c]
Agree that "the strength of this country today is mostly based on the success of American business."	82	66[c]
Agree that "government regulation of business usually does more harm than good."	60	36[b]
Agree that "labor unions have too much power."	60	19[c]

Statistical significance (based on chi-square):
[a] significant at .05 level
[b] significant at .01 level
[c] significant at .001 level

nomically liberal as the general population. Americans as a group endorse the idea of spending more federal money on the homeless, the environment, health care, and public schools; an even larger percentage of Hollywood opinion leaders are willing to increase the budget to satisfy those needs. The motion picture and television elite is more supportive of the idea of raising taxes, less admiring of American business, more favorably inclined toward government regulation of business, and less suspicious of labor unions than is the public in general.

When we consider that the Hollywood sample is composed mainly of the successful and well-to-do, these findings are remarkable. Wealthy people, as zillions of surveys have confirmed, tend to be economic conservatives. Indeed, it can be argued that any other ideology is irrational for them. By supporting more taxes and more spending, for example, the members of the Hollywood elite are obviously endorsing policies that strike at their own pocketbooks. By favoring government regulation of business, they are endorsing in the abstract a policy that they would be likely to oppose if it were applied specifically to them. What may be on display here is the only concentration of educated, wealthy, powerful economic liberals in the country. The first paradox of Hollywood's politics is that even its wealthy citizens endorse an ideology far more appropriate to the poor and oppressed.

Before attempting to explain this phenomenon, however, we should examine other policy positions. There isn't necessarily a connection between economic and social liberalism. The Times Mirror poll replicates the findings of many other surveys in its conclusion that a large number of Americans, although liberal on economic questions, are decidedly conservative on social issues. They are, for example, supportive of government spending on health and welfare but opposed to gay rights and in favor of prayer in school.

Not so these Hollywood opinion leaders. They are at least as liberal on social as on economic questions, and on several issues are far more left-wing than the general population. As Table 6.3 shows, Hollywood leaders are overwhelmingly pro-choice, opposed to the suppression of unpopular ideas, and accepting of interracial dating. They are far more tolerant of homosexuality (this is, remember, an expression of personal values, not company policy) than is the public and much less concerned about communism. Consistent with liberals in general, the one issue on which they appear willing to invite government regulation of personal behavior is in the area of gun control, for they are almost uniformly hostile to the National Rifle Association.

In the area of foreign policy, world events were in such a state of flux during and preceding the period in which the surveys were administered that I do not have much confidence in the results. The collapse of communism in Eastern Europe, the change in Soviet policy toward the United States, and the invasion of Kuwait by Iraq all operated to throw opinion into disorder. Because of the datedness of the questions, I have not included these results in a table. For what it is worth, however, Hollywood opinion leaders showed themselves just as liberal on these measures as on the others. They were consistently pro-peace, supportive of negotiation over confrontation, and suspicious of U.S. meddling beyond its borders.

DETAILS

Because this sample of opinion leaders is overwhelmingly but not unanimously liberal, we should ask whether the results show ideological differences based upon income. Although most of these respondents are financially comfortable, not all are, and it is logical to wonder if the wealthier among them lean to the right on economic or other questions.

They do not. On none of the questions do rising levels of income correlate with different answers. Not even when they are asked if they support a federal tax increase do the rich in this sample answer any differently than the merely middle class. In fact, simply looking at the responses to the economic

TABLE 6.3   Social Liberalism: The American Public and Hollywood Opinion Leaders, 1990

	American Public (percent)	Hollywood Opinion Leaders (percent)
Favor changing the laws to make it more difficult for a woman to get an abortion	41	9[a]
Favor a constitutional amendment permitting prayer in public schools (Times/Mirror, 1987)	74	16[a]
Agree that "it's all right for blacks and whites to date each other."	53	97[a]
Agree that "books that contain dangerous ideas should be banned from public school libraries."	53	6[a]
Agree that "AIDS might be God's punishment for immoral sexual behavior."	42	6[a]
Describe themselves as		
a religious person (1987)	62	24[a]
an anti-communist	69	37[a]
a supporter of the women's movement (men only)	46	75[b]
a supporter of the National Rifle Association (1987)	35	9[b]
an environmentalist	59	71
a supporter of gay rights (1987)	12	68[a]

Statistical significance (based on chi-square):
[a] significant at .001 level
[b] significant at .01 level

questions, one would think that the respondents were a sample of poor people from some urban ghetto or Appalachian village, not a gathering of the relatively wealthy.

However, small but noticeable differences can be observed between the sexes. Because only nine of the thirty-five respondents are women, it is not possible to compare their answers with the men's in a statistically significant way. Nevertheless, the data establish that the females are, if anything, even more liberal than the males. All the women (as opposed to 80 to 90 percent of the men) endorsed increased federal funding for the homeless, the environment, health care, and public schools. Given their status as careerists, it is not startling that all the women in the sample strongly oppose making abortion more difficult. (Three of the men held anti-abortion views.) It is perhaps more surprising that all nine women were united in opposing prayer in public schools, banning books containing "dangerous ideas" from public school libraries, and viewing AIDS as a possible divine punishment for immoral sexual behavior. Women are also slightly more supportive of the "peace" movement of the late 1980s and slightly more anti-business. In fact, almost every conservative response in the survey, few as they were, came from men.

Because women are continuing to move into positions of authority within the motion picture and television industries, these differences suggest that in the future, liberal values may dominate Hollywood even more than they do now. This, however, is not necessarily a sure thing. The women in this survey are pioneers in a formerly man's world. As part of a social vanguard, they can perhaps be expected to be more radical than the sisters who will follow them. Nevertheless, this survey does suggest strongly that the continued sexual integration of the Hollywood power structure will not diminish the industry's leftist perspective.

WHY LIBERALISM?

The conventional wisdom, then, is not mistaken. The people who create American screen entertainment operate in an environment that is without doubt permeated by liberal social and political attitudes. Given the fact that liberalism is normally the ideology of the poor, the downtrodden, the despised, and the outsiders, it is puzzling that these comfortable, influential, respected insiders should endorse it. What could explain such anomalous opinions?

Social scientists, looking at these remarkable differences of opinion between Hollywood and the rest of the nation, might conclude that the differences are actually an illusion. These scientists might argue that the apparent differences are really an artifact of the fairly high educational level of the Hollywood respondents. This suggestion would be fruitless, however. When the results of this survey are subjected to statistical controls, Hollywood's educational attainments do not account for its liberalism. We must look elsewhere for an explanation.

There are, in general, three theories about why Hollywood is dominated by liberalism. The first comes from within the industry. People in Hollywood generally explain the phenomenon as being a natural outgrowth of the artistic life. Artists, they suggest, must have empathy with other people. With empathy comes compassion, and with compassion comes liberalism. Thus Barry Diller, chairman and chief executive officer of 20th Century Fox, suggests, "This creative process forces you to be somewhat humanistic. ... It comes with the work."[12] (Note that Diller, a career executive, seems to be identifying himself with artists. This is a provocative point to which we shall return.) Director Arthur Hiller agrees that there is a connection between the artistic career and left-wing politics. "I think that most creative people are liberal. Part of being creative is having feelings. I'm not saying that other people don't, but the creative community lives on its feelings a lot more, so you care more, maybe that touch more for the oppressed or various causes."[13] Producer David Wolper concurs. "A guy making automobiles, social consciousness isn't part of his everyday life. [But] people working in Hollywood discuss it in scripts, they talk about it all day."[14]

There may be something to this theory. Artists must be emotionally sensitive. Moreover, it is true that a worker spending all day making automobiles has no need to think about ideas, whereas a Hollywood artist cannot escape them. Yet this interpretation of the political leaning of Hollywood is unsatisfying. For one thing, it is self-serving, and we should always be suspicious of explanations based upon the moral superiority of the explainer. For another, self-assertion is at least as important a component of the artistic temperament as empathy, and self-assertion does not usually imply compassion for others. In addition, Hollywoodites have earned an international reputation as people who are quite capable of pursuing their individual and collective self-interest with ruthless, unsentimental calculation. Although it is plausible that Diller, Hiller, and Wolper are largely motivated by altruism, it is impossible to believe that most people in the industry are dominated, either in their personal lives or in their political outlook, by empathetic concern for other people. To understand Hollywood liberalism, then, we will have to look elsewhere than to the selfless humanism of artists.

A second explanation for Hollywood's liberalism is based on the assumption that people who create television programs and motion pictures are part of a "new class" composed of employees in the information and public service industries. Observers who make this argument claim that workers in these newer sectors of the economy are hostile to older, powerful institutions such as business, the military, and religion. As Ben Stein wrote in *The View from Sunset Boulevard*, "TV people are ... a class that once was powerless, dominated by other classes. ... They realize that other power centers must be denigrated and humiliated if they are to take the top positions. ... So the people who make television create characters and situations that attack their class enemies." As part of this assault on American power centers, Hollywood people ally themselves with underdog groups such as the poor and ethnic minorities.[15]

Again, there is some plausibility to this explanation for Hollywood liberalism. It is indisputable that the media are now an extremely powerful institution (or set of institutions) in the economy and society of the United States. In addition, there is some evidence that people in other media institutions such as journalism share a liberal political stance, and the "new class" hypothesis offers an explanation as to why this would be so.[16]

As with the first explanation, however, the new class theory is not completely satisfying. For one thing, the notion of a new class is a rather muddled idea because it does not make clear exactly who is supposed to be a member of the class or what their attitudes are supposed to be.[17] There is no clear picture of who makes up the group: Is it moguls, executives, distributors, independent producers, celebrity artists, obscure artists, agents, or all of them that are allegedly attempting to "create characters and situations that denigrate their class enemies"?

Second, the notion of a class implies that its members are conscious of its existence, recognize the existence of other, rival classes, and cooperate to further its interests against the interests of other classes. It is difficult to imagine, however, any group of people acting less like the members of a class than the entertainment "media elite." Although they do recognize that they form a community in some sense, they are so riven with personal and professional conflicts that it strains credibility to imagine them as participating in some sort of concerted action. Besides the cutthroat competition that characterizes business relationships and the personal resentment that arises from the employment situation, there are the various hostilities that arise over structural conflicts of interest. Independent producers resent the studios, both the studios and the independents execrate the networks, the unions are suspicious of the employers' labor practices, exhibitors detest distributors and vice versa, artists abhor the producers, and everybody complains that his or her work is mutilated and insulted by the philistines who control the money supply. It is impossible to accept that such a feuding group imagines itself an institution and that it acts cohesively in opposition to other institutions.

I believe that the pattern of liberalism evident in Hollywood beliefs, values, and actions can better be explained by examining the forces *within* the Hollywood community rather than by hypothesizing an imagined conflict between people in the industry and institutions *outside* that community. That is, people in Hollywood do not see themselves as part of a media elite in relation to other elites. Their lives and their ideologies are formed from individual rather than social struggle. There are, I think, three important forces causing so many among them to adopt a liberal outlook on life and politics. First and most important, because the existential situation of artists in Hollywood is one of eternal frustration, resentment, and paranoia, even the successful among them come to adopt the perspective of social outsiders. Although objectively their lives may offer wealth and adulation, subjectively they *feel* abused and exploited. The industry thus contains many millionaires who identify with the wretched of the earth. This is even more true of the great majority who are not successful. The spectacle of rich celebrities pronouncing themselves in solidarity with, for example, South African blacks may seem either hypocritical or weird to outside observers, but this feeling of solidarity is a genuine expression of psychological truth for Hollywood artists.

Reinforcing the feeling of being ill used is the ever-present economic uncertainty. Historically, in every democratic country, groups that traditionally suffer from extreme insecurity of income—one-crop farmers, fishermen, miners, lumbermen—usually vote in high numbers for leftist parties.[18] Any list of people with insecure incomes must include the actors, screenwriters, directors, and everyone else who ever came to Hollywood pursuing a dream and found themselves parking cars or waiting tables instead.

Artists are thus the most left-wing of Hollywood's citizens. The number of respondents to my survey are too small to establish statistical significance; however, dividing my sample into artists and non-artists (administrators, executives, journalists, etc.) yields some interesting divisions on the representative questions shown in Table 6.4.

Although the artists are clearly the most leftward part of the Hollywood community (at least on economic issues—there are no differences on social issues), the non-artists are also considerably more liberal than the public at large. This may be partly due to the fact that many people in Hollywood with jobs that are technically non-artistic nevertheless identify with artists. The earlier quotation from Barry Diller suggests such an interpretation. Because their own jobs are creative in the sense that they make decisions about creativity, executives such as Diller may come to consider themselves artists and thereby share many artistic attitudes. Or it may be that the sheer number of artists (and the fact that non-artists must constantly deal with them) means that the artistic point of view dominates the town's intellectual perspective.

Whatever the explanation, artistic liberalism seems to exert a strong influence over the general political outlook of Hollywood. It is not, however, the only force for left-wing politics. Hollywood contains a much higher percentage of Jews than does American society as a whole. Hollywood was virtually founded by Jews (the only important early industry business figure who was not Jewish was Walt Disney), and its important decisionmaking positions have been dominated by them ever since.[19] All of today's studio heads are Jewish. Fourteen of the thirty-five people in my sample of opinion leaders, or 40 percent, are of Jewish background. (About 2 percent of the general population of the United States considers itself Jewish.) If Jews as a group are more liberal than non-Jews, they could be expected to exert a leftward push on political opinion in Hollywood.

Such is indeed the case. As the classic outsiders in Western society, Jews have a long history of progressive political activity in Europe and the United States. Many researchers over the years have concluded, in the summarizing words of one scholar, "Jews are more liberal than any other white ethnocultural group" in the United States.[20]

This generalization is borne out by my sample, although the numbers are so small that we can place no statistical confidence in the results. Of eleven respondents opposed to a tax increase, only one is Jewish; of the five who would permit prayer in public schools, none is Jewish; of the four who are willing to call themselves conservative, none is Jewish; of the three who fa-

TABLE 6.4   Liberalism and Hollywood Artists, Hollywood Non-artists, and the American Public (in percent)

	Artists	Non-artists	American Public
Identifying as liberal	75	50	30
Favoring tax increase	75	56	30
Favoring more spending on homeless	92	81	67
Favoring government regulation of business	79	50	33

vor stricter abortion controls, none is Jewish; of the four who continue to be suspicious of the Soviet Union, none is Jewish. Although it seems clear that Hollywood would still be a liberal community even if it contained no Jews, the high proportion of Jews in the industry nevertheless reinforces its dominant tendency.

Finally, although it is difficult to support this assertion with evidence, it seems clear that the high percentage of homosexuals in the industry also adds to its leftward slant. For good reasons, gays feel themselves part of an oppressed minority. That consciousness leads to dissatisfaction with the status quo, which in turn leads to liberal philosophy and liberal voting.

Hollywood is thus dominated by people who have reasons to hold grudges against the "powers that be." This position is independent of their status as members of a "media elite"; indeed, it is in direct opposition to an elite consciousness. Because Hollywoodites feel oppressed, their ideology favors society's lower classes and endorses change in the prevailing economic, social, and political arrangements. Celebrities or struggling artists, they are liberals.

The industry's social institutions also tend to foster the liberal consciousness of the group. Research has shown that when people with a reason to vote left wing are able to communicate readily among themselves, their liberal leanings are reinforced.[21] In Hollywood, the constant shmoozing, award-giving, celebrity-eventing, and lunching that are part of the off-screen world of the industry facilitate the personal interaction that helps translate private grievances into social philosophies. A synergy arises in which personal outlooks multiply by peer confirmation, and many individuals come to have the same value system and interpretation of reality.

Although the resulting liberalism is a consensus, it is not unanimous. My sample confirms evidence available in the trade papers that conservatives, although a small minority, nevertheless exist in Hollywood. Ronald Reagan was unusual but not unique. With a few prominent exceptions, such as Reagan, Charlton Heston, and Arnold Schwarzenegger, the conservatives tend to keep quiet. They are so outnumbered that they are intimidated, and in addition, they are reluctant to offend the powerful liberals who dominate most of the important institutions. Hollywood's public activism, therefore, is even more liberal than its private ideology. This fact has many consequences for both the image of the industry and the organizing that takes place within its boundaries.

THE CONSEQUENCES OF LIBERALISM

We can now see that Hollywood is all of a piece. The risky economic situation, the nightmarish sociological circumstances, and the peculiar political ideology are not accidental and unconnected phenomena but parts of a social system that add up to a coherent whole. If unemployment were lower, if artists had more control over their work, if the market were more stable, if the audience were easier to predict, if the community were not so stress-ridden, if the place did not have so much glamour, then the people who lived there would have different lives, would see the world differently, and would possess different political values. As it is, Hollywood both attracts and produces an alienated citizenry, and such people tend to be liberal.

Despite the suspicions of conservatives, the nearly unanimous liberalism of Hollywood is not the result of a conspiracy. Whatever the source of their views, people in the film and television industries have every right to hold opinions and to express them to their fellow citizens. Besides, the important people in virtually every other industry are heavily conservative, at least on economic issues. They vote overwhelmingly Republican and provide that party with a luxuriant financial base. It is only fair that the liberals get some support too.

Still, because the entertainment media occupy such an important place in the national consciousness, it is disquieting that the people who create movies and television programs show so little diversity in their outlook. Most of us assume that ordinary people learn a great deal about life, love, business, and democracy from the entertainment media. If media products are purveying a one-sided ideology, their potential impact on our society and its politics is immense. If entertainment is conveying a species of disguised propaganda to a trusting public, then it is considerably more than a harmless diversion; it may even be dangerous. It is important, then, to try to discover whether the political perspective of Hollywood seeps into the product it offers the public.

This is not an easy question to answer. Although it might be presumed that liberal artists would choose to create liberal entertainment, they are mightily constrained by market forces. No one wants to labor over a didactic film or television program that the public will refuse to see; and financiers will certainly reject projects that smack of outright indoctrination, for such projects have the reputation of being surefire audience repellents.

Moreover, it is very difficult to study the question of political slant in screen entertainment because it involves ascertaining the meaning that artists

who create a film or television program intend it to convey and then survey-
ing the audience to discover whether that meaning was received. Attempting
either end of this research traps anyone in a quagmire of difficulty. Because
of the collaborative nature of screen entertainment, it is often impossible to
identify the author of a film or television program, and even when it is possible, the author is frequently unavailable for interviews, inarticulate, or not
honest with answers. If authors are hard to pin down, the consumers of entertainment are even more mercurial. Even when audiences are somehow re-
constructed in the laboratory, they often turn out to interpret what they see
in astonishing ways. In one famous research project, for example, some of
the people who watched the television series "All in the Family" interpreted
it as endorsing the bigoted opinions of its main character, Archie Bunker.[22] If
a message that seems as clear-cut as the one in this program can be interpreted in such a perverse manner, it is impossible to make any assumptions
about the meaning of other entertainments, most of which deliver a message
that is much more ambiguous than the message of "All in the Family." Consequently, there are only partial and provisional answers to questions about
the extent to which Hollywood's ideology colors its products. Through the
years, many writers have accused motion pictures and television programs
of containing all manner of hidden or manifest ideological messages. These
accusations usually turn out to spring from the fears of the writer: Conservatives see liberal propaganda, liberals suspect conservative indoctrination.
The "real meaning" of a film such as *Rambo: First Blood, Part II* can be interpreted as either left- or right-wing, without the millions who paid to see it
being consulted at all.[23] This does not mean that screen entertainment
carries no ideological message—only that we have not yet learned how to
measure it properly.

There was one research project, however, in which an effort was made to
apply social science methodology to the question of whether motion pictures
have become more liberal over the years. The authors of that study concluded that from the 1940s to the 1980s, films tended to become more permissive of nontraditional sexual behavior, more favorable to minority citizens, and more negative toward both the military and business.[24] Although
these conclusions must be taken with a grain of salt (partly because they
were not based on any kind of audience research), they are consistent with
intuition. These conclusions reflect the social and political attitudes that
would be expected if the industry's ideological biases were affecting its products. (I am not aware of any comparable study in regard to television programs.)

Although there is no good evidence that television presents a liberal bias,
there is abundant proof that on certain issues, some Hollywood producers
are attempting to move it in that direction. As we will see in Chapter 7, television entertainment is increasingly viewed within the industry as a vehicle

of "educational" programming. Although it is impossible to say that the medium has been a tool of propaganda in the past, there is no doubt that some in Hollywood will try to use it as one in the future.

METHODOLOGICAL APPENDIX

In 1987 the Times Mirror Company, in cooperation with the Gallup Poll, launched a massive effort to survey American social and political attitudes. The Gallup organization used a "nationally representative sample" of 4,244 adults chosen in accord with standard statistical methodology. Their goal was to probe the public's religious, social, and political attitudes, factual knowledge about public affairs, personal security, and specific issue positions.[25] In 1990 the survey was repeated, with most of the original questions reappearing. In a fine display of generosity, the Times Mirror Company has made this huge data bank available to scholars.

Because the Hollywood "community" is so ambiguous, I had to somehow define clearly the type of people whose opinions I would gather. I decided to try to gather the views of those people who might be said to have the most influence on the ideological tone of the community. Those who have some clout over the content of films and television (and the more the better) and/or those who are active in social and political causes (so that they can be presumed to have some influence over the thinking of others) qualified as opinion leaders.

After years of research to secure the names of those who either head important organizations or are very active in social causes (or both), I compiled a list of fifty-eight of these opinion leaders. The thirty-five people I managed to survey constitute 60 percent of this group. The respondents included chief executive officers of three of the major studios, the presidents of all five of the artists' trade unions, the chief executives of five of the most important trade associations (both motion picture and television), the leaders of four of the most active interest groups, the editor or publisher of the three most important trade papers, plus an assortment of citizens whose intense participation in social and political groups and causes makes them influential. Two of the three men generally regarded as the most powerful in the industry were included in the survey.

Because my survey was administered by a single scholar rather than by a squad of paid interviewers, it took longer to complete than the second Times Mirror survey, in which interviewing lasted from late 1989 to May 1990. Three of my respondents were interviewed in the summer of 1989, twenty-six in June, July, and August 1990, and six around Christmas 1990. Consequently, although neither dataset is collected from a single point in time, the "center of gravity" of the Times Mirror study is the spring of 1990 and mine is the summer of 1990. This makes them generally comparable.

Because most of the 1987 Times Mirror questions were repeated in the more recent survey, the distribution of opinion in Hollywood on various questions can be compared directly to the distribution of opinion among the general population on identical questions. There are a few exceptions, for Gallup did not repeat every 1987 question in the second survey. Most important, Gallup failed to repeat the general ideological question: When it comes to politics, do you usually think of yourself as a liberal, a conservative, or what? Because this question gets at an important concept, I have included the results from a similarly worded 1990 National Opinion Research Center survey along with the 1987 Gallup results in the table with my 1990 Hollywood findings.

All the selected questions were asked exactly as they were written in the national survey. In the presentation of results in the tables, however, I have often collapsed the data or paraphrased questions to simplify the display.

The thirty-five Hollywood respondents, part of an elite group, differ from the public in a number of ways. They are generally well educated, most having attended college for at least some time and several having earned graduate degrees. Because they are successful in a business that confers large monetary rewards, they tend to be at least well-off and in a few cases rich. Two-thirds of them earn more than $100,000 per year; one-third garner more than $500,000; and two are worth over $100 million.

As in most groups of powerful business people, males dominate; only nine in the group are women. In addition, the group reflects Hollywood's large Jewish population: fourteen, or 40 percent of the sample, come from that background. Nine have a Protestant background and an equal number Catholic; three are unclassifiable. The respondents are overwhelmingly white anglo. Two are of Asian background, one is black, and one Latino.

7

Political Activism

ONE OF THE PARADOXES OF HOLLYWOOD'S POLITICS is that the restless dissatisfaction that is part of the atmosphere of the industry furnishes the motive force for large numbers of its residents to become ideal democratic citizens. People in Hollywood may be paranoid, frustrated, and envious, but they are not apathetic. Even successful artists have a great deal of spare time between projects, and the less successful have more. For some, the combination of idleness and frustration leads to despair and self-destructive behavior. An amazingly large number of Hollywoodites, however, pour their energies into public activity rather than private vice. Motion picture and television people—especially artists—combine shmoozing and politics to such an extent that the whole industry sometimes seems to be engaged in an ongoing series of town meetings.

Democratic government is based on the notion that ordinary men and women will participate in the political process. Good citizens contribute at least some of their spare time to parties and groups whose purpose goes beyond merely defending the personal interests of their members. Clearly, then, democracy is alive and well in Hollywood. The town hums with meetings, caucuses, fund-raisers, and planning sessions.

The extent of some artists' involvement in groups and politics is astounding. For example, Boxes 7.1 and 7.2 list some of the activities of producer Marian Rees and actor Charlton Heston. Each has an unusually heavy work schedule, yet they both manage to volunteer time to a wide array of organizations both inside and outside the entertainment industry. Although Heston is unusual in that he is a political conservative, he is typical of his colleagues in his hyperactive participation in causes, charities, clubs, and campaigns.

The general ideological tone of these causes is easy to characterize. Although there are a handful of individuals, such as Heston, who volunteer to help conservative organizations, they are too few to sustain any sort of group life. As a result, all the organized activity in Hollywood is left-wing. This activity ranges from the conventionally liberal to the unabashedly radical. Because artists (rather than executives, who have less free time) domi-

Box 7.1 Citizen Rees

Marian Rees is an independent producer specializing in motion pictures for television. Among her many films have been *The Shell Seekers* (1989), *Foxfire* (1987), *Love Is Never Silent* (1985), and *The Marva Collins Story* (1981). She was associated with the television series "All in the Family" and "Sanford and Son" and the theatrical films *Come Blow Your Horn* and *Divorce, American Style* among others.

Membership in Professional Associations

1. Academy of Television Arts and Sciences: First vice-president and Board of Governors, 1983–1984; Secretary, 1981–1982; Activities committee, 1978–1984
2. American Film Institute: Advanced film studies board
3. Hollywood Radio and Television Society
4. Hollywood Women's Coalition: Steering Committee
5. Humanitas Children's Award: Board of Trustees
6. National Council for Families and Television: Appointed council member
7. The Caucus for Producers, Writers, and Directors: Steering Committee
8. The Center for Population Options Board
9. UCLA/ATAS Archive Board
10. National Association of Cable Programming
11. Producers Guild of America: Board member
12. Procter and Gamble "Great Women" Series: Advisory Board
13. Women in Film: President, 1988–1990

Membership in Civic Organizations

1. Gwen Bolden Foundation: President and board of directors
2. YWCA Council
3. The Committee of Professional Women in Los Angeles: Philharmonic Association
4. Alternative Living for Aging: Board of Trustees

SOURCE: "Career Resume," obtained from office of Marian Rees Associates, Inc.

BOX 7.2 CITIZEN HESTON

Charlton Heston is an actor who first appeared on screen in the motion picture *Dark City* in 1950. Since that date he has appeared many times in film, including starring roles in *The Ten Commandments* (1956), *Ben Hur* (1959), *Planet of the Apes* (1968), and *Treasure Island* (1990). He frequently appears on the stage both in the United States and abroad.

The following is a partial re-creation of his calendar of activities for September 1990. Personal plans and business activities that do not pertain to public service or political participation have been omitted.

Date	Time	Activity
5	10 AM	Interview with professor from San Diego State University on the subject of interviews and interviewing
	1 PM	Record narration on film (*America the Beautiful,* produced for release later in the year)
9		To Chavez Ravine and Dodger Stadium to plant trees and do a spot for Arbor Day and the ecology
10		Depart for Hillsdale College (Michigan); "Firing Line" panelist
11		Accept Freedom Award from Hillsdale; return to L.A.

(continues)

nate in these groups, the tendency to take extreme positions is increased. The organized Hollywood voice thus not only speaks from a one-dimensional perspective but actually exaggerates the already leftward tendency of the community.

In the late 1980s, conservative activist David Horowitz moved to Hollywood and attempted to organize right-wing artists into a political club. After several futile years, he gave up and instead founded the Committee on Media Integrity. With a membership largely from outside of Hollywood, the committee criticizes screen entertainment from a conservative perspective. So although there are some individuals, like Horowitz, who break the progressive

12	9 AM	Tape drug spot for Nancy Reagan–sponsored group
13	9 AM	Tape anti-smoking interview
15	7:30 AM	Fly to Atlanta for political fund-raiser for Representative Newt Gingrich; fly to Montgomery
16		Representative Bill Dickinson events and interviews in Montgomery
18	6 PM	Limo to Bonaventure Hotel for Bush/Senator Pete Wilson event; give the Pledge of Allegiance
19	9 AM	Record Lou Rawls spot for Negro Colleges of America
26		Cancel trip to Chicago due to filming glitches around the Air Force One, *Flight II* film to be shot aboard with the president
28	5:30 AM	Flight to Washington, D.C.
	9 AM	Meet with Senator Phil Gramm
	10:30 AM	Meet with Representative Newt Gingrich
	12:45 PM	White House interview with President Bush to finish narration for Air Force One film

SOURCE: Charlton Heston's office

mold, there is no organizational counterweight to balance the leftward hegemony of Hollywood's political groups.[1]

But not every cause, liberal or otherwise, finds supporters. Hollywood tends to become enamored of only certain kinds of issues. Those that have been most prominent in the 1980s and 1990s, that is, the sorts of movements that have a good chance of attracting entertainment industry volunteers, include the following.

1. *Civil liberties.* Artists feel themselves and their work threatened at every turn by censors, fundamentalist Christians, bluenoses, and busybodies. Needless to say, they consider the process of creating motion pictures and television to be an expression of free speech. As a result, they tend to be abso-

lutist defenders of the First Amendment to the U.S. Constitution, which guarantees freedom of speech and press. The Hollywood/Beverly Hills chapter of the American Civil Liberties Union is thriving and wealthy; flocks of celebrities attend most of its meetings.

2. *Abortion.* Hollywood is intensely pro-choice. In six years of reading the trade papers, I have not come across a single statement by anyone in defense of the pro-life position nor any indication of organized activity on its behalf. The views of the women in the industry on abortion can perhaps be explained by their own career orientation. For the men, however, it is obviously ideology, not personal situation, that accounts for their attitudes.

3. *Environmentalism.* Hollywood's groups endorse every liberal perspective and position on the environment. Although there is controversy within the scientific community about the existence of global warming due to the burning of hydrocarbons, in Hollywood it is considered a fact beyond dispute. Hollywood also opposes pesticides, waste incineration, and disposable diapers; it holds business responsible for such problems as acid rain, oil spills, the death of dolphins in the tuna industry, and the destruction of the world's rain forests and supports recycling, solar power, threatened and endangered species, preservation of wetlands, and energy conservation.

4. *The homeless.* Hollywood supports all government programs to alleviate the problem, regardless of cost.

5. *Nukes.* Hollywood opposes both nuclear power and nuclear weapons. This is partly a manifestation of environmentalism (the goal being to eliminate the need for nuclear and fossil fuels, to obtain more energy from solar collectors, and to reduce energy needs through conservation). But it is also a reflection of Hollywood's hostility toward centralized public utilities and the military.

6. *Handgun control.* Hollywood favors handgun control.

7. *AIDS.* Hollywood supports more money for AIDS research and opposes all restrictions on the personal liberties of homosexuals.

8. *Apartheid.* Hollywood embraces the African National Congress (ANC), the radical wing of the anti-apartheid movement that has roots in Marxist revolution (the ANC has officially moderated its position in recent years). However, Hollywood ignores the more moderate movement, Inkatha. When Nelson Mandela, leader of the ANC, visited Hollywood in June 1990, more than 960 of the industry's luminaries, including studio heads, network executives, major agents, and a huge number of stars, attended a testimonial dinner for him. The dinner raised more than $1.2 million for the ANC.[2] When Chief Mangosuthu Buthelezi, head of Inkatha, visited the United States a year later, he was not even invited to Hollywood.

9. *Central America.* Until the victory of Violetta Chamorro in Nicaragua's presidential election of 1990, Hollywood endorsed the Marxist Sandinista government and vigorously opposed U.S. support of the Contra rebels who

were fighting a guerrilla war against the Sandinistas. Hollywood organizations also gave aid and comfort to the Marxist rebels fighting to overthrow the government of El Salvador and opposed official U.S. support for that government. One might expect that there would be at least some people in Hollywood who preferred not to help subject the Central American population to Communist rule, yet I was unable to find a single organization in the entertainment industry that endorsed the official U.S. policy in that area.

These are the causes and issues that engage Hollywood's emotions. Those issues that do not draw organized support within the industry are equally telling. For example, there are no groups in the industry that make it their business to praise the U.S. military, or lobby against abortion, or support a balanced federal budget, or oppose tax increases, or reward anti-Communist activity, or sympathize with small farmers, or strengthen the traditional family, or, in a general way, celebrate business. The town is devoid of organized effort on behalf of any conservative cause.

Along with their left-wing character, the popular Hollywood issues and causes tend to share certain other characteristics. First, Hollywood causes are not the bread-and-butter issues that occupy political interest in the rest of the country. The fin-syn issue, for example, is of very great importance to the livelihood of almost everyone in the city. Producers, whose pocketbooks are most directly affected by the FCC's rules, are very conscious of the political situation. But other artists who are affected almost as much are uninterested. Ask them what they think about fin-syn; their eyes glaze over, and they mutter something about not following such a technical issue. These are the same people who feel comfortable chatting about the South African legislature or the chemical composition of acid rain.

Second, aside from their nonfinancial character, Hollywood's issues are remarkable for not directly impinging on the people who feel so intensely about them. The issue of civil liberties is obviously relevant to members of the motion picture and television industries, and the abortion issue directly affects the lives of Hollywood's females. The other issues, however, are of only indirect relevance at best. Some of the causes, such as environmentalism and antinuclearism, have a tangential impact, in the sense that they affect everyone on the planet. Others, such as the homeless and the foreign policy issues, have no direct personal bearing on any of the people who become so exercised about them.

In other words, most of Hollywood's activism goes into a *symbolic* politics that is very different from the direct economic involvement that characterizes much of "politics as usual" in the rest of the country and the world. It is not that symbolic issues derive no support anywhere else. Both environmentalism and the antinuke bias are popular generally, and opposition to apartheid is evident in all black communities. Where they are important, however, these issues are part of a complex discussion of public policy that includes many pocketbook issues as well. In Hollywood, however, symbolic issues are the only ones that can draw a crowd.

Symbolic political issues have certain characteristics. First, unlike bread-and-butter issues, they are hard to compromise. When two groups disagree on the amount of subsidy an industry should receive, for example, their leaders can always split the difference and declare the resulting figure a victory. But it is much more difficult to compromise on, say, the public policy of abortion.

Second, symbolic issues tend to engage the emotions at a deep, unconscious level that makes rational discussion difficult. People tend to adopt extreme positions on them and demonize everyone who fails to agree with their point of view. This also makes compromise difficult.

Third, symbolic issues tend to be seen in moral rather than economic terms. Not only does this reinforce the tendency to condemn people who disagree but it also discourages the consideration of costs. In all the documents and statements that have come out of Hollywood about the need to switch from fossil fuels to solar, for example, there is nothing that suggests that anyone has considered what the national price tag for such a change would be or who would pay it. Because the celebrities who advocate such policies are wealthy, the economic impact of any of their favored courses of action is pretty much irrelevant to them. They are therefore at liberty to ignore costs when recommending behavior to the rest of the country and to judge politicians who worry about costs as morally deficient.

With symbolic politics comes the need to make symbolic statements—manifestos that have no practical relevance to anything but create emotional satisfaction in the speaker and enrage observors of other ideological persuasions. Such was the situation, for example, during actor Martin Sheen's tenure as the honorary mayor of Malibu, California. The town's business leaders elected Sheen in April 1989. The post is one with no actual power; it was created by the Malibu Chamber of Commerce to wring publicity out of the fact that so many celebrities live in the expensive beach town. Most honorary mayors accept the title as one more award and then keep quiet. Sheen, however, promptly declared Malibu a "nuclear-free" zone and a few days later requested that the community become "a sanctuary for aliens and the homeless." Nothing, of course, came of these pronouncements (except an impeachment movement within the Chamber of Commerce), but they created a publicity stir and no doubt made many Hollywoodites feel as though a blow had been struck for justice.[3]

At the center of this symbol-obsessed Hollywood town meeting are several dozen successful artists, most of them actors, who contribute their time, money, and names to many left-wing causes and candidates. Some of the most active and influential are shown in Table 7.1.

TABLE 7.1   Hollywood Artists and Their Political Causes

Name	Profession	Recent Causes
Robert Downey, Jr.	actor	civil liberties, environmentalism
Jill Eikenberry	actress	pro-choice, Dianne Feinstein for governor (CA), Leo McCarthy for senator (CA), Hollywood Women's Political Committee (HWPC)
Morgan Fairchild	actress	pro-choice, AIDS, Jim Hightower for agriculture commissioner (TX), environmentalism, Kathleen Brown for treasurer (CA), Leo McCarthy for senator (CA), HWPC
Jane Fonda	actress	environmentalism, pro-choice, anti-apartheid, Leo McCarthy for senator (CA), HWPC
Kris Kristofferson	actor	civil liberties, anti-apartheid
Norman Lear	producer	civil liberties, Leo McCarthy for senator (CA), environmentalism, Ann Richards for governor (TX)
Michael Ovitz	agent	Bill Bradley for senator (NJ), Robert Mrazek for U.S. House (NY), civil liberties, anti-apartheid
Sarah Jessica Parker	actress	environmentalism, civil liberties, Leo McCarthy for senator (CA), HWPC
Barbra Streisand	actress	pro-choice, environmentalism, Ann Richards for governor (TX), antinukes, Leo McCarthy for senator (CA), HWPC
Alfre Woodard	actress	pro-choice, Leo McCarthy for senator (CA), anti-apartheid, HWPC

Many other actors specialize in a cause—Robert Redford, Meryl Streep, and Ted Danson in environmentalism, Cecily Tyson in the homeless, Elizabeth Taylor in AIDS, and so on. But because everyone who is successful knows nearly everyone else at the same level, and because frantic shmoozing is constant at the social as well as the political level, the overall effect is of one perpetual loud buzz of effort to affect public policy.

Although in one respect Hollywood politics thus resembles the classical notion of an ideal democracy, in others it is the sort of communal activity no democratic theorist ever imagined. The spectacle of rich, famous, intensely disaffected liberals throwing their weight behind symbolic left-wing causes is surely a unique force in the history of political participation.

If this eccentric politics occurred among people in another, less visible and affluent community (say, a sawmill town or a mining camp), it would be of interest primarily to the citizens directly involved and perhaps to political scientists. Because Hollywood is a town full of rich celebrities, however, its political style and views resonate far beyond its boundaries. The politics of celebrities is inevitably part of the politics of the nation. The question is, How big an impact does Hollywood have on the practical governance of the rest of the country?

HOLLYWOOD'S INFLUENCE ON ELECTIONS

Across the political spectrum—conservative or liberal, Republican or Democratic—the general rule is that the most important single resource in American politics is money. People, interest groups, and industries that donate money to candidates generally find that their contributions purchase sympathy for their problems and attention to their arguments. Because Hollywood is a town with oodles of money and strong political views, it is logical to wonder if its money has been used in an attempt to bring government policy in line with its views.

The answer is that the town has attempted to influence policy for decades but so far has very little to show for it. In the 1930s and 1940s, a significant percentage of the total donated to the Democratic Party, especially for presidential campaigns, came from Hollywood. Despite incomplete records, it is fairly clear that at least 10 percent of the contributions to Franklin Roosevelt's 1944 campaign originated with people in the motion picture industry. Among the largest contributors to FDR were members of the Warner family, owners of one of the major studios. Yet the Roosevelt Justice Department was in that year in the middle of a suit against the studios that would culminate four years later in the Paramount decree, which would destroy the studios' vertical integration. Moreover, when the studios (including Warner Brothers) attempted to acquire television stations to make up for the theaters they were losing, the Justice Department, under Democratic President Harry Truman, prevented them from doing so.[4]

More recently, Washington has demonstrated that Hollywood's money does not necessarily buy influence. Lew Wasserman of MCA (parent of Universal), for example, became a very important contributor to Democratic candidates in the 1960s. Wasserman virtually ran President Lyndon Johnson's 1964 campaign in the western states. After the victory, Johnson offered him the cabinet post of secretary of commerce, which he declined. Four years later, however, Johnson's Department of Justice forbade MCA to merge with Westinghouse. Wasserman not only continued his personal contributions to Democratic candidates into the 1970s and 1980s but also became the central organizer of corporate Hollywood's support of that party. Yet in the 1970s, the Carter Justice Department forbade MCA to join with three other studios and the Getty Oil Company in forming a cable competitor to HBO. In 1983,

Congress, with one house controlled by the Democrats, refused to acquiesce in a lobbying campaign led by MCA to pass a law either outlawing the VCR outright or forcing consumers who bought one to pay a royalty to the studios. In other words, although it would be foolish to claim that Hollywood's money has never affected public policy, there are abundant examples to support the claim that Washington has frequently felt free to ignore the town's generosity.[5]

Nevertheless, Hollywood remains a major source of money for Democrats and a minor source for Republicans. Studio executives, generally more moderate than artists, maintain regular connections to campaigns. Along with Wasserman, Michael Eisner, chairman of Disney, and Barry Diller, chairman of Fox, can be relied upon to organize fund-raisers for Democrats. Frank Mancuso, former chairman of Paramount, and independent producer Jerry Weintraub are traditionally Republican supporters.[6]

The general feeling among activist artists, however, is that neither party is liberal enough. In an effort to rectify this situation, left-wing Hollywood organized in the 1980s in an attempt to coax the Democratic Party in a more progressive direction. There were two prime movers of this activity: the Hollywood Women's Political Committee (HWPC) and producer Norman Lear.

The HWPC got its start at a fund-raising brunch given by several prominent women in the spring of 1984 to support the California chapter of the National Organization for Women. Delighted with the success of the brunch, the organizers decided to turn their energies toward helping the Democratic ticket of Walter Mondale and Geraldine Ferraro. After that debacle, the women resolved that a long-term, serious approach to the transformation of American politics was needed. They each donated $2,500 and began applying their money and celebrity status to the support of their principles. In 1988 they hired Margery Tabankin, former director of VISTA under the Carter administration, to be executive director.[7]

From its founding through 1990, the HWPC garnered about $5 million for various causes and candidates. In the most spectacularly successful of the organization's efforts, Barbra Streisand single-handedly raised $1.5 million in the fall of 1986 by singing at her home for a large group of the industry's most important people. That money helped the Democrats regain control of the Senate in the 1986 elections, a contribution that has not been forgotten by the party. The HWPC has been prominent in organizing a number of prochoice marches and rallies; it managed Nelson Mandela's visit to Hollywood in June 1990; it lobbied intensively against budget cuts to or restrictions on the National Endowment for the Arts; and it participates in a smaller way in several other causes.[8]

Since the famous Streisand concert, Democratic candidates have regularly trouped to Hollywood to voluntarily subject themselves to questioning by HWPC members in hopes of collecting the pot of gold at the end of the ideological rainbow. The results of this series of meetings has been decidedly mixed, from the standpoints of both Hollywood and the candidates. The HWPC's favored presidential hopeful in 1988, Gary Hart, self-destructed through personal indiscretions. The eventual Democratic nominee, Michael Dukakis, was noticeably cool to the HWPC (in one widely reported encounter, actress Whoopi Goldberg lectured Dukakis on his duty to the republic). Several other candidates were offended at the group's evident feeling of superiority toward both the candidates and the common people. A number of Democratic congressional and gubernatorial candidates supported by the HWPC have been accused of having "gone Hollywood" by their opponents, and some, fearful of such an attack, have refused its endorsement.[9] A special problem for HWPC is that one of its members, Jane Fonda, has never been forgiven by many Americans for her vocal support for the North—the enemy—during the Vietnam War. Many candidates would just as soon be endorsed by Saddam Hussein as by a group associated in the minds of voters with Fonda.[10] For all its high profile as a fund-raising organization, therefore, the Hollywood Women's Political Committee cannot be said to have purchased much influence over the politics of the Democratic Party.

Although no one questions his patriotism, similar problems have been encountered by Norman Lear. He founded the local branch of the American Civil Liberties Union (ACLU), serves as president of the ACLU Foundation, founded People For The American Way, cofounded the Environmental Media Association, and is so active in politics that it is a wonder that he ever gets any work done. In the 1980s he began gathering groups of friends at small dinners and inviting candidates for the presidency and Congress to come meet, eat, discuss issues, and perhaps earn many thousands of dollars in contributions.[11]

Despite the fact that Lear and his friends, using money as a lure, have managed to interrogate almost every prominent Democratic office-holder, the results have not been satisfactory. The dinners have earned their hosts a reputation for intolerance, smugness, arrogance, and lack of appreciation for political reality. Journalist Ronald Brownstein quoted an aide to Senator Joseph Biden, emerging from one of the Lear dinners, as having said, "We have just participated in the greatest demonstration [of the need for] public finance [of campaigns] I have ever seen." Moreover, Lear has not demonstrated a knack for picking winners, backing both Dukakis' run for the presidency and Leo McCarthy's failed bid for a California Senate seat the same year.[12]

Looking at the histories of the Hollywood Women's Political Committee and Norman Lear, one might conclude that the entertainment industry, for all its money and effort, has been a negligible force on the national scene. That assessment would be inaccurate, however. Wherever there is money to be gained, politicians will bend their behavior to get some of it. Such is the case with Vice-President Albert Gore.

In 1985, then-Senator Gore's wife, Tipper, joined with a number of other wives of politicians to form the Parents Music Resource Center. The group was dedicated to persuading the music industry to put warning labels on the packaging of albums, compact disks, and tapes to alert parents if the songs inside contained explicitly sexual lyrics. Shortly thereafter, Senator Gore participated in hearings held by the Commerce Committee into the possibly damaging effects that listening to such lyrics might have on impressionable young minds. Tipper Gore testified at these hearings.[13]

Although there were no concrete measures proposed at the hearings, the entertainment industry smelled censorship and instantly went bananas. The music, television, and motion picture industries joined in a giant coalition to smother the censorship threat in its infancy. Organizations were put together, money was raised, and volunteers went out on the talk-show circuit to warn the populace of the alleged threat to free speech. Tipper Gore became ensconced in Hollywood's "rogue's gallery" along with the blacklisters of the 1940s and 1950s.

Meanwhile, husband Albert had decided to run for the Democratic nomination for president in 1988. Like the other hopefuls, in 1987 he made the trek to Hollywood in search of celebrity support and campaign contributions. Unlike them, he discovered every door shut to him, every ear averted, and every pocketbook tightly zipped. Hollywood was ready to give millions to Third World Marxists, but not a penny to a senator whose wife had questioned the wholesomeness of rock music.

After months of fruitless entreaties, Albert Gore capitulated. In November 1987, he and his wife addressed a meeting of prominent show-business leaders and, in essence, apologized for the 1985 hearings. Gore denied that he had wanted them in the first place, blaming them on his colleagues John Danforth of Missouri and Paula Hawkins of Florida, both Republicans. While defending the notion of labeling packages so that parents can learn what their children are buying, the Gores both vigorously denied any intention of imposing censorship on any aspect of the entertainment industry.

It didn't work. Although he continued as a strong candidate for the Democratic nomination for months afterward, Gore failed to attract any appreciable contributions from Hollywood. Whether that fact was responsible for his ultimate failure to achieve the 1988 nomination, of course, is impossible to say.

After the humbling of the Gores, there were no further inquiries into popular music on Capitol Hill. Although Tipper Gore continued to argue for the labeling of albums, she was always careful to add that she opposed government censorship. Meanwhile, Albert Gore attempted to build a Hollywood constituency by becoming one of the most knowledgeable American politicians on environmental problems.

Their efforts to rehabilitate themselves in Hollywood's eyes were only partly successful. When Democratic presidential candidate Bill Clinton chose Senator Gore to be his running mate in 1992, the praise from the entertainment industry was not unanimous. "[Gore's] a terrific candidate," stated Michael Medavoy, chairman of TriStar Pictures. "With his environmental record and his knowledge of foreign relations, I think he's a really good balance for Bill Clinton." Others were not so ready to forgive. "The attack on the arts may 'only' involve calls for stickering, monitoring and other restrictions today, but the agenda of Tipper and her friends is censorship, and we'd better recognize it right now," wrote Mark Leviton to *Daily Variety*. He also warned of her "potential influence on the campaign," and, presumably, the White House.[14]

For all the seeming futility of liberal Hollywood's participation in campaigns, then, the Gore episode reveals that it does have some effect. Politicians will not only court the wealthy activists, but modify their policy stands in the hope of being rewarded with contributions. It is impossible to determine whether this trimming of sails has had any noticeable effect on public policy, but it is conceivable that it could be important in the future.

HOLLYWOODIZING PUBLIC OPINION

For those who are frustrated with trying to influence policy directly through access to politicians, there is also the hope of indirectly affecting it by first helping to form public opinion. Because people learn things from their entertainment, every story is a potential vehicle for ideological messages. As with any art, the attitudes of the artists have always seeped into screen entertainment, and any motion picture or television program could be analyzed with a view to exposing its latent political content. But there was no overt, systematic attempt to employ the screen to influence public opinion until Norman Lear decided to put its power to use in the 1980s.

Lear, undoubtedly the most important single force in television in the 1970s, had become rich, famous, and powerful, producing such hit series as "All in the Family," "Maude," "Good Times," and "Mary Hartman, Mary Hartman." Always an active liberal, late in the decade he grew concerned about the rise of the religious right in the United States and was especially bothered by the evidently successful attacks of such organizations as the Moral Majority on liberal Democrats in the 1980 congressional elections. That year, he began working on a documentary about TV evangelists but became so disturbed by their mixture of religion and right-wing politics that he dropped the film and decided to make a television commercial attacking them. Deciding that he needed an organization to sponsor such an ad, he founded People For The American Way.[15]

Lear is Jewish, but deciding that People For should represent all faiths, he recruited prominent Catholics and Protestants to be on its executive board. John Buchanan, former eight-term member of the U.S. House from Alabama, became its chairman, and on its board sat Father Robert Drinan, former president of Boston College and former member of the U.S. House from Massachusetts; M. William Howard, former president of the National Council of Churches of Christ; Barbara Jordan, former member of the U.S. House from Texas; and actor Martin Sheen. Lear provided $100,000 of his own money to get the organization started; it now has a budget of more than $10 million and about 270,000 members.

At first, People For concentrated on running TV commercials attacking the religious right and pleading for toleration. Prominent actors and directors volunteered to work for the union minimum wage in these ads. In one of them, Danny DeVito and Joe Bologna play a pair of wall painters who get into a discussion about religion and politics. The dialogue goes like this:

> Bologna: I thought it out, Mac; I'm voting for Kimberly.
> DeVito: Kimberly? That flake? I'm voting for a good Christian, Stanton.
> B: K's a Christian, too.
> D: The hell he is. Not the way he votes.
> B: What's how he votes got to do with it?
> D: Look, don't be a dope. Anybody can say he's a good Christian. But I'm saying, it takes one to know one.
> B: What's that supposed to mean?
> D: Look, we're good Christians, aren't we?
> B: Yeah.
> D: All right, if we were senators, we'd know how we'd vote on everything, right?
> B: Yeah.
> D: That's how you can tell a good Christian, because he'd vote the way we'd vote. Got it?
> B: But if we were senators, how do you know I'd vote the same as you?
> D: Hey, I thought you said you were a good Christian!
> Voiceover: When the founders wrote our Constitution, they placed a ban on religious tests for public office. They didn't take their freedom for granted. Don't take your freedom for granted.

In about 1986, People For decided to expand its activities to include efforts to defeat the confirmation of some of President Reagan's nominees to the federal administration and bench. For example, it helped defeat the nomination of Christian fundamentalist Herbert Ellingwood as assistant attorney general in charge of choosing candidates for judgeships, and it mounted an unsuccessful campaign against the confirmation of Daniel Manion as judge in the Seventh Court of Appeals. People For truly came into its own as a national force, however, in the campaign against the confirmation of Robert Bork to the Supreme Court in 1987.

Like those of any intellectual, Bork's views on constitutional questions are both subtle and constantly evolving. Simplifying for the sake of clarity, however, we can characterize Bork as a conservative in the sense that he generally opposes government intervention in economic life but supports it in personal life. In addition, he is usually opposed to the extension of new personal rights that are not specifically mentioned in the Constitution (the most hotly contested of which is the right to an abortion).[16] Given these views, his nomination provoked intense opposition from black, labor, environmental, and feminist groups, which combined forces to attempt to defeat Bork in the senate.

People for the American Way made itself this coalition's research center and launched a $1.2 million advertising and direct-mail campaign to persuade the public to lobby its representatives to reject Bork. The centerpiece of this campaign was a television commercial, narrated by actor Gregory Peck, attacking Bork's opinions and urging viewers to contact their senators:

[On the screen, a family climbs the steps of the Supreme Court building.] Voiceover: There is a special feeling of awe that people get when they visit the Supreme Court of the United States, the ultimate guardian of our rights as Americans. That's why we set the highest standards for our highest court justices, and that's why we're so concerned. This is Gregory Peck.

[The screen image changes to a picture of Bork on the left and the Constitution on the right.] Robert Bork wants to be a Supreme Court justice. But the record shows that he has a strange idea of what justice is. He defended poll taxes and literacy tests, which kept many Americans from voting. He opposed the civil rights law that ended 'whites only' signs at lunch counters. He doesn't believe the Constitution protects your right to privacy. And he thinks that freedom of speech does not apply to literature and art and music. Robert Bork could have the last word on your rights as citizens. But the Senate has the last word on him. Please, urge your senators to vote against the Bork nomination, because if Robert Bork wins a seat on the Supreme Court, it will be for life—his life, and yours.

The Senate rejected Bork. Once again, there is no way to tell just what role People For The American Way, and the Peck commercial in particular, played in the outcome. Political scientists William Haltom and Patti Watson examined the issue and concluded that the whole lobbying and publicity campaign against confirmation probably shifted the votes of only three senators against Bork and that he would have been rejected even without it.[17] Nevertheless, three votes out of one hundred is not an insignificant percentage, and if People For can claim responsibility for even one of the three senators' votes, it has cause to consider itself a force in American politics.

More important, however, the campaign against Bork was *perceived* by politicians, journalists, interest groups, and by Bork himself to be very important to the outcome.[18] President Reagan called it an attack based on "innuendos, mistruths, and distortions ... a lynching," and Patrick McGuigan, director of the conservative Judicial Reform Project, said that the political right was determined to "go on the warpath. ... If this means translating the subtleties of jurisprudence into hard-hitting one-liners that touch people's hot buttons, we're ready."[19] Whatever the truth, People For The American Way will go down in history as one of the knights that helped to slay the Bork dragon.

The Peck attack on Bork was only a television commercial, a one-minute performance. If such a short message could be so evidently powerful, however, then the obvious next step was to begin fashioning full-length entertainment that advises the population how to think and behave.

THE ENVIRONMENTALISM CAMPAIGN

As the 1980s waned, Hollywood became obsessed with an issue that provided the motive to take the process of forming public opinion one step further. Environmentalism swept through the entertainment industry. Stars began to go on talk shows to discuss that they had added solar panels to their homes or that they were now driving electric automobiles. Interviewers found them distressed about the depletion of the ozone layer, concerned about endangered species, and worried about global warming. In the Times Mirror survey discussed in Chapter 6, Hollywood opinion leaders registered as very strong environmentalists, stronger than the American public in general.

And the public, in the view of Hollywood, was not evolving fast enough in its views on the subject. In the late 1980s, many people in the industry independently came to the conclusion that they would have to assist ordinary citizens to become educated about the necessity for ecological action. In the words of Norman Lear, it became imperative for him to begin to "help Americans understand changes needed in behavior and lifestyles" in order to save the planet.[20]

In April 1989, in cooperation with actor Robert Redford, Disney chairman Michael Eisner, and others, Lear founded the Environmental Media Association (EMA). On the board of directors of this organization are many of the truly big names in the industry: studio heads (Robert Daly of Warner Brothers), network honchos (Robert Iger of ABC), superagents (Michael Ovitz of Creative Artists Agency), producers (Grant Tinker), heads of trade associations (Jack Valenti), and celebrity actors (Don Johnson). EMA operates out of Lear's ACT III offices in Culver City and is sustained by voluntary contributions from its board members.[21]

The main purpose of EMA is "to encourage films, television programs and other creative projects to incorporate environmental themes." In this it has been phenomenally successful, especially in regard to television programming. It has held seminars on environmental problems for the Writers Guild of America, MTM Enterprises, Warner Brothers Studios and the writers of at least twenty-five television series.[22] Out of these educational sessions have come environmentalist themes, sections of dialogue, and whole plotlines that have been broadcast into America's living rooms. Among the messages that can be traced to EMA's influence are the following.

1. In an episode of "thirtysomething," Hope (Mel Harris) became involved in a community effort to stop a waste incinerator. Characters discussed the advantages of cloth diapers, fretted about pesticides, and wore environmental tee shirts.[23]

2. A short-lived series, "Earth Force," featured a small group of environmental activists (led by actors Gil Gerard and Joanna Pacula) who were backed by the unlimited funds of a giant corporation. The characters roamed the globe, stamping out evil in the guise of pollution and polluters.[24]

3. In an episode of "Murphy Brown," the main character (a television reporter played by Candice Bergen) bet her newsroom crew that she could lead an ecologically responsible life for one week.[25]

Thanks to EMA, therefore, American television has become an arena for forming public opinion on this one issue. The most impressive evidence, however, of Hollywood's determination to educate the public on environmentalism and of EMA's participation in that intention was the two-hour "Earth Day Special," sponsored by Time Warner and broadcast by ABC on April 22, 1990. This program was a series of sketches, lectures, and pep talks featuring three dozen celebrities from the worlds of film (Jane Fonda, Bette Midler, Jack Lemmon), television (Bugs Bunny, Dana Delany, Kermit the Frog), popular music (Quincy Jones and the Toxic Rappers), sports (Pat Riley), and science (Dr. Carl Sagan). The "Earth Day Special" was an opportunity for these celebrities to urge Americans to lead a more ecologically responsible life and to criticize corporate America for its toxic habits. The entire casts of the television series "Cheers," "The Cosby Show," "The Dating Game," "The Golden Girls," "Jeopardy!" and "Married ... with Children" appeared to lend moral support. EMA received credit as "production consultants" on the show. [26]

Although Lear and EMA are the most visible examples of Hollywood's determination to propagandize on behalf of the earth, others are also proceeding independently. Ted Turner has produced a variety of documentaries for his cable stations WTBS and TNT. One of these, "Ancient Forests: Rage over Trees," so angered the logging industry that it persuaded advertisers, by threatening boycotts of their products, to withdraw their support. Turner telecast the show anyway, sans sponsors. Motion picture producer David Zucker, who opposes sequels on principle, nevertheless agreed to do *The Naked Gun 2 1/2: The Smell of Fear* because he was convinced that it could be a vehicle for opposing nuclear power and advocating solar power. David Simon, the producer of television's "My Two Dads" (which has featured a variety of environmentalist messages), proclaimed, "In the 60s we were fighting the people in power. Now, *we're* 'the man.' All these ex-radicals are in government, in the media. This is true activism. It's really thrilling to be able to do something."[27]

No doubt it is thrilling for Turner, Lear, Bugs Bunny, and everyone else in Hollywood who is participating in the industry-wide movement to help form public opinion on an important political issue. The rest of us, however, might put aside our thrills for a moment and reflect upon the questions this raises for our self-government.

As citizens, Hollywoodites have every right to express their opinions and join any national dialogue on public policy. Moreover, the advocacy television of the 1980s and 1990s is surely superior to the cautious blandness of the 1960s, in which few recognizable human conflicts, especially of a public nature, ever appeared. The problem is not that entertainment is now taking stands, but that the ideological bent of its messages is so one-sided.

Watching American television or motion pictures these days, viewers will never get the impression that many environmental issues are hotly contested, either scientifically or politically. Discussing his network's carrying of the "Earth Day Special," Robert Iger, president of ABC Entertainment, wrote, "I firmly believe that the demand for a cleaner and safer environment is not a political position nor is it an attempt to advocate a specific policy."[28]

In its blandly reassuring style, Iger's statement is typical of Hollywood's approach to environmental concerns: Ignore crucial questions of implementation and costs and pretend there is no controversy on the subject. *Of course* everyone wants clean air and water, safe power, healthy forests, and lots of wild animals. The question is, How do we get them? What policies are best? What are the tradeoffs involved in a choice among policies? Who will win and who will lose if we shut down our nuclear plants and make a national commitment to solar power? What are the arguments against the theory that the planet's climate is warming? Why has it been so hard to get a handle on the problem of toxic wastes? By ignoring the hard questions, Hollywood leaves the false impression that environmental problems could be solved easily, if only we had enough collective will and if only a few bad guys could be eliminated.

Moreover, although Iger speaks truthfully about not advocating specific policies, the "Earth Day Special" was nevertheless clearly anticorporate in tone. Even Hollywood leftists admit this is true—indeed, they are happy about it. Although refraining from discussing concrete political issues, therefore, the program managed to leave one clear message: When the earth is the victim, business is the villain. The bad guys who must be defeated reside in the boardrooms of American corporations. The liberal mindset that colors all Hollywood thinking thus distorts its portrayal of the problem of the environment as much as on any other issue.

In brief, it is not Hollywood's willingness to embrace national problems in movies and on television that is disturbing. It is the relentless one-dimensional viewpoint that dominates the films and television that come out of the industry.

If Hollywood were not so monolithically liberal, it might be able to produce programs that portrayed environmental problems from a variety of viewpoints. Among those perspectives might be one that argued that business could be the solution rather than the problem. Offered a pluralism of perspectives, the audience might be able to form judgments about the evidence for and against such scientific problems as global warming or nuclear waste disposal. Exposed to arguments from several sides, viewers would be able to make rational choices about, for example, whether the logging industry is a threat to the spotted owl. Instead of informing public opinion, however, Hollywood's simplistic, one-sided approach to the environment can only confuse citizens about the choices they will be asked to make, thereby further degrading national discussion of ecological problems.

Hollywood will behave similarly in regard to other issues besides environmentalism, now and in the future. If, as I have argued, the industry's overwhelmingly liberal outlook is rooted in its political economy, then it is unlikely to change. The anxiety and paranoia that make nearly everyone feel oppressed created a left-wing community in the 1930s. Despite the decline of motion pictures, the rise of television, the advent of cable, the death and rebirth of the vertically integrated studio system, and myriad other changes over five decades, the sociological situation is pretty much the same today. Hollywood was liberal then, it is liberal now, and it will be liberal tomorrow.

If Hollywoodites were content to hold their opinions privately, this would be of small consequence. As this chapter has demonstrated, however, the industry spawns dozens of celebrity activists, people who are determined to use the great factory of ideas in which they work to influence the political outlook of millions of their fellow citizens.

At this point, Hollywood's existential problem becomes everybody's. A shrill, one-sided liberalism dominates its attempts to "educate" the public about important issues. The good citizenship that compels activists to participate in the national dialogue ends by turning them into propagandists. American entertainment becomes a vehicle for conveying the ideas of a tiny and unrepresentative elite.

If the future promises an increasing attempt to "Hollywoodize" the American political process, then, the potential consequences are not encouraging. An endless series of sitcoms preaching an unchallenged left-wing gospel will be the outcome if Hollywood is left to its own devices. And it will be. It is hard to imagine the political economy of the industry changing to such an extent that it brings different people with different outlooks into power. Nor is it likely that government will attempt to change the situation. The First Amendment to the Constitution protects motion pictures from government meddling. Although the Federal Communications Commission has the authority to regulate broadcasting, it scrupulously avoids attempts to dictate the content of television programs (with a few exceptions, such as forbidding obscenity, which are not relevant to the point here).

With the ongoing fragmentation of video delivery systems leading to the prospect of every American home wired for hundreds of channels, many observers have hoped that viewers would soon be offered a profusion of programming choices. Paradoxically, the outcome may instead be even greater political conformity. The proliferation of buyers for their products merely gives individual producers greater freedom to realize their own ideological visions in their work. And because those visions are remarkably similar, the result is likely to be not a multiplicity of outlook, but simply more outlets through which the reigning liberalism can express itself. The final irony of Hollywood politics is that the explosion of programming choices that promises so much diversity is instead likely to result in an even more monotonous political message.

8

Internal Politics in Hollywood

*T*HE FACT THAT HOLLYWOOD is almost unanimously liberal in national political ideology does not mean that it lacks internal conflicts. On the contrary, the suspicion and resentment that typify relations among individuals in the industry also frequently describe dealings between groups. The town is characterized by a more-or-less permanent set of antagonisms that have by now assumed the shape of political cleavages. Although they originate within the industry, however, they consist of quarrels that transcend Hollywood. The squabbles over Affirmative Action, labor relations, and artists' rights are internal Hollywood quarrels that are of interest far beyond the boundaries of the entertainment industry.

AFFIRMATIVE ACTION

Hollywood is largely peopled by young white males. Surveys conducted by various organizations in the late 1980s documented that the industry's work force barely begins to reflect the ethnic and gender composition of American society. Only 15 percent of television producers, 25 percent of writers, and 9 percent of directors are women. Nearly two-thirds of network entertainment executives are male, and at the rank of vice-president and above, 80 percent are men.[1] Of the 170 members of the American Society of Cinematographers, exactly one is a woman.[2] In 1990, only 11 of the 207 feature-film directing jobs went to females.[3] Although there is less documentation for the percentage of minority workers in the industry, it is clear that their level of employment in Hollywood also does not reflect their proportion of the general population. A 1989 study by the Writers Guild, for example, reported that blacks, Hispanics, and Native Americans together constituted only 2 percent of working writers.[4] Although no one seems to keep track of the employment of Asian-Americans in Hollywood, there is no doubt that their numbers are similarly low.

Statistics on the number of older people working in Hollywood are even more difficult to obtain. Many industry veterans, however, report that "ageism" is a growing problem in Hollywood. Leonard Stern, president of the Producers Guild of America, characterized the prevailing prejudice: "Right now, youth is mistaken for talent."[5] Actor Marvin Kaplan, president of the Los Angeles local of AFTRA, summarized his frustration at the waste of his experience when he recounted, "I wrote a casting director a letter: 'Taking your advice, I got into a car accident and am now a new face.'"[6] George Kirgo, president of the Writers Guild of America West, reported that he had been recently informed by a producer that he was too old to be hired as a writer on a TV movie because it is believed that older people cannot write love scenes. Kirgo underscored the absurdity of such an assumption by protesting that "some of us have kept diaries!"[7]

Beginning in the 1960s, federal and state governments began to pass laws encouraging companies to recruit minorities and females and discouraging them from forcing retirement on older workers. By the late 1970s, major firms in most industries had programs in place to diversify their work force and had discontinued mandatory retirement. They did this partly because they might lose government contracts and partly because they faced class-action suits if they did not change their policies. But in Hollywood, neither television nor motion picture producers rely on government contracts, and artists are reluctant to sue for fear of being labeled trouble-makers. The dread of ruining one's career forever inhibits the unemployed from making noise. Besides, rejection is constant in the industry even without discrimination entering into it; the town is full of young white males griping about being unable to sell their screenplays. In the pervasive ambiguity of failure, it is impossible to establish a specific animus against oneself. Uncertainty discourages lawsuits.

Moreover, the nature of the business itself, rather than any conscious discrimination, handicaps women and minorities. As liberals, Hollywood decisionmakers are in fact in favor of equal access to employment. But their habitual mode of operation—making deals with their friends—disadvantages people who are members of groups less likely to have personal relationships with a player. As Marcy Kelly, president of Women in Film (WIF), sums up the plight of all nonyoung, nonwhite, nonmales trying to get started in films and television, "You may have all the skills in the world and be much more qualified, but they're going to hire someone else because that's who they play tennis with."[8]

Besides, there are reasons for outcomes besides discrimination. In a report on a survey of women's employment in Hollywood, Sally Steenland reports that one female executive "was on the fast track before she had children. Work was her life; in fact, she was prepared to divorce her husband if he impeded her career. But having a baby changed her priorities. 'Now I have a job, not a career,' she says. 'I don't work weekends, I don't travel; I'm not on the fast track.'"[9] Given the well-documented tendency of women to be more family-oriented and less career-driven than men, it may be that the low percentage of females in the industry is at least partly due to a natural selection of the aggressive and ambitious, rather than to discrimination by the powerful.

Similarly with minorities. Addressing the issue of the low percentage of minority writers, Herb Steinberg, spokesman for the major studios, pointed out that the authors of scripts are usually identified to readers only by the name on the cover. "If it's a good story, it's a good story. There's nothing on the cover [of a script] saying it was written by a black, a white, a male, a female, or someone in polka dots."[10] Under these circumstances, if an executive or producer picks a script written by a white male, it is because, without being identified as such, the white male did the best job. That being so, economics and social justice decree that the the white male deserves the contract. Part of the failure of minorities to advance in Hollywood may thus be due to their lack of qualifications for particular jobs.

No doubt the outcome of employment decisions in Hollywood are the result of a combination of various factors. Possibly there is some outright discrimination. Certainly the reliance on shmoozing and friendship cliques operates to freeze out talented people who would otherwise be successful. Without question, however, Hollywood is also a meritocracy in which failure can credibly be attributed to an applicant having more ambition than ability. In the haze of ambiguity, pinning down the rationale behind any one decision, or even many choices, is an impossibility. Individuals who are attempting to get their foot in the door can only keep trying.

And organized groups that make it their business to advance the interests of women or minorities (I am aware of no such groups representing older workers in Hollywood) are therefore faced with the nearly insurmountable challenge of changing the entrenched employment practices of the industry. Not that they haven't tried. Representatives of the Los Angeles chapter of the National Black Media Coalition (LABMC), the National Association for the Advancement of Colored People (NAACP), Women In Film , and the Association of Asian Pacific American Artists (AAPAA), among others, meet regularly with studio executives to try to persuade them to institute affirmative action programs.[11]

Other organizations also try to help. Beginning with the Screen Actors Guild (SAG) 1980 agreement, all the artists' unions have negotiated language in their contracts establishing equal opportunity as a desired goal, and several have established institutions to attempt to encourage the employment of minorities. SAG requires signatory companies to submit periodic reports on their progress and employs an affirmative action coordinator to keep track of the data and remind producers of their obligations. The Writers

Guild runs a writers' training program that permits employers to hire first-time minority screenwriters at one-fifth the union minimum scale. The guild also operates a service that submits scripts written by minority members to production companies. The American Film Institute runs a directing workshop for women, which has graduated more than one hundred female directors.[12]

The results of these efforts have been mixed. Among actors, blacks are now actually overrepresented on the screen in proportion to their numbers in the population. Women, however, especially those over forty, are considerably underrepresented, and the members of other minorities are practically invisible. The percentages of women among directors, writers, and producers represent a dramatic increase from twenty years ago, when females comprised less than 1 percent of all three professions. Activist women, however, generally regard the present numbers as intolerably low. The Writers Guild, in its effort to bring minority talent to the attention of producers, has sent out more than 600 scripts by new minority writers; but as of the October 1989 press report, not one had resulted in employment.[13]

Activists examining this evidence are apt to interpret it as proving that the glass is half empty rather than half full. Many of them advocate some sort of congressional or Federal Communication Commission mandate that would require employers to hire a certain percentage of women and minorities for positions in both television and motion pictures, from script prompter all the way up to studio head. The fact that such a quota system is not only extremely unlikely in a political sense, but would probably be declared unconstitutional by the courts, does not deter them. Eternal frustration induces people to become unrealistic in their demands.

LABOR AND MANAGEMENT

Just as the screen entertainment industry is peculiar among American businesses, so are its relations with its workers. In most industries, a relatively stable, organized business establishment deals with a relatively stable, organized work force. Not so in film and television. Because most projects, even those under the auspices of the studios, are put together from scratch, the employer in each case is apt to be a new entity. Not only that, but because one company may finance a project, another make it, and still another distribute it, just who the "employer" is, in a legal sense, is apt to be rather vague.

If management is somewhat ambiguous, labor is positively evanescent. The transient nature of employment, in which even million-dollar stars are hired only for a single project, makes keeping track of workers over the course of their careers extraordinarily difficult. The National Labor Relations Board (NLRB), quite happy to deal with "sensible" industries such as automobile manufacturing and coal mining, approaches a nervous breakdown when asked to umpire management/labor relations in an industry in which nobody stays put. In the 1970s, the Directors Guild of America (DGA) was attempting to organize production assistants who, like nearly everyone else in Hollywood, worked free-lance. The dispute went to the NLRB. That organization, upon investigation, decreed that under its rules about who could vote in a union election, *no one* in the profession of production assistants was eligible. The DGA did begin to represent the production assistants, but no thanks to the NLRB.[14]

Further, the industry's reliance on a complex, constantly evolving technology not only divides the work force into a kaleidoscopic mélange of professions but also frequently changes their relationship to one another. This means, among other things, that Hollywood deals with more unions than do most industries. In the late 1980s, it was not uncommon for there to be members of more than twenty guilds and unions on a typical movie set.[15] It also means that the various unions are frequently in conflict with one another over jurisdiction because the evolving technology constantly changes the tasks the workers are supposed to be doing. Thus the advent of sound in the 1920s, of television in the 1940s, of cable in the 1970s, and of the videocassette recorder in the 1980s all set unions against one another in jurisdictional fighting that has been acrimonious and, in the early days, frequently violent. This quarrelling is characteristic both of the artists' guilds, which are called "above the line" (an accounting term) in industry vernacular, and of the craft unions, which are called "below the line" (see Table 8.1).

The unions have legitimate functions. In the days before unionization, producers sometimes worked their employees sixteen hours a day without overtime. Workers had no retirement pensions and no health insurance, and companies evinced no interest in the workers' welfare once they had ceased to be useful. Employees were subject to arbitrary firing without recourse, and artists were traded around among studios very much as though they were slaves. Their safety on the set did not appear to concern their employers. Somebody has to protect workers from such abuses, for it is clear that management cannot be trusted to restrain its own tendency to regard them as mere tools.

Although they originally arose to protect workers from the tyranny of the moguls, once safely esconced in a contract with the studios, Hollywood unions have tended to misbehave. As Table 8.1 shows, there is significant overlap in the jobs represented by the guilds and unions. Both SAG and AFTRA represent actors. The International Alliance of Theatrical and Stage Employes (IATSE) and the International Brotherhood of Electrical Workers (IBEW) represent electricians. IATSE, IBEW, and the National Association of Broadcast Employees and Technicians (NABET) represent camera opera-

TABLE 8.1 Major Hollywood Unions

Unions	Number of Locals/Branches	National Membership	Professions Represented
"Above the line" labor			
American Federation of Television and Radio Artists (AFTRA)	30	77,000	Actors, newscasters, announcers, disk jockeys, puppeteers, extras
Directors Guild of America (DGA)	3	10,000	Directors, assistant directors, unit production managers, associate directors, stage managers, production assistants
Screen Actors Guild (SAG)	21	73,000	Actors, singers, stunt performers, dancers, extras, voice-overs, puppeteers, pilots, models
Writers Guild of America West (WGAW)	1	9,000	Writers in motion pictures, TV, and radio
"Below the line" labor			
International Alliance of Theatrical Stage Employees (IATSE)	800	61,000	Art directors, story analysts, cartoonists, set designers, set decorators, scenic artists, art craftpersons, set painters, electricians, grips, make-up artists, hairstylists, editors, costumers, camera operators, others
International Brotherhood of Electrical Workers (IBEW)	1400	14,000	Announcers, radio technicians, camera operators, mot pic editors, electricians, film processors, audio persons, film technicians, others
National Association of Broadcast Employees and Technicians (NABET)	49	13,500	Newswriters, radio producers, film editors, camera operators, stage managers, others

SOURCE: Adapted from Curtis J. Matheaus, "Lights! Camera! Contract!: The Impact of Technology on Entertainment Unions," Master's thesis, University of Texas at Austin, 1990.

tors. Defining the jurisdiction of each individual union becomes an abstruse project that invites featherbedding and poaching.

Attempting to make as much work for their members as possible and defend the jobs they control from encroachment by rivals, the unions contrive complex rules that waste human energy and drive costs through the roof. In an article on Hollywood labor relations, John Eisendrath recounted, "If a scene calls for a fire in a fireplace, a member of the American Federation of

Guards must be present to tend it. One stagehand (a 'grip') moves furniture. Another stagehand (a 'gaffer') moves lights. Teamsters musn't handle the equipment they deliver. Hair stylists aren't allowed to touch makeup. When a location is overseas, all members of the International Alliance of Theatrical and Stage Employes (IATSE) must fly first class."[16]

The result is that union shoots, which means anything produced by the studios, are far more expensive than they could be. Producer Don Simpson reported on his experience at Paramount that "we have figured that a picture like *Beverly Hills Cop* ... that cost over ten million dollars, we could have made it for six and half or seven million dollars if we didn't have to worry about the unions."[17] The situation is similar on television.

As a consequence, studios contract out as much work to nonunion technical shops as possible. Studios also try to finance the work of independent producers, who frequently refuse to sign union contracts (at least at the craft level—it is impossible to make a film or television series with nonunion artists and create anything but an amateurish product). Perhaps half of the work that ultimately appears on television and motion picture screens is thus shot with nonunion "below-the-line" labor.

Management's increasing tendency to employ nonunion workers is of course the chief concern for craft-union leaders in modern Hollywood. Leaders of the artists' guilds, however, have a different sort of problem. For the past half century, their chief worry has been the issue of "residuals." Back in the days when Hollywood produced nothing but motion pictures to be shown in theaters, the employment problem for the actors, writers, and directors was fairly simple. They attempted to get jobs in which they were well paid and well treated, and when those ended they tried to get another. They had some reason to feel optimism in this quest because new movies were constantly being made. When the run of a film ended, it pretty much disappeared from the marketplace. The ceaseless manufacture of new movies to fill the void in the market meant the continuous creation of new jobs.

With the arrival of television, however, the situation changed. Television repeatedly broadcast not only its own programs but also old films. Artists saw the small screen occupied with their former efforts, still generating revenue for the producers, but now denying them employment. And so, early in the history of television, the artists' guilds began to demand that their members receive compensation whenever a television program or motion picture was rebroadcast. In a series of strikes in the 1950s and 1960s, actors, writers, and directors won the right to receive residuals, or payments, every time their work appeared on the screen.

By the 1980s, residuals payments from television made up a very large part of the income received by members of the artists' guilds. At the same time, however, new delivery systems were introduced that had the potential to generate lucrative incomes for producers but were not covered by guild contracts. All the guilds wanted to share in the new income streams from cable, from videocassette sales, from satellite broadcasts, and so on. Yet no one in the unions or among the producers could forecast how much money would come out of the new technologies, what formulas might extract enough of the revenue to be fair to the artists without discouraging investment by the producers, or how those revenues were to be collected so that no one would suspect fraudulent accounting. Negotiating in a swamp of ignorance, management was afraid it would inadvertently give away too much, while labor feared it was missing its chance at the golden goose. The result was an atmosphere of suspicion that pervaded the negotiations of the 1980s.

This atmosphere was made even more tense by an evident antiunion push by management. During the 1970s and 1980s, corporations all across the country increased their efforts to bust unions.[18] In Hollywood, long-term observers invariably argue that the acquisition of several studios by conglomerates introduced a more hostile tone into labor negotiations. Speaking of the difference between dealing with the old moguls and dealing with the new hired negotiators, one veteran writer-producer explained, "In the past, we dealt with primitive types, wild men. But they were our own. They may be out to kill you at the negotiating table, but we all went out for dinner together afterwards. We were, roughly speaking, colleagues. Now it's the new management, the studios and networks owned by Coca-Cola, Gulf and Western, General Electric. They *really* play hardball."[19] Using the legitimate issue of runaway costs as a rallying cry, management began to attempt to roll back benefits in every contract negotiation.

The conjunction of the guilds' determination to win residuals from the emerging technologies combined with everybody's ignorance about how to do that, and management's resolve to get control over spiraling costs made the 1980s a bruising decade for labor relations in Hollywood. The decade began with a bitter two-month strike by the Screen Actors Guild and AFTRA over the issue of residuals from motion pictures made for cable—a walkout that the unions were widely regarded as having lost.[20] In 1983, management formed the Alliance of Motion Picture and Television Producers (AMPTP), a centralized bargaining organization that allowed it to bring a united front against the unions which had to bargain one at a time. During the next five years, Hollywood was constantly in a state of nervous exhaustion over negotiations that were right on the brink of collapse and in fact produced six more strikes. All of this rancor, however, was basically just a prologue to the terrible confrontation of 1988 in which a war between the Writers Guild of America West and the AMPTP virtually shut down the industry for five months.

Employment opportunities for screenwriters are about the same as for every other profession in Hollywood: bleak. Although several hundred of the Writers Guild's 1988 members of 9,000 were rich, only about 2,500 earned enough to support themselves solely from writing.[21] The great majority of screenwriters were thus a part of the eternal Hollywood mob of the permanently discontented.

Additionally, however, writers are traditionally at the bottom of Hollywood's artistic hierarchy. They seldom get the sort of big money that goes to successful directors and actors, they are not idolized by the public or press, and their work is often altered without their consent. As Joan Didion has observed of her profession, "Writers do not get gross from dollar one, nor do they get the Thalberg Award, nor do they determine when or where a meeting will take place; these are facts of local life known even to children."[22] In a town in which frustration and paranoia are endemic, since the 1930s writers have ranked as the group most resentful of its treatment at the hands of the powers that be.

It is not a coincidence that the writers have always composed the most militant labor organization in Hollywood. In the 1930s and 1940s, the Screen Writers Guild was the most hospitable union to Communist infiltration. By 1955, for example, 106 writers, 36 actors, and 11 directors had been blacklisted for refusing to testify to their Communist Party membership before the House Committee on Un-American Activities.[23] The SWG's radical reputation so destroyed its effectiveness that it dissolved itself and merged with several other organizations to form the Writers Guild of America (West and East) in 1954.[24] Not much tamed by the transformation, the West writers (the WGAW) struck in 1960, 1973, 1981, and 1985.[25]

That last walkout set the stage for 1988. The 1985 strike had been a fiasco. The issue had been residuals from videocassette sales, and the WGAW had been internally divided on whether a strike was appropriate.

This internal division was becoming chronic in the artists' unions as more and more of their membership fell into the category "hyphenate." Hyphenate members are those writer-producers, actor-producers, and director-producers who begin their careers as artists but graduate, with success, to management. As artists (employees) they remain members of the unions, but as producers (management) they see conflicts from the point of view of the bosses. During a strike such as the writers' walkout in 1985, they can argue loudly against the union's position, creating perplexity and irresolution among the membership.

This internal conflict marked the decisions of the WGAW in 1985. Confused by hyphenate arguments, its members voted to return to work after only two weeks on the picket line, agreeing to give up most of their demands. The guild became a laughingstock in the industry. No doubt this encouraged management to regard the WGAW as a pushover and resolve to defeat it even more resoundingly when the contract expired three years later.[26]

In the interim, however, the WGAW had changed. Shortly after the unsuccessful strike, it hired a new executive director, Brian Walton. In the 1985 guild elections, a group of reform-minded writers had been elected to the board. In 1987 it elected a new president, George Kirgo. By 1988, therefore, the guild had a new leadership that was determined to be nobody's patsy again, hyphenates or no hyphenates.[27] With worker and management representatives thus resolved to impose their wills on each other, the union and the AMPTP moved into negotiations in the spring of 1988.

The issue, once more, was residuals. Producers insisted on an agreement that would roll back payments on one-hour television programs. Besides rejecting this, the writers demanded improved residuals on foreign broadcasts of syndicated shows. Neither side budged in the negotiations, and the strike began on March 7.[28]

Again, the WGAW experienced problems from its hyphenates. Their argument was that the unemployed and underemployed majority of the guild membership were voting to impose a strike on the writer-producers, the backbone of the guild's financial health. Every week the trade papers contained several letters from hyphenates attacking the guild's leadership for being more concerned with the idle majority than the productive minority. ("We who pay most of the guild's dues and strike costs," wrote Stephen Bochco to *Daily Variety* on July 18, "and keep the health insurance fund solvent, are victims of taxation without representation.") Twenty-one dissidents actually filed a complaint against their own union with the NLRB because it would not allow them to resign and go back to work.[29]

This time, however, the guild leadership had anticipated the complaints and had embarked on a member-education project to counter the hyphenate arguments. Further, in Walton and Kirgo they had forceful and articulate spokesmen who made effective debating points in the articles that filled the trade papers. Despite the few dissenters, therefore, the great mass of the membership held firm. Scripts stopped flowing to producers and networks. Dialogue went unwritten. Programs had no stories to put on the screen. Hollywood stopped.

If the industry had needed a reminder of the central part writers play in making films and television, this was it. Without stories, there was nothing for anyone else to do. All through the spring and into the summer, actors, hairstylists, and cinematographers sat at home. Secretaries, truck drivers, and janitors were laid off. The networks postponed their fall season, thereby losing several hundred million dollars in advertising. The studios, not turning out product for the theaters and the webs, lost a similar amount. Universal Studios' commissary closed for want of business. Secondary industries like restaurants and typing services saw their business plummet. Requests for financial assistance to the Motion Picture and Television Fund increased by 90 percent over the year before.[30] The secret fear of everyone in Hollywood—"I'll never work again!"—seemed to be coming true.

Meanwhile, the writers, losing about $500,000 a week in pay, were not enjoying themselves either.

After the initial breakdown of negotiations, the AMPTP refused to return to the bargaining table for twelve weeks and declined to submit the dispute to arbitration. The most likely explanation for this stubbornness is that management expected the WGAW membership to cave in as it had in 1985. When the producers finally realized that the guild was going to hold its ground, they returned to the table, but no progress was evident for another month. Then, in June, management blinked, offering a formula for foreign residuals that conceded most of what the writers demanded. At this point, the writers fumbled an opportunity. Believing that they had the AMPTP at the point of surrender, they voted down the offer. The rest of Hollywood gasped in disbelief and despair. The strike went on.

After another six weeks of shutdown and intransigence, both sides conceded that whatever they had to gain from continuing to disagree was small in comparison with the losses piling up all around them. In the first week of August, therefore, the leadership of the WGAW accepted a contract that was only marginally different from the one that had been rejected in June. They agreed to a sliding scale for residuals from one-hour shows, that, given the economics of the business, amounted to a cut. However, management agreed to pay foreign residuals based on the gross earned by each television program. It was, in short, a compromise.[31] Although a few militant writers claimed that the contract was unfavorable and that they should hold out for better, they were overwhelmed by the belief of their peers that enough damage had been done and that a further holdout would be self-destructive. The membership voted by 84 percent to ratify the agreement.[32] After twenty-two weeks of enforced idleness, Hollywood sighed and went back to work.

Even from the hindsight of only a few years, it is clear that this strike was a watershed. The industry-wide trauma of five months without work had a broadly educational effect. Leaders of both management and the unions decided that the adversarial system of dealing with labor disputes had become a monster that was threatening to devour the industry. Changes had to be made.

Soon after the end of the strike, representatives from the AMPTP began meeting regularly with labor leaders to discuss the problems and perspectives of each side. This method of continuous contact between employers and employees allowed each to deal with the problems of the other in an atmosphere of mutual good will rather than in the confrontational mode that had characterized contract negotiations. This changed the tone of interaction between the two from one of clear hostility to one of cautious cordiality.

The results of the new attitudes have been striking. In early 1989 the AMPTP reached an agreement with the IATSE that adjusted contract provisions to make shooting at night and on weekends less expensive. Although the IATSE thus agreed to some cuts in its members' pay in the short run, the benefits in the long run have been dramatic. With union shoots not costing so much, the studios began to rely less on nonunion production, and IATSE studio employment shot up 23 percent from 1987 to 1990, resulting in an increase in wages of $87 million.[33]

Even more impressive was the method by which the AMPTP and the two actors' unions resolved their negotiations in the spring of 1989. Only half a year after the end of the writers' strike, the looming expiration of the actors' contract had the industry praying for a settlement without a walkout. To the astonishment and delight of everyone, the parties announced even before negotiations were scheduled to begin that they had come to an agreement. In what might be termed an "anticipatory compromise," the actors had conceded to a more flexible workweek and a revision in the residuals formula for one-hour television series; in return, they received an increase in minimum wage, pension and health benefits, guest-star fees, and basic cable and foreign TV residuals.[34] Hollywood practically fainted with joy, and the leaders of the unions became wildly popular with their membership. Ten months later, the directors followed the actors' lead, reaching an agreement with the AMPTP five months in advance of the expiration of their contract.[35]

But the biggest surprise was yet to come. In December 1990, the Writers Guild announced that it had negotiated a contract extension with the AMPTP. The 1988 contract, instead of expiring as planned in 1992, would run until 1995. In order to head off problems that a rapidly evolving industry might cause such a long-term agreement, a "contract adjustment committee" had been created that would allow mutually agreed-upon amendments to the contract during its term. In essence, management and labor had devised a means of eliminating the traditional, confrontational, crisis-inducing manner of writing contracts and replacing it with an institutionalized form of continuous reciprocal adjustment. There was some opposition to this agreement from within the union, and some people raised questions about its legality; but when the members voted in its favor 2,017 to 698, they settled the matter decisively.

There has not been a strike in Hollywood since 1988.

It would be too strong to say that industry labor relations are now sweetness and light. There are still disagreements. For example, the Screen Actors Guild has been trying to acquire representation of West Coast extras for a solid decade but has been blocked at every turn, sometimes by dissenters within its own ranks, sometimes by AMPTP maneuvers. This situation seems unlikely to change. Nevertheless, labor disputes are now definitely less frequent than they used to be and less intense when they do occur. The basic, fundamental fact of employment in Hollywood—there is not enough of it—cannot be changed, and so there is nothing that can be done about the permanent reserve of discontent that underlies workers' attitudes. To the extent that tractable problems exist, however, they are now being dealt with in a rational manner in an atmosphere of comity.

This change in labor relations, together with the industry's response to the AIDS epidemic, suggests an important fact about Hollywood's ability to cope with its grim sociological situation. Faced with a crisis, its citizens are able to work together creatively to keep the industry functioning. In 1988, it became clear to everyone that the customary methods used by unions and management to deal with one another had become self-destructive. No longer within tolerable limits of conflict, these methods were threatening to destroy the industry. The result was an institutional adjustment that, without relieving the fundamental hostility of the two sides, nevertheless made it possible for them to live together in peace.

This suggests an important corollary to the political economy of Hollywood: Individually, people in the industry may be anxious, frustrated, and paranoid, but as a group they are not suicidal. They can cooperate to pursue collective defense despite their private enmities. In Hollywood, dissatisfaction may be permanent, but warfare can be avoided.

ARTISTS' RIGHTS

Sometimes, however, combat is unavoidable. The second greatest cause for ill feelings among artists in Hollywood, after the unemployment problem, has always been the lack of control over their own work. Because film and television are collaborative media, and because they are controlled by investors, the actors, writers, and directors who work in these media have never enjoyed the kind of personal autonomy for which artists yearn. Artists live to create. They pick their professions because in them they feel that they will be allowed to express their inner visions. Artists love their work the way parents love their children, the way addicts love their drugs, the way saints love their gods. They are fanatically selfish in their need to bring something into being on the screen *their* way.

But the whole experience of working in Hollywood is one of being thwarted in the pursuit of personal goals. Read any account of making a film or a television show and you will be treated to a roster of clashing opinions, of dreams squelched by lack of money, of genius stifled by circumstance, of art betrayed by philistines. To stay sane in Hollywood, artists must accept the tragic fact that even their very best work must inevitably be a compromise.

Artists do accept it, but they don't like it. Even those who have come to terms with the system harbor a simmering resentment against the fools and vulgarians who have defiled their visions in the past and will undoubtedly do so in the future.

This resentment is much greater among those who work in motion pictures than those who work in television. Anyone who works in television must accept the fact that the medium's low budgets and extreme time limitations militate against artistic freedom. These are the reasons that television work ranks far below movie work in the Hollywood status hierarchy. Motion pictures offer at least the potential for personal accomplishment, while TV is seen as pretty much a lost cause. Successful film artists, of course, are generously paid for their willingness to put up with Hollywood's lack of respect for their need for autonomy. But this extrinsic compensation only seems to intensify the indignation they feel when their efforts to attain intrinsic satisfaction are blocked.

In the early history of the motion picture industry, this bitterness was experienced before the project was finished. Artists might have felt outrage at the way they were deflected from completely realizing their dreams while a film was being shot; but once it was finished, they at least felt some pride in having partially succeeded in fashioning a product that was worthwhile. Each completed motion picture was a testament to the manner in which they could ultimately prevail despite the imperfections that were forced upon them. Once completed, a film was beyond the tinkering of barbarians.

Then came television. Networks and stations blithely punched holes in movies in order to insert commercials, omitted whole scenes to fit the film into time slots, snipped out sections of scenes that they deemed unfit for home entertainment, and substituted new words for profane dialogue. Artists did a slow burn while the results of their labors were chopped, dubbed, and expurgated.

They were legally helpless. In many other countries, notably those on the continent of Europe, artists are recognized as having some control over their work, regardless of the wishes of the official owner. In those countries there is a tradition of *droit d'auteur,* or author's right, which means that an artist retains a legal interest in his or her work forever, distinct from economic rights and interests. In discussions of this concept in the United States, *droit d'auteur* is usually translated as "moral rights," to convey the notion that artists rightfully have a general claim over the children of their imagination. In the Anglo-American legal system, however, it is traditionally the holder of the "copyright" who exerts absolute control over the work of art. If an artist was merely an employee on a project and holds no copyright, he or she has no say in how the fruits of that project are treated ever afterward. There are no moral rights. Because the studios retained the copyright on old films, they could sell or lease them to television with the understanding that they would be altered in whatever way was most convenient and profitable.[36]

A Hollywood artist once challenged in court the absolute freedom of studios and networks to work their wills with a motion picture. In the 1960s, director George Stevens sued to prevent the editing for television of his classic 1951 film, *A Place in the Sun.* It appeared that Stevens had a strong case because his contract stipulated that he alone would have the right to edit his pictures. The courts held, however, that for NBC to cut and alter scenes to make them more suitable for television did not violate Stevens's contract because that contract applied only to the process of creating a film before it was completed; anything done to it afterward did not constitute editing.[37]

In so holding, the judges demonstrated their ignorance of the nature of filmmaking in general and of the function of the director in particular. The essence of a motion picture is the arrangement of a multitude of shots into a narrative. Everything that goes into making each individual shot—the amount of light, the angle of light, the type and volume of the sound, the colors of the scene, the distance of the camera from the object being photographed, the camera angle, the motion contained within the shot—is the result of a deliberate choice, usually made by the director. Further, once the thousands of individual shots are taken, their arrangement—which ones will be used, how long each one will be, and in which order they will be found—is also a question of choice, again, usually the director's. The artistic essence of a film consists in just this stream of thousands of decisions by the person or persons in charge as they strive to take a multitude of sensory impressions and fashion them into something that is intellectually coherent and emotionally satisfying. To claim that a film is a collaborative effort is only to say that more than one person may have participated in the choices that went into its creation; that does not touch the status of the film as an artistic whole.

Plainly, then, to modify the film after the fact by altering either individual shots or their arrangement is to substitute a new set of choices for the original set, thus destroying the film as an artistic creation. When NBC changed *A Place in the Sun* by editing it for television, it recreated the film and thereby, without question, violated Stevens's contract.

The fact that the courts did not see it this way, however, completely discouraged other directors from bringing complaints of artistic butchery to the legal system. If Stevens, with a clear contract, could not prevent tampering with his creations, then others who worked under less favorable contracts hadn't a prayer. And so directors and others simply got used to the fact that viewers would see adulterated versions of their work on television.

But then came the 1980s. Advancing technology created still more ways for people who had not participated in the original creation of a film to alter it retroactively. Companies became able to stretch or compress the duration of a scene, meanwhile compensating electronically for the change this induces in the pitch of the actors' voices. The practice is useful for networks trying to shoehorn movies into television time slots. Needless to say, it destroys the rhythm and timing the actors and director attempted to put into the film. There is also "panning-and-scanning," in which a scene that is too wide for a television screen can be redone to fit the dimensions of the box. If two characters sitting at either end of a canoe are having a conversation, for example, the viewer's eye can be made to center first on one, then on the other, as if the camera had originally moved between the two of them. This reedits the cinematography, as if the original director had wagged the camera back and forth instead of having it sit still. With these two techniques, technicians are able to wrest the function of the director away from (often long-dead) artists and, in effect, shoot a new movie under the credits of the old.[38]

Although time alterations and panning-and-scanning are considered abominations by artists, they reserve their most intense fury for the third arrow in the quiver of electronic alteration, "colorization."

When a black-and-white motion picture is to be colorized, it is first transferred to a videotape—the process does not touch the original copy. Using a computer, technicians then turn the taped version into a color film. The colorized version does not look like a "real" movie to the sophisticated eye because lighting for black-and-white films is different from the lighting needed for an original color movie. To the educated eye, colorized films contain too many pastels and "incorrect" lighting angles.[39]

To the unsophisticated eyes of most viewers, however, colorized films are more interesting than the dull old black-and-white movies they are no longer willing to watch on television. Colorization has therefore been an economic bonanza to owners of film libraries from the days of the studio system. Ratings of colorized versions of black-and-white classics are invariably much higher than for showings of the originals, and these improved ratings allow the broadcast stations or cable systems showing them to collect more in advertising revenue. It costs between $180,000 and $500,000 to colorize a film, which may generate millions in extra income. The first colorized movie, *Miracle on 34th Street,* had garnered about $30,000 a year for the MGM library in the two decades in which it was occasionally broadcast in the original black-and-white. In the two years following its colorized debut in 1986, however, it earned $350,000. *Yankee Doodle Dandy* attracted about 5 million home viewers nationally when it was first televised in color compared to about 3.5 million who watched it when it was shown in black-and-white the previous year.[40] Given this economic picture, a number of media entrepreneurs, including cable mogul Ted Turner, have invested millions in colorization, and by now dozens of mutant films can be encountered on television in a typical week.

To Hollywood artists, however, the economics are irrelevant. "I've spent many years fighting an uphill battle to protect my most valuable asset: my good image," testified actress Ginger Rogers to a U.S. Senate subcommittee in 1987. "I've learned the hard way that actors have few—if any—rights over the use of our work. And that is why I'm here today. This computerized cartoon coloring is the final indignity. It is the destruction of all I have worked to achieve."[41] She spoke for the artists in general. All the guilds have taken positions opposing colorization. A 1987 opinion survey of 1,200 motion picture critics reported that 86 percent of them were against the process.[42]

It is among the directors, however, that the most intense opposition to colorization is found. In most cases, the interests they feel they are defending are not personal. The great majority of directors who worked under the studio system in the days when black-and-white photography was the norm are now dead; the younger directors who are currently active shoot almost exclusively in color. The directors see, then, not an attack on them personally but an assault on their art. After all the insults and humiliations they have learned to suffer working in Hollywood, colorization is an intolerable affront—even the work of dead directors is not safe from meddling by the princes of greed in the front office. The depth of outrage among directors at this evidence of the contempt in which their profession is held by their employers is impossible to exaggerate.

The DGA demands that the director, the principal screenwriter, and the cinematographer be recognized as the "authors" of a film and be given legally sanctioned moral rights over their work. The DGA also wants Congress to ratify U.S. assent to language in an international copyright treaty (the Berne Convention) that explicitly grants moral rights to artists. It wants colorization (and other retroactive interference with the creative process) to be outlawed or, failing that, to be subject to veto by a committee of directors, writers, and cinematographers.[43] Copyright holders of black-and-white films point to their unassailable legal rights under present U.S. law and dismiss these demands.

This controversy restates the classic Hollywood conflict of art versus commerce in a vivid way. It is also an issue, arising in the industry, that has implications for the nation. Should artists, whether working in film or any other medium, be recognized as having a moral interest in their work over and above economic ownership? Is legal ownership absolute? Is there a public interest involved that is distinct from the interests of the two parties? In order to consider these questions, it will be useful to summarize the arguments of the contending sides.

Arguments made by those in favor of colorization are clearly stated and powerful.[44] They include the fact that the original copy of a film is not touched by the colorization process and will always be around for those who wish to see it in its black-and-white purity. More important, proponents of the process point out that film is a collaborative art, and no one has the right to claim that he or she was responsible for a particular motion picture. Even more strongly, they scoff at the notion that the director, screenwriter, and cinematographer—or any group of artists—were the "authors" of a motion picture under the old Hollywood system, affirming that it was the *studios* that should be seen as the creators of those old black-and-white movies, the artists being merely hired hands. Because it was business organizations that were the artistic as well as economic authors of the motion pictures, then business should be permitted to continue to decide what is done with them.

Presenting themselves as the champions of classic films, colorizers argue that the new process has given companies an incentive to rescue old movies that were being allowed to disintegrate because it was unprofitable to restore them. According to executive Rob Word, "When I was approached to work for Hal Roach Studios, I was thrilled because of my love for Laurel and Hardy. The first thing we did was discover in the vaults all the films that were deteriorating, paralleling the general lack of public interest in black and white films. These movies were filmed on combustible nitrate stock. ... There has been no economic reason, up until recently, to preserve those films. ... The conversion of black and white to color has suddenly provided companies with an economic incentive to restore these films."[45]

Finally, colorizers invoke the free market to portray themselves as humble servants of the people and the directors as arrogant elitists attempting to dictate national tastes. According to Roger Mayer of the Turner Entertainment Company, "At issue here are simply matters of taste and choice. Some of us may not like sushi or *Finnegan's Wake* or ... the colored version of *The Maltese Falcon* or Shakespeare's *Hamlet*. None of us, I would trust, would consider legislation to *proscribe* what we dislike and what others may enjoy. ... Let us allow no one to mandate what the public may see and judge for itself."[46]

Directors regard most of these arguments as beside the point. To them, making a black-and-white film into a color version and then showing it under the original title while giving credit to the original artists is simply perpetrating a fraud. "Black and white photography is not color photography with the color removed," stated Sydney Pollack. "It is not better or worse in general, but it is *different*. It is a *choice*. ...*Changing what you see is altering what the film is.*"[47] Martin Scorcese agreed. "A lot of film directors use color as a statement. In using a certain color in a frame, you create an emotional and intellectual response in an audience. ... When you colorize, you change these responses."[48] Offering a concrete example from his own work, Fred Zinneman reported that he deliberately shot his classic 1952 western *High Noon* in black-and-white, even though color was available. "My notion was that the picture should look like a newsreel of the period, if movie cameras had existed in the 1880s. ... Floyd Crosby—the cameraman—and I studied a lot of stills from that period, especially the Civil War photos by Matthew Brady. ... I will always believe that this style—the white sky, the flat lighting and the grainy texture—had a lot to do with the impact of the movie. Color would have softened it, made it look trivial—in short, would have *corrupted* it."[49] Other directors have added their testimony to the argument that their use of black-and-white photography involved deliberate choices that would be negated by colorization.[50]

As for the contention of the colorizers that directors were only employees in the studio system and therefore have no claims to authorship, present-day directors retort that Michelangelo was also a hired hand, yet nobody is proposing to paint colors on the statue of David. To the argument that television audiences are larger for colorized movies than they are for the originals, the directors reply that market forces should not justify the mutilation of anyone's work. "If audiences who have grown up on mindless television were so desensitized that a movie like *It Happened One Night*, which has been delighting people in black and white for generations, now had to be viewed in color to be appreciated," fumed Woody Allen, "then the task would be to cultivate the audience back to some level of maturity rather than to doctor the film artificially to keep up with lowered tastes."[51]

In regard to the argument that colorization furnishes the incentive to rescue old movies, directors acknowledge that preservation is a worthy goal but insist that it is a separate problem. Saying that films must be colorized in order to be preserved reminds them of the Vietnam War commander who argued that it was necessary to destroy a village in order to save it. Directors endorse a major effort to find and restore old movies, but not at the expense of the artistic heart of the films.

The directors' most important rebuttal, however, is focused not so much on motion pictures as on the nation. Reminding us that films are part of our cultural history, they suggest that it is a betrayal of our common heritage to allow their display under false pretenses. In a report in 1986, the Directors Guild argued that the new technologies were allowing a falsification of the historical record: "We believe that 'colorization' represents the mutilation of history, the vandalism of our common past, not merely as it relates to film but as it affects society's perception of itself. 'Colorization' is a rewriting of history, which we believe is inherently dangerous. We believe that ... no civilization worthy of the name can afford to promulgate lies about itself."[52]

In my own judgment, this argument is unanswerable and makes the directors' battle one that should be supported by everyone concerned with the public interest. To change the original choices of the artists changes the film into something else. Colorizers do not even deny this. In order for a colorized motion picture to receive copyright protection, it has to be shown to contain "substantial variation" from the original work. Whenever they apply for a copyright, therefore, colorizers admit they have made a novel product.[53] Yet they display this newly manufactured film under the original title, listing the original artists in the credits. Every colorized film is thus a counterfeit, and the televising of such commodities constitutes a gigantic deceptive trade practice. The fact that many people are willing to watch these bogus productions is irrelevant, as is the fact that their authorship is ambiguous.

The directors, however, have not had much success persuading others to share this position. They are, of course, solidly opposed by corporate Hollywood, the networks, television stations, cable companies, and virtually the entire recording and publishing industries. Although the DGA is able to attract a fair hearing for its views because of its ability to marshall big-name directors to testify in any public forum, in a lobbying battle it is vastly outgunned. Moreover, for Congress to ratify the portions of the Berne Convention dealing with moral rights would shatter the foundations of American copyright law and introduce even more confusion into a legal area that is already semi-chaotic.

Given the magnitude of the forces arrayed against the directors, the wonder is that they have managed to make any headway. In 1988 they launched a major push to persuade Congress to ratify Berne, pass moral rights legislation, or in some other way restrain the technological altering of old movies. Although none of these outcomes was ever a remote possibility, Congress did pass a rather tepid compromise, the National Film Preservation Act, in September of that year.[54] This law established the National Film Preservation Board (NFPB) as an adjunct to the Library of Congress. A thirteen-member commission composed mostly of representatives from Hollywood's artists' guilds and major trade associations, the board was given the task of recommending twenty-five "culturally and historically significant" motion pictures per year to the Librarian of Congress. Assuming that the librarian took its advice, the titles would then be placed on the National Film Registry, and anyone who wished to "materially alter" them would have to label them as such.[55] The law contained a "sunset" provision mandating that it would need to be renewed every three years.

In the three years after the NFPB began operating in 1989, it afforded film buffs across the nation a good deal of fun discussing the relative merits of the seventy-five movies that were chosen. It did nothing, however, to stop or even slow the modification of old motion pictures. The Librarian of Congress angered moral-rights advocates by defining the "material alteration" of a film narrowly, so as to exclude just about any change except colorization. For their part, colorizers were happy to label the altered films they presented on television, considering the labels a form of advertising.[56]

Despite its innocuous nature, the National Film Preservation Act proved to be surprisingly unpopular with Congress when it came up for renewal in 1991. James Billington, the Librarian of Congress, disliked having to deal with the wrangling representatives from Hollywood and felt that his office "should not be responsible for enforcing labeling requirements. Individuals who feel their rights are violated when films are altered should seek redress by other means."[57] Congressional representatives hated being caught in an emotion-laden argument between Hollywood artists and producers and preferred to appropriate money for film preservation (which everyone could support), meanwhile allowing the labeling requirement to slide into oblivion. Even the American Civil Liberties Union weighed in against the NFPB, arguing that it was unconstitutional because it required "a private party to place a label with specific government-mandated wording on a product like motion pictures protected by the First Amendment."[58] Finally, the directors, the original force behind the NFPB, felt that it functioned only to distract attention from the ongoing desecration of old films. And so, with even its original sponsors having deserted it, the NFPB was allowed to die an unlamented death.

The issue, however, will not go away. Hollywood artists, especially the directors, are mad as hell and determined to do something about what they consider to be a gigantic collective insult from corporate America. Given the economic forces at work, however, the corporations cannot be expected to concede that artists are entitled to anything other than their paychecks. And so, unlike the labor relations problem, the issue of artists' rights appears to be intractable.

If the outcome to the struggle depended only on lobbying power, the artists would not have a chance. They are outnumbered and outfinanced, and the opposition has both tradition and law on its side. But in the long run, the artists' position may be stronger than it appears to be now. Artists possess two intangible but crucial advantages: the power of an idea and the skill to publicize it. Already they have recruited a variety of intellectuals to their side, and a spate of scholarly articles have appeared arguing for the modification of U.S. copyright law.[59] Some journalists have also taken up the cause of moral rights.[60] Over the years, if they are persistent, the directors may find a significant portion of public opinion swinging their way. An intra-Hollywood squabble may become a national political issue. If that happens, corporate power will no longer be decisive.

9

Censorship and Self-Expression

ENTERTAINMENT IS A RISKY BUSINESS in the political as well as the economic and psychological senses. Other industries face threats to their investments because of consumer indifference, but few of them encounter active hostility to their products. People may not like a shoe style, but they usually do not claim that it insults their ethnic group. A coal mining company may be accused of polluting a local stream but never of befouling the moral climate of the country. Consumers sometimes object to children's toys on the grounds that they are physically dangerous but not because they think that the toys are inspired by Satan.

In the television and motion picture industry, however, such accusations are a normal part of the business. Sex and violence have always been principal components of stories in every culture and medium. The extraordinary psychological vividness of screen entertainment, however, seems to magnify the threatening aspect of these two dramatic staples. The stuff of entertainment is fantasy, and fantasy always contains instruction in values and behavior, if only implicitly. Parents are perennially concerned that their children will learn the wrong things while enjoying themselves in front of their magic screens.

Moreover, Hollywood's stories usually contain good guys and bad guys, and the bad guys must have specific characteristics—a certain complexion, a certain accent, a certain age, and so on. Since the industry began, many people have been concerned that ordinary viewers would tend to make generalizations about groups based on the individual characterizations they saw on the screen. The depiction of a criminal Italian, a greedy Jew, or an immoral priest can often provoke the charge from representatives of these groups that the industry is instilling pejorative and false images in millions of minds. Since the United States is a pluralist society with hundreds of racial, religious, national, economic, and lifestyle groupings, it is to be expected that just about any product will make the members of some group think that they are being targetted for disapproval.

Nor should these two worries be lightly dismissed. In a society in which rates of murder, rape, births to unwed mothers, and general violence have been rising steadily for decades while school performance has been falling, and in which relations between ethnic groups are frequently tense, it is legitimate to wonder if screen entertainment contributes to these problems. And if the conclusion is reached that Hollywood does help to worsen the moral climate and civic atmosphere, it is just as legitimate to try to do something about it. One does not have to be a prude or a Puritan to see the realistic concern expressed by the author of a 1988 editorial in *The New Republic* magazine who said, "What has degraded so many of the young ... is the sense, actively encouraged by our popular culture and propagated by the incessant images of our mass media, that nothing is true and everything is permitted."[1] For citizens who think they see a threat to their faiths, their country, or their values on the screen, it is but a short step to try to gain control over the source of the danger, through government means or otherwise. From its first decade, therefore, Hollywood has existed in an environment bristling with potential censors. To the economic risks inherent in any commercial undertaking, motion pictures and television thereby add the constant danger of ideological interference.

The industry, of course, pleads innocent to all charges of moral corruption and group insult. Before we discuss its defense, however, it will be useful to cast an eye back on the history of dissatisfaction with the entertainment media and look at some of the battles that have been fought between Hollywood and those who would censor it.

THREE CULTURAL BATTLEFIELDS

In the spring of 1915, D. W. Griffith released his motion picture *The Birth of a Nation* to a stunned and delighted world.[2] It was the first "movie" in the sense that we think of the term—the first long film to tell a complex, coherent story. Although Griffith did not invent the close-up, crosscutting, rapid-fire editing, the iris shot, the split-screen shot, realistic and impressionistic lighting, or a roster of other cinema techniques, no previous director had employed them together in the service of a powerful narrative. Griffith was the first, in other words, to realize the potential of the motion picture both as mass entertainment and as an art form.

The Birth of a Nation was a huge critical and financial success. Although the industry's primitive accounting methods at that time make it impossible to reconstruct the exact income of the movie, some estimates peg its total box-office gross at more than $60 million. Given inflation and population growth, this would be roughly equivalent to $1.5 billion today. President

Woodrow Wilson, after seeing the film in the White House, remarked, "It is like writing history with lightning."[3] Griffith became an instant celebrity.

Yet since the day of its release, the film has been accompanied by a chorus of outrage. And no wonder. It is based on a novel and play by Thomas Dixon called *The Clansman*. It tells the story of a white family with northern and southern branches torn asunder by the Civil War. After the war, in which one of the family's sons is killed, its southern branch endures humiliation at the hands of carpetbaggers and freed blacks until the family, the South, and presumably the nation are saved by another son, who founds the Ku Klux Klan. The principal goal of all the male black characters in the film appears to be to marry white women. The movie features a scene in which a mulatto ex-Union army sergeant pursues a virginal young white woman onto a precipice with the avowed intent of forcing her into marriage. To avoid this fate, she casts herself over the cliff to her death. At the climax of the movie, gangs of blacks and carpetbaggers besiege good Southern citizens, but the KKK, led by our hero, rides to the rescue and saves the innocents amidst much slaughter of the evildoers.

This movie was not a racist document merely in passing or as some melodramatic afterthought. Its central message was consciously and explicitly to reunite the North and South after the schism of civil war (the title would have been more correctly rendered as *Rebirth of a Nation*) by creating a sense of historical mission among whites to cooperate in the subjugation of blacks. Along these lines, Griffith boasted that one of his purposes "was to create a feeling of abhorrence in white people, especially white women, against colored men."[4] Unified by this mutual antipathy, whites would forget the wounds of war and rebuild a united, harmonious society. Of course, this united society would not include blacks, who were, by implication, to be stripped of the rights of citizenship and returned to a state not unlike slavery.

Although Griffith's grander aims were not realized, there is reason to believe that his artistic polemic had effect. There were more blacks lynched in 1915 than in any previous year in the century. In the 1920s the Ku Klux Klan frequently offered screenings of *The Birth of a Nation* as a sort of super-recruiting poster, and its membership grew into the millions. Some social science experiments with children have offered evidence that suggests that viewing the film creates anti-black prejudice in its viewers.[5]

None of this would come as a surprise to the National Association for the Advancement of Colored People. In alliance with appalled white liberals and public officials concerned about potential disturbances of the peace, the NAACP attempted to prevent the showing of the film everywhere it had a chapter. W.E.B. Dubois, a black sociologist and one of the NAACP's founders, argued, "We are aware ... that it is dangerous to limit expression, and yet, without some limitations civilization could not endure."[6] Under this rationale, the organization filed dozens of lawsuits, some of which were temporarily successful. From 1915 to 1973, there were at least twenty-eight court actions involving the movie, a few of which, in the early years, resulted in its being banned from some areas of the country. At least five city councils passed censorship ordinances specifically aimed at Griffith's film. State censorship boards prohibited its showing in Kansas and Maryland. In 1918 Governor James Cox banned it within Ohio. *The Birth of a Nation* is still occasionally shown today, usually in university communities, and can be relied upon to engender opposition from those who think that American race relations are bad enough already.

Racism, however, is not the only topic that many people think does not deserve to be celebrated on the screen. In November 1972, two episodes of "Maude," a program from Norman Lear's stable of CBS situation comedies, threw the television industry into an intense controversy with the Catholic Church over the issue of abortion.[7]

The Maude character was a strong-minded woman in late middle age who was married to her third husband. In the first episode, she discovers that she is pregnant. After an intense bout of soul-searching and discussion with her spouse, she decides to have an abortion. In the second episode, she carries out her intention.

The programs sparked hundreds of angry phone calls and thousands of letters to Lear and the network. On November 21, the day of the second broadcast, Monsignor Eugene V. Clark of the Archdiocese of New York wrote Richard Jencks, president of the CBS Broadcast Group, accusing the network of "open propaganda for abortion."[8] Shortly thereafter, the National Council of Catholic Bishops filed a protest with CBS, asking for equal time to present the anti-abortion position. They demanded that the network devote two additional episodes of "Maude" to stories "supporting the right to life of unborn babies," specifically "a sequel in which Maude is pregnant and has a baby."[9]

When the network refused, protesting groups lodged a formal complaint with the Federal Communications Commission, claiming that by running the program CBS had violated the FCC's Fairness Doctrine. This rule, aimed primarily at news and public affairs programs, requires broadcasters to give time to opposing groups when presenting one side of a controversial issue.

While the FCC considered the petition, both pro-choice and pro-life forces waged a battle for public opinion and political power. Catholic leaders urged their parishioners to launch a letter-writing campaign and a boycott of the products of eight corporations whose ads had appeared in the controversial episodes. Leaflets were handed out, urging the faithful to contact their local CBS station managers and inform them "that you will not allow your children to watch [channel X] as long as they continue to carry 'Maude.'"[10] Meanwhile, pro-choice groups were organizing their own letter-writing campaign, targetting stations, the network, the FCC, and advertisers. To encourage Norman Lear, the Los Angeles office of Planned Parenthood held a testimonial dinner for him at the home of UCLA Chancellor Charles Young.

In June 1973, the FCC denied the petition to punish CBS for violation of the Fairness Doctrine. That rule, the commission said, insisted on a balanced coverage of issues within the schedule of a station but not within each program. Thus fortified, the network rebroadcast the offending episodes in August. This decision cost it considerably. All of the show's sponsors pulled out, creating the rare sight of an American television entertainment program presented without commercials. Thirty-nine of the network's 198 affiliate stations refused to carry the show.

Although the specific controversy over "Maude" faded, its reverberations remain. The Catholic Church began to form lobbying groups to bring direct and indirect pressure to bear on the television industry to offer more acceptable programming. On the specific topic of abortion, however, the Church had already made its impact, for prime-time television did not feature a program centering around the subject again for more than a decade.

Abortion is a secular issue with religious overtones. In 1988, however, Hollywood produced a motion picture that many Christians believed to be a direct attack on their faith. After having been kicked around among several studios for three decades, in 1988 Nikos Kazantzakis' novel *The Last Temptation of Christ* was brought to America's theaters by Universal.[11] Directed by Martin Scorcese, the film aroused indignation among millions of Christians world-wide for three reasons. First, Jesus' character as portrayed in the film was that of an anxious neurotic, not at all like the somber but self-assured messiah who dominates the New Testament. Second, the film took great liberties with the wording of key passages in the Gospels, so that the Sermon on the Mount, for example, becomes hopelessly muddled, and Jesus' basic message is lost. Third, in an extended fantasy sequence in which Jesus imagines what his life would have been like had he chosen to live it as an ordinary mortal, he is shown in one fairly explicit scene engaging in sexual intercourse with his wife, Mary Magdalene.

To say that most Christians were offended by this movie would be a pale understatement. One Protestant minister, Dr. Jack Hayford, summed up the reaction of many when he charged that it "casts as mentally unbalanced the man who established the teachings that became the guideposts for an entire civilization. It's an outright distortion of history and a devastating assault on the personal values of hosts of people."[12] Both the Roman Catholic and Mormon churches condemned the film and urged their members not to see it. Wherever it played around the world, there were demonstrations against it and occasionally some mild violence. Either because their management was offended by the film or because they hesitated to insult so many potential customers, several American theater chains refused to exhibit it and some videocassette rental chains announced that they would not carry it

when it was released for home viewing. Although a few liberal Protestant religious leaders praised the movie, their opinions were drowned in the flood
of denunciation.

In the United States a campaign to make Universal withdraw *The Last
Temptation of Christ* from exhibition had two prongs. In the first, demon-
strators in the Los Angeles area attempted to embarrass the studio's executives, especially Lew Wasserman, into pulling it. The protestors showed that
they were sophisticated in battles of publicity and that they believed that the
way to fight images was with counterimages. In one media event, for example, hundreds of marchers "began at Sunset Blvd. and proceeded up the
street to Wasserman's Foothill Drive home, led by a barefoot, wigged actor
wearing a bloody sheet and carrying a full-size cross. The Christ figure then
kneeled in front of Wasserman's home, and a protestor in a business suit
...placed his shoe on the kneeling man's back and spread bloodied hands
above him."[13] These spectacles were a frequent occurrence in Hollywood in
the summer of 1988.

The second prong of the attack was less sophisticated and petered out
quickly. Some groups of citizens sued to have the film suppressed because of
its alleged blasphemy, and a few municipalities attempted to ban it. Lower
courts unanimously held, however, that Scorcese's and Universal's freedom
of expression were constitutionally protected, and the Supreme Court
agreed. Any effective barriers to the motion picture's display were therefore
psychological, not legal.

Whether because of the tumult and commotion against *The Last Temptation of Christ* or not, the film barely broke even at the box office. It has not
been broadcast on network television. It does a fairly lively business in video
rental stores, however, and may make the studio a decent profit eventually.
Given the trouble Universal had to endure for such a meager return, however, studios will undoubtedly be less likely in the near future to produce motion pictures containing unorthodox religious themes. The real effect of the
campaign against *The Last Temptation of Christ,* then, like the outcome of
the attack on "Maude," is not that it suppressed the particular product in
question but that it effectively discourages similar products in the future.

ARGUING FREEDOM OF ARTISTIC EXPRESSION

Like the members of any other industry, people in motion pictures and television strenuously oppose most government interference in their enterprises.
Unlike citizens involved in other businesses, however, they believe that they
enjoy constitutional protection from most such intrusion. The First Amendment of that document decrees, "Congress shall make no law ... abridging
the freedom of speech, or of the press," and the Fourteenth Amendment

applies the interdiction to the states. People in Hollywood invariably assert that these passages together guarantee a "freedom of expression" that applies to artistic endeavors and that therefore they should be immune to all efforts to suppress or alter their activities. Executives endorse this constitutional view implicitly, but it is held even more intensely by artists. Their lives already consist of constant battles against ignorant and mean-spirited meddling by financiers, executives, and other artists. Having to overcome the weight of philistinism within the industry in order to realize some shred of their personal visions in their films and television programs, artists have no sympathy with forces outside the industry that then want to control their products. Hollywood artists regard all efforts to influence the content of entertainment as one more facet of the gigantic conspiracy that is attempting to thwart their work and leave them poor and unrecognized forever. The dirtiest word in Hollywood, even worse than "blacklist," is "censorship."

The industry is therefore a fertile breeding ground for organizations defending an absolutist interpretation of the First Amendment. The American Civil Liberties Union is probably the most active and well-supported political group in town. People For The American Way is its frequent collaborator. In addition, many people in the industry join organizations with names such as the National Campaign for Freedom of Expression and the Creative Coalition whenever they feel that censorship threatens, which is most of the time. On any given day, the trade papers are likely to report on some gathering in which prominent members of the community warn against the tide of suppression of ideas that is sweeping the country and urge that America adhere to the principles of the First Amendment in order to save itself from a tyranny of the mind.

Hollywood's argument for freedom from outside control consists of two parts. First, it makes the traditional claim that because the free circulation of ideas is crucial to democracy, speech and press must be unfettered. Second, it asserts that motion pictures and television, because they are electronic extensions of speech and press, similarly deserve complete liberty.

The first part of this contention, the rationale for freedom of speech and press, is straightforward and unassailable. Competition in ideas is essential to democracy. In a society in which the people govern themselves, they must be allowed to examine differing views of the public interest and evaluate competing prescriptions about how to achieve it. Private citizens must therefore be at liberty to express themselves on issues of public policy within certain very wide bounds, such as a prohibition on libel and slander. The First Amendment is the very cornerstone of American democracy, and any country that does not have some similar guarantee of the circulation of ideas cannot be considered a free society.

The second part of the argument takes a bit more intellectual stretching. Artists maintain that when the First Amendment mentions "speech and press" as protected activities, it is really outlining a general *freedom of expression* that must be protected. According to this view, art, which includes television and motion pictures, is just as much a forum for expression of ideas as are speech and the press. The form of address is irrelevant; a stump speech, a novel, a newspaper editorial, and a movie are all differing forms of the same essential activity.

When the hubbub over *The Birth of a Nation* was at its height, D. W. Griffith released a statement, titled "A Plea for the Art of the Motion Picture," which nicely encapsulated this philosophy. It read:

> We do not fear censorship, for we have no wish to offend with improprieties or obscenities, but we do demand, as a right, the liberty to show the dark side of wrong, that we may illuminate the bright side of virtue—the same liberty that is conceded to the art of the written word—that art to which we owe the Bible and the works of Shakespeare.[14]

The strategy has not changed in the decades since. In the midst of the violent reaction to *The Last Temptation of Christ,* Universal Studios took out ads in national newspapers and the trades, making essentially the same syllogism: The First Amendment protects freedom of expression; art is expression; therefore, artists have the right to produce whatever they want.[15]

When the motion picture industry first made this argument, in reaction to the activities of a local censorship board in 1915, the Supreme Court disagreed that films deserved First Amendment protection. Deciding that "the exhibition of moving pictures is a business pure and simple ... not to be regarded ... as part of the press of the country or as organs of public opinion," it upheld the board's powers.[16]

Over the course of the next few decades, however, American intellectual currents evolved in a more libertarian direction, and D. W. Griffith's assertion of a right of artistic freedom became the orthodox view. In 1952, in the *Miracle* case, the Court reversed its 1915 position and ruled that films were a "significant medium for the communication of ideas" and as such were protected by the First Amendment.[17] For forty years, therefore, motion picture content, except for pornography, has been immune from government regulation.

As the *Last Temptation of Christ* example illustrates, however, groups of annoyed citizens continue to try to force their way into the creative process anyway. The risk of a return of censorship, however small, is real. Hollywood's perception that it is continually threatened from outside is thus accurate, if exaggerated. There is just enough genuine possibility of a renewed censorship to feed the film industry's paranoia and keep the ACLU's coffers full.

SELF-REGULATION OF MOTION PICTURES

In another sense, however, the argument over censorship and the First Amendment is misplaced because it assumes that Hollywood stubbornly resists any influence from ordinary citizens. In fact, for all their noisy opposition to interference, both the motion picture and television industries have always expended considerable effort attempting to avoid giving offense to outsiders. Historically, their strategy can be summarized as one of adopting self-regulation to forestall outside censorship. The fact that various groups in society continue to be offended by what appears on the screen does not mean that those industries make no efforts to restrain themselves; rather, it is evidence that you can't please everyone.

In 1922 America was in the midst of a national paroxysm of moral indignation over the content of motion pictures and the alleged behavior of movie folk who, then as now, had a reputation for adventurous living. Censorship legislation had been introduced in more than half the states when the industry asked Will Hays, former chairman of the Republican National Committee and postmaster general of the United States, to head the newly formed Motion Picture Producers and Distributors of America.[18] The MPPDA had two purposes: to establish a voluntary Production Code that would restrain the producers' tendency to create ever more licentious entertainment; and to act as a public relations agency, convincing the outside world that Hollywood was cleaning up its act. Hays did his job successfully for twelve years, but in the midst of the Depression, the voluntary censorship system collapsed as the producers attempted to retrieve their declining box-office receipts by pumping up the sex-and-violence quotients of their films. This new, rougher style of movie caused an outcry among the nation's moral guardians, and in 1934 the Catholic Legion of Decency made preparations to urge the Church's parishioners to boycott all theaters. If successful, this desertion by a portion of its remaining audience would have spelled disaster for an industry whose income had already fallen by a third in five years.[19]

The producers responded to the threat by putting teeth into the voluntary guidelines that granted the Hays Office, as it had come to be called, the power to levy $25,000 fines for violations of the Code. Henceforward, any picture produced by the major studios, which included about 98 percent of all American movies, had to run a gauntlet of examination in the Hays Office in order to win a seal of approval without which it could not be released.

Not only were portrayals of sex and violence toned down considerably under the Production Code, but scripts containing references to any ethnic group or occupation were also scrutinized for potentially offensive characterizations. The self-censorship was so complete that Joseph Breen, the

Code's chief enforcer, once remarked that in Hollywood movies under his authority, "A villain can be only a native-born white American with no college, no fraternity, no political affiliations, no profession, and no job."[20] Further, the Code imposed a rigid and rather prissy set of moral conventions on all American films. Suicide and divorce were seldom encountered. Anyone who had committed evil acts in the past, especially of a sexual nature, had to be punished in the course of the story; there was no possibility of overcoming a wicked personal history. All references, implied or otherwise, to sexual intercourse, even between husband and wife, were forbidden. Profanity was prohibited (Rhett Butler's "Frankly my dear, I don't give a damn," caused a mini-scandal in 1939); also prohibited were characters who were prostitutes, shots of toilets or the sexual organs of animals, the sound of a human burp, and any suggestion of homosexuality. In Hollywood under the Code, actors and actresses kissed with their mouths closed.[21]

The artists who had to work under the studio system of self-censorship naturally held it in contempt and attempted to evade its strictures. Almost every production became a tangle of negotiation, with the artists trying to wheedle and maneuver their own preferences into the script and Joseph Breen and his assistants objecting to dozens of points of plotline and dialogue. Writers would purposely produce a script that they knew would be far too racy to be acceptable under the Code, so that in the course of bargaining with Breen they might grudgingly "compromise" by giving up some nonessential dialogue, thereby saving what they really valued in the story. Producers spent weeks arguing with Breen's censors, attempting to convince them that certain scenes were essential to the plot. Historical accounts of Hollywood during the studio era document the enormous amount of time and effort the artists spent wrestling with those whom producer Val Lewton called "Joe Breen and his merry men."[22]

And yet out of this struggle between the conventional, unimaginative minds of the self-regulators and the desires of the artists for autonomy emerged a cinema that dominated the world market and is still looked upon with nostalgia. Scholars invariably regard the 1930s and 1940s as the Golden Age of American motion pictures. Essays by historians about the New Hollywood, with its much greater artistic freedom, almost always argue that its movies are generally inferior to the products of the old studio system. It appears that the struggle between artists and censors under the old arrangement may actually have been good for movies and that there may be worse things in entertainment than self-restraint.

Be that as it may, the system did not last. The disintegration of the studio system in the 1950s unleashed a mob of independent producers who refused to submit their films to the Hays Office, and that institution declined into extinction. The Supreme Court's *Miracle* decision in 1952 prevented government agencies from stepping in where the MPPDA left off. By the late 1960s, explicit sex and gory violence were difficult to avoid on the nation's theater screens.

Despite judicial interdictions against government interference with motion picture content, the new freedom raised a great outcry among the populace. Because another twist of the political dial might always bring a different, less tolerant philosophy to the Supreme Court, film producers could not rely on the legal atmosphere remaining so permissive. Once again, Hollywood moved to calm the citizens and head off potential efforts to impose external controls by instituting self-regulation.

Because it could no longer demand script changes from its producers, the industry opted this time for truth-in-labeling. In 1968, Jack Valenti, head of the new Motion Picture Association of America, huddled with Louis Nizer, the organization's general council, and devised a series of "ratings" for freshly released movies. The two then sold the idea to the important production, distribution, and exhibition segments of the industry. Under the new system, American producers and importers of foreign features would submit their films before release to the MPAA's Code and Rating Administration (CARA), where each movie would be given a symbol designed to inform consumers of its content. Presumably, parents would then assume the censor role that was no longer within the power of the industry. A rating of "G" meant that the film was suitable for general audiences (that is, families with children). "PG" meant that parental guidance was suggested because the movie contained some material probably not suitable for pre-teenagers. A rating of "R" indicated that consumers under the age of seventeen would not be admitted unless accompanied by a parent or guardian. "X" meant that the film was clearly intended for adults and that no one under the age of seventeen would be admitted.[23] Beginning in 1984, the category "PG" spun off a "PG-13" rating, indicating that the film was not suitable for viewers under the age of 13.

Although the institution of the CARA rating system did not eliminate all grumbling about the moral tone of American films, it quieted most serious public complaints. The MPAA's other constituency, however, its own artists, became increasingly restive with the labeling program and the way it evolved.[24] All of CARA's ratings except "X" were copyrighted by the MPAA, meaning that although "G," "PG," and "R" could be applied to films only by that organization, "X" could be slapped on anything by anyone. Because "X" meant "adult," producers of pornographic films quickly began to apply it to their own wares, using it as an advertisement. It became impossible for consumers to distinguish ahead of time between an adult but nonpornographic X-rated movie (1973's *Last Tango in Paris,* for example) and a simple porn film. Consequently, all X-rated motion pictures came to be considered porn. Ordinary, family-oriented theaters would not show them, and most newspapers would not accept ads for them. But this meant the kiss of death for a nonporn Hollywood film that received an "X" rating. Such a movie would not be booked into mainstream theaters because it was presumed to be porn and not booked into "adult" theaters because it was not "hot" enough. In order to avoid the "X," filmmakers were forced to ask CARA what changes they could make that would allow them to achieve the "R." The organization that had been instituted merely as an information source for parents had become, by the 1980s, the authority that many producers and directors had to please in order to sell their wares. Adrian Lyne had to cut so much out of his 1986 film *9 1/2 Weeks* in order to earn an "R," for example, that the movie lost crucial scenes and became incomprehensible. The labeler had evolved into a censor.

Here again was the classic frustration of the Hollywood filmmaker: Events were conspiring to rob him or her of autonomy. Through the 1980s the artists' resentment smoldered, until by the end of the decade it burst forth into open opposition. In 1990 several distributors of foreign films (*Tie Me Up! Tie Me Down!,* for example) refused to submit their movies to CARA, releasing them unrated. When these films nevertheless found enough independent theaters willing to defy the MPAA and exhibit them anyway, it encouraged further defections. Meanwhile, director Mark Lipsky was starting an insurrection, organizing directors and writers to apply pressure to Jack Valenti and the MPAA to alter the system. Some of the most prominent artists in the industry called publicly for a reform of the system. The artists' unions joined the fray. The implicit threat behind the publicity was that the artists would simply begin to ignore CARA. If enough of them did this, the rating system would fall apart, because theaters could not afford to refuse the products of the most successful filmmakers.

The artists' contention was that there should be an additional rating, an "A," that would be applied to adult-but-not-pornographic films. Valenti resisted. The ratings system, he contended, was too complicated as it was; to add another symbol would damage its utility by rendering it too cumbersome. Moreover, to ask CARA to divide "adult" films into the pornographic and the serious would be requiring it to make artistic judgments. "An A would be a serious artistic film with aberrational behavior in it. The X would be nonserious, nonartistic film. We can't make those judgments. That's for critics to make."[25]

This argument, of course, makes no sense at all. In putting any rating on a movie, whether "G," "X," or anything in between, CARA automatically renders an artistic judgment. If Valenti had truly wanted to avoid judging films, he would never have gone into the labeling business. The MPAA, in other words, had no rational response to the clamor for a new "A" rating. As a result, the rebellion continued, and the outcome was foreseeable.

In September 1990, the MPAA announced that it was junking the "X" rating. Henceforward, films submitted to CARA that were considered adult would be given an "NC-17" rating. No children under 17 would be admitted to a theater showing such a motion picture. Because the new designation would be copyrighted, it would not be available to pornographic films. Their producers would still be free to apply the "X" to their wares, which would presumably eliminate the confusion between serious and unserious adult films. *Henry and June,* a decidedly adult but nonpornographic account of the relationship between Mr. and Mrs. Henry Miller and Anaïs Nin in Paris in the 1930s, became the first movie to receive the new rating.[26] In addition, CARA began to issue brief explanations as to why a film had received an "R" rating, thus helping parents to make more informed decisions.

As a compromise between Hollywood's twin needs for artistic freedom and box-office success, the new ratings scheme was a failure. As far as most citizens were concerned, "NC-17" was just a fancier version of "X," or in other words, a label meaning "pornography." As with "X," many theaters refused to show "NC-17" films, many newspapers and radio stations rejected ads for them, and many video chains and department stores declined to carry them when they were released on cassettes. Thus denied outlets, such films were almost guaranteed to fail commercially. In order to avoid the stigma of the new label, filmmakers were forced to bargain with CARA and then cut their movies in order to gain an "R" rating. By two years after the directors' rebellion that had forced the MPAA to modify the ratings system, it was clear that the insurrection had been based on a faulty premise. The problem had not been that the public could not distinguish between artistic and nonartistic "X" films. The problem had been that the public did not want to see dirty movies, however they were labeled.[27]

SELF-REGULATION OF BROADCAST TELEVISION

Although the details are much different, the television industry has also found ways to regulate itself. Of all forms of communication, broadcasting has received the most limited First Amendment protection from government regulation. The Supreme Court has ruled on several occasions that the right to broadcast is not comparable to the right to speak, write, publish, or make movies. Many people have argued over the years that this distinction has no sensible basis and that radio and television should be accorded the same First Amendment immunities as all other forms of expression. The courts have disagreed, holding that because the broadcast spectrum is limited, the government has an obligation to insure that it is allocated and used according to national needs. As a result, the Federal Communications Commission has the authority to see to it that the broadcasting industry pursues the "public interest, convenience, and necessity."[28]

Despite this lack of independence, however, the broadcasting industry suffers very little from government interference. Generally, FCC content rules forbid only obscene language and subject matter and require that news and public affairs programming achieve a general balance. In the 1970s the FCC yanked the license of a Mississippi television station because of its racist programming and employment practices, but that was a rare and extreme action. As the "Maude" episode illustrates, government rule-making has not prevented the networks from occasionally broadcasting a show with intensely controversial subject matter. The *threat of interference*, of course, always hangs over the industry and undoubtedly induces a certain caution in programming. Nevertheless, the real censorship of television entertainment comes from elsewhere.

As a commercial medium that cannot yet sell tickets to consumers, broadcast television relies on outside sponsors for its revenue. The purpose of television, as far as its executives are concerned, is to sell audiences to potential advertisers. If those advertisers think that there is something about the program that will offend people enough to make them resent the product associated with it, they will refrain from sponsoring it. As NBC Vice-President Gerald Jaffe once observed, "With the audience, you could get very high ratings with frontal nudity, penetration, torture, and people being cut up with chainsaws. But Congress would shriek, and so would advertisers. It would make a hard sell for Hamburger Helper."[29]

Accompanying their desire to avoid offending sponsors directly, station and network executives also prefer that shows not be indirectly troublesome. There is no telling what sort of ruckus will cause advertisers to flee from a certain program, and so as far as the executives are concerned, the blander the show the better. Television therefore has a stake in appeasing organized groups that have the potential to make a lot of noise.

The stations, and especially the networks, have evolved several institutions for mediating between themselves and potential trouble. Within the networks there are departments that go by different names but collectively are known as the "broadcast standards offices" (BSOs). These offices perform the same function as the Hays Office in the movies' old studio system: They are the internal censors that try to ward off the external censor. Each network BSO keeps a list of "don'ts" and drives producers and writers crazy by objecting to language, situations, and plot points that do not conform. As with films in the 1930s, each program is the product of a tortured series of negotiations between the artists trying to do it their way and the broadcast standards office attempting to keep them within official guidelines.

Just as important, the networks now have routinized contacts with a swarm of advocacy groups that has arisen in the last two decades to try to influence television programming. There are groups concerned about violence, about family values, about sexual lifestyles, about their particular race, religion, or cultural heritage, about over-commercialization, about children, about senior citizens, about the handicapped, about various diseases, about organized labor, and about sundry environmental issues. According to researcher Kathryn Montgomery, by the early 1980s more than 250 such organizations had been involved in efforts to modify the messages on America's TV screens.[30]

Most of these groups remain outside the Hollywood power structure and attempt to affect the content of the screen by putting pressure on advertisers or by lobbying the FCC or Congress. On the right, for example, CLEAR-TV (Christian Leaders for Responsible Television), formed by the Reverend Donald Wildmon in 1989, monitors programs and, when it finds examples of profane or anti-Christian messages, threatens to boycott the products of its sponsors.[31] On the left, Action for Children's Television has achieved considerable influence with Congress in its crusade to control the commercialization of what is known in the trade as "kidvid."[32]

Other groups have so burrowed into the fabric of Hollywood that they can virtually be considered parts of the industry. The networks maintain regular contacts with representatives of the major ethnic-defense organizations, for example. Any script dealing with black themes is first circulated unofficially among important black Los Angeles politicians as well as among leaders of the NAACP and the National Black Media Coalition (NBMC). Their objections and suggestions, if any, become incorporated into edicts handed down by the broadcasts standards offices, and thereby enter into the negotiations with artists that accompany the development of any program. Similar access is enjoyed by the Association for Asian Pacific American Artists, Nosotros, and other groups.[33]

The result is that when artists are developing a program for television, they are continually reminded that they are not alone. Reflecting on his hundreds of productions in more than forty years in Hollywood, David Wolper reported, "I cannot think of a subject matter that I did that somebody didn't object to."[34] Despite the aggravation these objections caused, however, Wolper managed to persevere and produce some of television's most celebrated programs ("Roots," for example). His is the individual experience that stands for the whole.

CONCLUSION

In both motion pictures and television, there is a continual process of adjustment, negotiation, and compromise between artists, corporate officials, and concerned citizens in the larger society. No one likes this system. Artists regard it as one more interference on top of the multitude of intrusions they must already suffer. Corporate officials would rather not be bothered with it; they would prefer to be free to get on with the task of making money. And citizens feel that their opinions are too little considered and that an out-of-control industry is proceeding on its arrogant path. If so many people are so dissatisfied with the system, perhaps it's not such a bad thing.

This system of negotiation and compromise inevitably contains biases. Hollywood's liberal political slant influences the sorts of stories its citizens want to tell and colors the way they interpret objections to those stories. *The Birth of a Nation* could never be produced in contemporary Hollywood. No artist would work on it; no studio would be associated with it; no distributor would touch it; no theater would show it. But *The Last Temptation of Christ* could never have been produced in 1915. Then, the film industry could put out a film intensely offensive to blacks but not to Christians. Now, it is the other way around.

So the system is not perfect. What is? Hollywood is a continual battleground of commercial interests, ideological perspectives, personal ambition, and social pressure. The process of adjustment among all of these forces is messy, time-consuming, expensive, and agreeable to no one. It is, in other words, very like the process of democracy itself. Furthermore, the alternatives to the present ugly system are even less appealing. Complete freedom from all social control would unleash this immensely powerful media machine on a population already insufficiently able to defend itself. Yet government censorship would not only merely exchange one set of biases for another but would probably also kill the golden goose of commercially popular entertainment at the same time. The best prescription I can offer for improving American screen entertainment, then, is that we should continue to allow the combatants to fight it out.

Notes

CHAPTER I

1. Information on actors' earnings from David F. Prindle, *The Politics of Glamour: Ideology and Democracy in the Screen Actors Guild* (Madison: University of Wisconsin Press, 1988), 11; information on the tax bill and Heston's lobbying from author interview with Charlton Heston, September 30, 1991; and *Daily Variety,* June 30, 1986, 2; August 19, 1986, 1; December 11, 1986.

2. Information on Mandela dinner from author interview with Charlton Heston, September 30, 1991; and *Los Angeles Times,* "Metro" section, June 30, 1990, 1.

3. Harold L. Vogel, *Entertainment Industry Economics: A Guide for Financial Analysis,* 2nd ed. (New York: Cambridge University Press, 1990), 63; University of Texas *Daily Texan,* February 14, 1991, 3.

4. Vogel, *Entertainment Industry Economics,* 114.

5. Todd Gitlin, *Inside Prime Time* (New York: Pantheon, 1985), 35, 43.

6. Author interview with Sydney Pollack, December 21, 1990.

7. Brennan quoted in *Daily Variety,* March 6, 1991, F6.

8. Hortense Powdermaker, *Hollywood: The Dream Factory* (Boston: Little, Brown, 1950), 289.

9. Goldenson quoted in Laurie Nadel, "Television's Quiet Giant: Leonard Goldenson," *Vis a Vis,* March 1991, 72.

10. Neil Gabler, *An Empire of Their Own* (New York: Anchor Books, 1988), 258–259.

11. John Gregory Dunne, "Foreword," *The Studio* (New York: Limelight Editions, 1985).

12. Joan Didion, *The White Album* (New York: Pocket Books, 1979), 158–159.

13. Spielberg quoted in Mark Litwak, *Reel Power: The Struggle for Influence and Success in the New Hollywood* (New York: William Morrow, 1986), 101.

14. For discussions of the insecurity of executive jobs, see Mark Litwak, *Reel Power,* 65–66; and Steven Bach, *Final Cut: Dreams and Disaster in the Making of "Heaven's Gate"* (New York: New American Library, 1986), 417.

15. Prindle, *The Politics of Glamour,* 10–11.

16. Bach, *Final Cut;* Stephen Farber and Marc Green, *Outrageous Conduct: Art,*

Ego, and the Twilight Zone *Case* (New York: Ivy, 1988); Julia Phillips, *You'll Never Eat Lunch in This Town Again* (New York: Random House, 1991), 244–349.

CHAPTER 2

1. Norman H. Garey, "Elements of Feature Financing," in Jason E. Squire (ed.), *The Movie Business Book* (Englewood Cliffs, N.J.: Prentice-Hall, 1983), 100–110.

2. Peter S. Myers, "The Studio as Distributor," in Squire, *The Movie Business Book*, 275–309.

3. Nat D. Fellman, "The Exhibitor," in Squire, *The Movie Business Book*, 314–322.

4. Harold L. Vogel, *Entertainment Industry Economics: A Guide for Financial Analysis*, 2nd ed. (New York: Cambridge University Press, 1990), 116–120.

5. John Eisendrath, "Hollywood Jackpot," in *Los Angeles Times Magazine*, September 4, 1988; William Lafferty, "Feature Films on Prime-Time Television," 251; Tino Balio, "Introduction to Part II," 292–293; Michele Hilmes, "Pay Television: Breaking the Broadcast Bottleneck," 310; Bruce Austin, "Home Video: The Second-Run 'Theater' of the 1990s," 321; all in Tino Balio (ed.), *Hollywood in the Age of Television* (Boston: Unwin Hyman, 1990).

6. Hilmes, "Pay Television," 297–318.

7. Suzanne Mary Donahue, *American Film Distribution: The Changing Marketplace* (Ann Arbor, Mich.: UMI Research Press, 1987), 16–20.

8. Tino Balio, "Struggles for Control: 1908–1930," 114; and J. Douglas Gomery, "The Coming of the Talkies: Invention, Innovation, and Diffusion," 210; both in Tino Balio (ed.), *The American Film Industry* (Madison: University of Wisconsin Press, 1976); Donahue, *American Film Distribution,* 17; Barry Langford and Douglas Gomery, "Studio Genealogies: A Hollywood Family Tree," in "The Image Factory," *Gannett Center Journal*, Summer 1989, 158–161, 164–165.

9. Robert A. Hammond and A. Douglas Melamed, "Antitrust in the Entertainment Industry: Reviewing the Classic Texts," in "The Image Factory," *Gannett Center Journal*, Summer 1989, 141.

10. *Daily Variety,* August 15, 1988, 2; February 6, 1990, 120; February 7, 1991, 3.

11. *Daily Variety,* February 6, 1990, 92, 98; *Wall Street Journal,* September 15, 1989, B4.

12. *New York Times,* March 25, 1991, C1; *Daily Variety,* April 23, 1990, 1; Harold L. Vogel, *Entertainment Industry Economics,* 116–120.

13. *Fortune,* "Loew's, Inc.," 291; and Ernest Borneman, "United States Versus Hollywood: The Case Study of an Antitrust Suit," 336; both in Balio, *The American Film Industry;* Peter S. Myers, "The Studio as Distributor," 282; Raphael D. Silver, "Independent Distribution: Midwest Films," 294–300; and Paul N. Lazarus, "Distribution: A Disorderly Dissertation," 306–307; all in Squire, *The Movie Business Book; Daily Variety,* March 13, 1991, 3.

14. Myers, "The Studio as Distributor," 282; Lazarus, "Distribution," 303, 306.

15. Paul N. Lazarus, *The Movie Producer* (New York: Barnes and Noble, 1985),

158; Lillian Ross, *Picture: John Huston, M.G.M., and the Making of "The Red Badge of Courage"* (New York: Limelight, 1952, 1984), 173–180.

16. Todd Gitlin, *Inside Prime Time* (New York: Pantheon, 1985), 31–46.

17. Norman H. Garey, "Elements of Feature Financing," in Squire, *The Movie Business Book*, 100–101; *Daily Variety,* August 10, 1990, 4.

18. Garey, "Elements of Feature Financing," 101.

19. Author interview with Alvin Rush, July 18, 1990; Vogel, *Industry Economics,* 117; Alan Landsburg, "The Independent Producer," in Steve Morgenstern (ed.), *Inside the TV Business* (New York: Sterling, 1979), 59; *Daily Variety,* September 10, 1990, 1; *Wall Street Journal,* February 9, 1989, 1; September 18, 1989, B1.

20. *Los Angeles Times,* March 23, 1990, F1.

21. Quoted in Martin Kasindorf, "Can't Pay? *Won't* Pay!" *Empire,* June 1990, 50.

22. Vogel, *Entertainment Industry Economics,* 123–124.

23. *Daily Variety,* August 9, 1990, 3; *Los Angeles Times Calendar,* April 9, 1989, 3.

24. Gordon Stulberg, "Film Company Management," in Squire, *The Movie Business Book,* 123; Aljean Harmetz, "Now Playing: The New Hollywood," *Screen Actor,* Winter 1988, 13.

25. *Daily Variety,* March 20, 1991, 1.

26. *Daily Variety,* March 25, 1991, 1.

27. Richard Corliss, "Box-Office Brawn," *Time,* December 24, 1990, 53; Silvie Schneble and Tristine Rainer, "Financing and Foreign Distribution," in Squire, *The Movie Business Book,* 123; *Economist,* November 3, 1990, 74; *Daily Variety,* February 6, 1991, 6.

28. Simpson quoted in Mark Litwak, *Reel Power: The Struggle for Influence and Success in the New Hollywood* (New York: William Morrow, 1986), 86.

29. *Daily Variety,* February 14, 1991, 10.

30. *Daily Variety,* February 28, 1990, F14.

31. Rod Granger and Doris Toumarkine, "The Un-Stoppables," *Spy,* November 1988, 88–94.

32. Arkoff quoted in Aljean Harmetz, *Rolling Breaks and Other Movie Business* (New York: Alfred A. Knopf, 1983), 135.

33. Goldberg quoted in Litwak, *Reel Power,* 310.

34. I am grateful to Joseph Slate of the University of Texas at Austin English Department for furnishing me with most of this information; see also Roberta Kent, "Exploiting Book-Publishing Rights," in Squire, *The Movie Business Book,* 87–92.

35. Bill Barol, "Batmania," *Newsweek,* June 26, 1989, 73; *Wall Street Journal,* January 5, 1990, B4.

36. *Wall Street Journal,* January 5, 1990, B4.

37. Jane Hall, "Aladdin's Lamp Goes Dark: The Deregulation of Children's Programming," *Gannett Center Journal,* Winter 1988, 21.

38. *Daily Variety,* January 4, 1991, 54.

39. Army Archerd's column, *Daily Variety,* March 20, 1991, 2.

40. *Daily Variety,* January 4, 1991, 54.

41. *Daily Variety,* January 4, 1991, 1.

42. *Daily Variety,* March 8, 1991, 1.

43. Roger Corman, "It Came from Corman," *California,* August 1990, 66–69.
44. *New York Times,* October 15, 1990, B1.
45. Author interview with Leo Chaloukian, June 6, 1990; *Daily Variety,* June 27, 1990, 74.
46. *Daily Variety,* June 23, 1989, 1.
47. Hurd quoted in "It Came from Corman," 69.
48. Author interview with Barry Gordon, May 23, 1990.
49. On this point see Walter Adams and James W. Brock, *The Bigness Complex: Industry, Labor, and Government in the American Economy* (New York: Pantheon, 1986), 48–64.
50. *Wall Street Journal,* February 9, 1989, 1; quotation is from Tim Brooks and Earle Marsh, *The Complete Directory to Prime Time Network TV Shows,* 3rd ed. (New York: Ballantine, 1985), 574.

CHAPTER 3

1. Christopher H. Sterling and John M. Kitross, *Stay Tuned: A Concise History of American Broadcasting* (Belmont, Calif.: Wadsworth, 1978), 439.
2. Robert Vianello, "The Rise of the Telefilm and the Networks' Hegemony over the Motion Picture Industry," 204–218; and Douglas Gomery, "Failed Opportunities: The Integration of the U.S. Motion Picture and Television Industries," 219–228; both in *Quarterly Review of Film Studies,* Volume 9, Summer 1984.
3. Mark Christensen and Cameron Stauth, *The Sweeps: Behind the Scenes in Network TV* (New York: William Morrow, 1984), 74.
4. Barry Litman, "Network Oligopoly Power: An Economic Analysis," in Tino Balio (ed.), *Hollywood in the Age of Television* (Boston: Unwin Hyman, 1990), 125.
5. Erwin G. Krasnow, Lawrence D. Longley, and Herbert A. Terry, *The Politics of Broadcast Regulation,* 3rd ed. (New York: St. Martin's, 1982), 16–19.
6. *Ibid.,* 52–54, 87–121.
7. Michele Hilmes, "Pay Television: Breaking the Broadcast Bottleneck," in Balio, *Hollywood in the Age of Television,* 299; Krasnow, Longley, and Terry, *The Politics of Broadcast Regulation,* 176–191, 206–239.
8. Norman Horowitz, "Syndication," in Steve Morgenstern (ed.), *Inside the TV Business* (New York: Sterling, 1979), 73.
9. Gary Edgerton and Cathy Pratt, "The Influence of the Paramount Decision on Network Television in America," *Quarterly Review of Film Studies,* Volume 8, Summer 1983, 15–16.
10. Krasnow, Longley, and Terry, *The Politics of Broadcast Regulation,* 53; Sterling and Kitross, *Stay Tuned,* 383; Litman, "Network Oligopoly Power," 129; on the Nixon dispute with the networks, see Lucas A. Powe, Jr., *American Broadcasting and the First Amendment* (Berkeley: University of California Press, 1987), Chapter 8.
11. Paul Klein, "Programming," in Morgenstern, *Inside the TV Business,* 15–17; Sally Bedell, *Up the Tube: Prime-Time TV and the Silverman Years* (New York: Viking, 1981), 35.

12. Chayevsky quoted in *Newsweek,* October 17, 1988, 85.

13. Thomas Streeter, "The Cable Fable Revisited: Discourse, Policy, and the Making of Cable Television," *Critical Studies in Mass Communication,* Volume 4, June 1987, 174–200.

14. Jane Feuer, "MTM Enterprises: An Overview," in Jane Feuer, Paul Kerr, and Tise Vahimagi (eds.), *MTM: "Quality Television"* (New York: BFI, 1984), 6–7.

15. Edgerton and Pratt, "The Influence of the Paramount Decision," 17.

16. Loy Singleton, *Telecommunications in the Information Age: A Primer on the New Technologies* (Cambridge, Mass.: Ballinger, 1983), 8; Don R. Le Duc, *Beyond Broadcasting: Patterns in Policy and Law* (New York: Longman, 1987), 96–97; figures from Motion Picture Association of America; *Standard and Poor's,* January 11, 1990, M30.

17. *Los Angeles Times,* April 4, 1986, Part IV, 1; *Daily Variety,* June 27, 1990, 1.

18. Bedell, *Up the Tube,* 25; *Daily Variety,* April 24, 1991, 10; April 17, 1991, 1; *New York Times,* May 2, 1991, B1.

19. Harry F. Waters, "The Future of Television," *Newsweek,* October 17, 1988, 88.

20. *Daily Variety,* February 28, 1991, 3; January 11, 1991, 1; November 21, 1990, 1; November 19, 1990, 2; November 8, 1989, 1; May 22, 1989, 1.

21. *Wall Street Journal,* October 16, 1989, B1; February 7, 1985, 60.

22. *Daily Variety,* December 17, 1990, 1; September 27, 1990, 1; September 10, 1990, 5; June 20, 1990, 2; June 23, 1989, 1; March 21, 1989, 1; *New York Times,* October 1, 1990, C1.

23. *Daily Variety,* February 19, 1991, 1.

24. Carl Solberg, *Oil Power: The Rise and Imminent Fall of an American Empire* (New York: New American Library, 1976), 33–39; David F. Prindle, *Petroleum Politics and the Texas Railroad Commission* (Austin: University of Texas Press, 1981), 20 and passim.

25. Valenti quote in *Daily Variety,* November 10, 1989, 2; see also October 4, 1990, 1; June 23, 1989, 1; April 19, 1989, 1; March 21, 1989, 1.

26. Author interviews with Leonard Stern and Charles Fitz-Simons, June 28, 1990; *Daily Variety,* April 2, 1991, 2.

27. *Daily Variety,* June 29, 1990, 1; January 30, 1990, 1.

28. *Wall Street Journal,* March 30, 1990, A12; February 7, 1985, 60; *Daily Variety,* January 29, 1990, 6; "How to Lobby Washington, Hollywood-Style," *Newsweek,* March 25, 1991, 48.

29. Oxley quote from *Daily Variety,* February 8, 1991, 1; December 17, 1990, 42; *Wall Street Journal,* February 26, 1990, B5.

30. *Daily Variety,* February 13, 1991, 1.

31. *Daily Variety,* March 20, 1991, 1.

32. On Quello, see *Daily Variety,* January 17, 1990, 42; on Duggan, see *Daily Variety,* April 17, 1991, 3; on Thompson and Barrett, see "How to Lobby Washington, Hollywood-Style," *Newsweek,* March 25, 1991, 48.

33. *Daily Variety,* April 10, 1991, 1.

34. Valenti quoted in *Daily Variety,* April 10, 1991, 1; Murphy quoted in *Daily Va-*

riety, April 16, 1991, C19; analysis by Bill Carter in *Wall Street Journal,* April 10, 1991, C19.

35. *Daily Variety,* November 6, 1992, 1.

36. *Ibid.*

37. On BET and CNN, see *Daily Variety,* February 13, 1990, 1; May 12, 1988, 1; on rural programming, see *Daily Variety,* March 16, 1990, 1.

38. Cable Communications Policy Act of 1984—Amendments to the Communications Act of 1934; 47 U.S.C. Sec. 151 et seq., 601, 623–26 (1984).

39. On making and breaking promises, see Thomas W. Hazlitt, "Wired: The Loaded Politics of Cable TV," *New Republic,* May 29, 1989, 11–13; on Tennessee fee increases, see *Wall Street Journal,* December 11, 1989, B1; on mayors, see *Daily Variety,* March 7, 1991, 1.

40. On tiering, see *Wall Street Journal,* January 23, 1990, B1; on gobbling sports, see *Wall Street Journal,* January 9, 1990, B1; on public access, see *Daily Variety* April 25, 1991, 1.

41. On channel repositioning, see *Daily Variety,* October 26, 1989, 1; May 1, 1989, 1; March 2, 1990, 1; May 5, 1988, 1.

42. Author interview with Jack Valenti, May 22, 1989; see also *Daily Variety,* December 28, 1988, 1.

43. *Daily Variety,* February 13, 1990, 1.

44. *Ibid.*

45. *Ibid.*

46. *Daily Variety,* September 10, 1992, 1.

47. Thomas F. Baldwin and D. Stevens McVoy, *Cable Communications,* 2nd. ed. (Englewood Cliffs, N.J.: Prentice-Hall, 1988), 77; Waters, "The Future of Television," 90; *Wall Street Journal,* March 30, 1990, A10.

48. Mooney quoted in Waters, "The Future of Television," 90; see also *Daily Variety,* December 19, 1988, 1.

49. Hazlitt, "Wired: The Loaded Politics of Cable TV," 13.

50. Baldwin and McVoy, *Cable Communications,* 223.

51. *Daily Variety,* July 17, 1992, 1.

52. Hilmes, "Pay Television," 312; *Wall Street Journal,* February 21, 1990, B1.

53. *Wall Street Journal,* March 30, 1990, A10.

CHAPTER 4

1. Lillian Ross and Helen Ross, *The Player* (New York: Limelight, 1961), 87.

2. Otto Fenichel, "On Acting," *The Psychoanalytic Quarterly,* Volume 15, 1946, 144–147; Ronald Taft, "A Psychological Assessment of Professional Actors and Related Professions," *Genetic Psychology Monographs,* Volume 64, 1961, 334; Aljean Harmetz, *Rolling Breaks and Other Movie Business* (New York: Alfred A. Knopf, 1983), 22; David F. Prindle, *The Politics of Glamour: Ideology and Democracy in the Screen Actors Guild* (Madison: University of Wisconsin Press, 1988), 9.

3. For a fuller discussion of blacklisting and its consequences see Prindle, *The Politics of Glamour,* 52–62.

4. *Daily Variety,* December 5, 1988, 2.

5. *Daily Variety,* July 6, 1988, 3.

6. William F. Buckley, Jr.'s column, *Los Angeles Times,* January 28, 1990, Section M, 7.

7. Melnick quoted in Harmetz, *Rolling Breaks,* 50; see also Richard Zimbert, "Business Affairs and the Production/Financing/Distribution Agreement," in Jason E. Squire (ed.), *The Movie Business Book* (Englewood Cliffs, N.J.: Prentice-Hall, 1983), 178.

8. *Los Angeles Times Calendar,* March 18, 1990, 45.

9. *New York Times,* November 16, 1990, B7.

10. Leo Rosten, *The Joys of Yiddish* (New York: Pocket Books, 1976), 360.

11. Quoted in Will Dana, "The Last Boomtown, Starring the Kids from Wall St.," *M Inc.,* February 1991, 88.

12. Robert R. Faulkner and Andy B. Anderson, "Short-Term Projects and Emergent Careers: Evidence from Hollywood," *American Journal of Sociology,* Volume 92, Number 4, January 1987, 879–909.

13. Todd Gitlin, *Inside Prime Time* (New York: Pantheon, 1985), 115.

14. *Daily Variety,* February 6, 1991, 3; December 14, 1990, 1.

15. These data were gathered from stories in *Daily Variety* for the relevant period.

16. *Ibid.*

17. *Daily Variety,* April 26, 1991, 8.

18. *Daily Variety,* April 18, 1991, 8.

19. *Daily Variety,* February 11, 1991, 2.

20. *Daily Variety,* March 25, 1991, 8.

21. *Daily Variety,* April 5, 1991, 22.

22. Invitation to the 1991 Crystal Awards luncheon.

23. *Daily Variety,* April 19, 1991, 3.

24. *Daily Variety,* May 3, 1991, 6.

25. Program for the 1990 Golden Eagle Awards ceremony.

26. Author interview with Marc Allen Trujillo, July 25, 1990.

27. *New York Times,* March 26, 1991, B1.

28. *Wall Street Journal,* April 8, 1986, 1; advertising brochure for *Celebrity Register* 1990.

29. *Daily Variety,* July 19, 1989, 12.

30. *Los Angeles Times Calendar,* September 11, 1988, 28.

31. *Ibid.,* 30.

32. Mark Christensen and Cameron Stauth, *The Sweeps: Behind the Scenes in Network TV* (New York: William Morrow, 1984), 270.

33. *Wall Street Journal,* February 7, 1990, A1.

CHAPTER 5

1. I have been unable to find much literature on this topic, but for an assertion by one well-known expert on art, see Susan Sontag, *Against Interpretation and Other Es-*

says (New York: Dell, 1966), 290; for an article in a gay-oriented publication that takes for granted the high percentage of gays and lesbians in the industry, see James Ryan with G. Luther Whitington, "Homophobia in Hollywood," *The Advocate: The National Gay and Lesbian News Magazine,* Issue 573, March 26, 1991, 32–41.

2. On surveys asking questions about gays, see *The Gallup Survey,* April 21, 1987, 22; see also James L. Gibson and Kent L. Tedin, "The Etiology of Intolerance of Homosexual Politics," *Social Science Quarterly,* Volume 69, Number 3, September 1988, 587–591; for a summary of state laws, see Ann Giudici Fettner and William A. Check, *The Truth About AIDS: Evolution of an Epidemic,* rev. ed. (New York: Henry Holt, 1985), 228; on the results of gay rights referenda, see John D'Emilio and Estelle B. Freedman, *Intimate Matters: A History of Sexuality in America* (New York: Harper & Row, 1988), 347; on personal attacks on gays, see Lori Heise, "Responding to AIDS," in Lester R. Brown (ed.), *State of the World 1989* (New York: W. W. Norton, 1989), 129.

3. Kinsey cited in D'Emilio and Freedman, *Intimate Matters,* 291–292.

4. Vito Russo, *The Celluloid Closet: Homosexuality in the Movies,* rev. ed. (New York: Harper & Row, 1987), 139, 162, and passim.

5. *Ibid.,* 66, 133, 226.

6. *Ibid.,* 139, 162, and passim.

7. *Los Angeles Times Calendar,* December 2, 1990, F1.

8. Russo, *The Celluloid Closet,* 252.

9. Quoted in Mary Murphy, "Denial/Secrecy/Dread: The AIDS Scare," *TV Guide,* October 22–28, 1988, 8.

10. My informant about "The Homintern" would prefer not to be named; the quote about "The Gay Mafia" is in Murphy, "Denial/Secrecy/Dread: The AIDS Scare," 7.

11. On total number of deaths and infections, see "Mortality Attributable to HIV/AIDS—United States, 1981–1990," *Morbidity and Mortality Weekly Report,* Centers for Disease Control, Atlanta, Volume 40, Number 3, January 25, 1991, 41–43; on 1990 cases, see *The Advocate,* May 21, 1991, 64.

12. *New York Times,* November 26, 1990, A1.

13. *Daily Variety,* May 5, 1989, 3.

14. *Daily Variety,* February 25, 1991, 1.

15. Quoted in Murphy, "Denial/Secrecy/Dread: The AIDS Scare," 9.

16. *Daily Variety,* September 20, 1990, 14.

17. On the bubonic plague, see Barbara Tuchman, *A Distant Mirror: The Calamitous 14th Century* (New York: Ballantine, 1978), 103; on tuberculosis and cancer, see Susan Sontag, *Illness as Metaphor* (New York: Doubleday, 1989), passim; on leprosy, see Susan Sontag, *AIDS and Its Metaphors* (New York: Doubleday, 1989), 133; on syphilis, see Theodor Rosebury, *Microbes and Morals: The Strange Story of Venereal Disease* (New York: Viking, 1971), 167–168; on herpes, see D'Emilio and Freedman, *Intimate Matters,* 341.

18. Heise, "Responding to AIDS," 129.

19. Jon Rappoport, *AIDS Inc.: Scandal of the Century* (San Bruno, Calif.: Human Energy Press, 1988), 193; Randy Shilts, *And the Band Played On: Politics, People, and the AIDS Epidemic* (New York: Penguin, 1988), 311.

20. Tuchman, *A Distant Mirror,* 99.

21. Quoted in D'Emilio and Freedman, *Intimate Matters,* 355–356.

22. Author interview with Marvin Kaplan, August 21, 1990.

23. Quoted in Russo, *The Celluloid Closet,* 213.

24. Quoted in Murphy, "Denial/Secrecy/Dread: The AIDS Scare," 4–5.

25. Russo, *The Celluloid Closet,* xii.

26. Shilts, *And the Band Played On,* 544.

27. Midler quoted in Army Archerd's column, *Daily Variety,* September 17, 1991, 2.

28. Author interview with George Kirgo, August 6, 1990.

29. Kathryn C. Montgomery, *Target: Prime Time: Advocacy Groups and the Struggle over Entertainment Television* (New York: Oxford University Press, 1989), 86–94; the quotation is on page 93.

30. This and the following five paragraphs are based on accounts in *Daily Variety,* October 26, 1988, 1; and December 15, 1988, 3.

31. *Daily Variety,* October 26, 1988.

32. Quoted in Murphy, "Denial/Secrecy/Dread: The AIDS Scare," 6.

33. David F. Prindle, *The Politics of Glamour: Ideology and Democracy in the Screen Actors Guild* (Madison: University of Wisconsin Press, 1988), 166.

34. The following eight paragraphs are based on: author interview with Marcia Smith, June 13, 1990; *Weekly Variety,* September 27–October 3, 1989; *Hollywood Reporter,* September 26, 1989, December 4, 1989, and December 27, 1989; *Daily Variety,* September 29, 1989, October 10, 1989, and July 16, 1990.

35. *Daily Variety,* September 20, 1991, 2.

36. *Hollywood Reporter,* December 27, 1990, 26.

37. *Hollywood Reporter,* December 28, 1990, 40.

38. Thomas E. Backer, " 'We Take Care of Our Own': The Entertainment Industry Responds to AIDS," in Alan M. Glassman and Thomas G. Cummings (eds.), *Cases in Organizational Development* (Homewood, Ill.: Richard D. Irwin, 1991), 4.

39. *Ibid.,* 5.

40. *Ibid.,* 12.

41. *Ibid.,* 17, 18.

42. *Ibid.,* 19; *Hollywood Reporter,* December 28, 1990, 40.

CHAPTER 6

1. On Mayer's Republicanism, see Neal Gabler, *An Empire of Their Own: How the Jews Invented Hollywood* (New York: Doubleday, 1988), 115, 317; on campaign contributions in 1936 and 1944, see Louise Overacker, "Presidential Campaign Funds in 1936," *American Political Science Review,* Volume 31, 1937, 485, 488; and "Presidential Campaign Funds in 1944," *American Political Science Review,* Volume 39, 1945, 902, 909, 916–918.

2. Leo C. Rosten, *Hollywood: The Movie Colony, the Movie Makers* (New York: Harcourt, Brace, 1941), 160.

3. Quoted in Gabler, *An Empire of Their Own,* 328.

4. Overacker, "Presidential Campaign Funds in 1944," 902, 909, 911, 917-918.

5. Larry Ceplair and Steven Englund, *The Inquisition in Hollywood: Politics in the Film Community,* 1930–1960 (Berkeley: University of California Press, 1983), 67.

6. Ronald Brownstein, *The Power and the Glitter: The Hollywood–Washington Connection* (New York: Pantheon, 1990), 233–239.

7. Ben Stein, *The View from Sunset Boulevard: America As Brought to You by the People Who Make Television* (New York: Basic Books, 1979), 135–136.

8. Lowe quoted in Brownstein, *The Power and the Glitter,* 297.

9. The Media Research Center, *TV Inc.,* Volume 1, Number 1, April/May 1989, 1.

10. David Brooks, "More Kafka Than Capra," *National Review,* September 30, 1988, 29.

11. See John C. Pierce, Kathleen M. Beatty, and Paul R. Hagner, *The Dynamics of American Public Opinion: Patterns and Processes* (Glenview, Ill.: Scott, Foresman, 1982), 180–183.

12. Author interview with Barry Diller, January 11, 1991.

13. Author interview with Arthur Hiller, June 27, 1990.

14. Author interview with David Wolper, January 11, 1991.

15. Stein, *The View from Sunset Boulevard,* 135–136; see also Robert Lerner, Althea K. Nagai, and Stanley Rothman, "Elite Dissensus and its Origins," *Journal of Political and Military Sociology,* Volume 18, Summer 1990, 27–28.

16. Robert Lerner and Stanley Rothman, "The Media, the Polity, and Public Opinion," in Samuel Long (ed.), *Political Behavior Annual,* Volume 2 (Boulder, Colo.: Westview, 1989), 39–76.

17. Daniel Bell, "The New Class: A Muddled Concept, " in B. Bruce Briggs (ed.), *The New Class?* (New Brunswick, N.J.: Transaction, 1979), 169–190.

18. Seymour Martin Lipset, *Political Man: The Social Basis of Politics* (Garden City, N.Y.: Doubleday, 1963), 243–244.

19. Gabler, *An Empire of Their Own,* passim.

20. Everett Carll Ladd, Jr., "Jewish Life in the United States: Social and Political Values," in Joseph B. Gittler (ed.), *Jewish Life in the United States: Perspectives from the Social Sciences* (New York: New York University Press, 1981), 123.

21. Lipset, *Political Man,* 262.

22. Neil Vidmar and Milton Rokeach, "Archie Bunker's Bigotry: A Study of Selective Perception and Exposure," *Journal of Communication,* Volume 24, Winter 1974, 36–47.

23. For an interpretation of *Rambo* as liberal, see Stephen P. Powers, Stanley Rothman, and David J. Rothman, "Hollywood Views the Military," *Society/Transaction,* Volume 28, November/December 1990, 84; for an interpretation of the same film as conservative, see Michael Ryan and Douglas Kellner, *Camera Politica: The Politics and Ideology of Contemporary Hollywood Films* (Bloomington: Indiana University Press, 1990), 207, 214.

24. Stephen P. Powers, David J. Rothman, and Stanley Rothman, "Hollywood Movies, Society, and Political Criticism," *The World & I,* April 1991, 563–581.

25. *The People, the Press, and Politics,* Survey I Dataset, A Times Mirror Survey, The Gallup Organization, April/May 1987, 5.

CHAPTER 7

1. Author interviews with David Horowitz, July 1990, and Mark McIntire, June 28, 1991.

2. *Los Angeles Times,* "Metro" section, June 30, 1990, 1.

3. *Los Angeles Times Calendar,* May 25, 1989, 2.

4. On 1944 campaign contributions, see Louise Overacker, "Presidential Campaign Funds, 1944," *American Political Science Review,* Volume 39, Number 5, October 1945, 911, 916; on the Justice Department preventing the studios from acquiring TV stations, see Douglas Gomery, "Failed Opportunities: The Integration of the U.S. Motion Picture and Television Industries," *Quarterly Review of Film Studies,* Volume 9, Number 3, Summer 1984, 220.

5. On Wasserman, LBJ, and Carter, see Ronald Brownstein, *The Power and the Glitter: The Hollywood–Washington Connection* (New York: Pantheon, 1990), 212–224, esp. 222–223; on Congress and the VCR, see James Lardner, *Fast Forward: Hollywood, the Japanese, and the VCR Wars* (New York: New American Library, 1987), 287–296.

6. Ronald Brownstein, "Boredom is Trendy," *New Republic,* August 22, 1988, 17.

7. Julia Phillips, *You'll Never Eat Lunch in This Town Again* (New York: Random House, 1991), 445–448; Fred Barnes, "Flix Mix in Politix," *New Republic,* October 30, 1989, 20; author interview with Margery Tabankin, July 11, 1990.

8. Brownstein, *The Power and the Glitter,* 311; Barnes, "Flix Mix," 20; author interview with Margery Tabankin, July 11, 1990.

9. Brownstein, *The Power and the Glitter,* 353–354; *Daily Variety,* October 18, 1983; on Whoopi Goldberg, see "Ms. Smith Goes to Hollywood," *The Economist,* November 3, 1990, 36.

10. *The Economist,* November 3, 1990, 36.

11. Brownstein, *The Power and the Glitter,* 352–357; *Daily Variety,* September 19, 1988, 3.

12. Biden aide quoted in Brownstein, *The Power and the Glitter,* 354; on Dukakis, see Brian Sullam, "The Cash Campaign," *New Republic,* March 14, 1988, 12; on McCarthy, see Brownstein, "Boredom is Trendy," 17.

13. This and the following four paragraphs are based on material found in *Daily Variety,* December 17, 1987, 1; and November 3, 1987, 1.

14. Medavoy quoted in *Daily Variety,* July 10, 1992, 1; Leviton's letter in *Daily Variety,* July 27, 1992, 15.

15. This and the following four paragraphs are based on material in *The Wall Street Journal,* April 8, 1988, 1; Ann Reilly Dowd, "Winning One for the Gipper," *Fortune,* November 9, 1987; and documents and videotapes supplied by People For The American Way.

16. This summary is based on an unsigned analysis of Bork's views, "The Case Against Bork," *New Republic,* October 5, 1987, 7–8.

17. William Haltom and Patti Watson, "Sealing Judge Bork's Doom: The Role of the Usual Suspects," unpublished paper presented at the convention of the Western Political Science Association, Newport Beach, California, March 22–24, 1990.

18. *Ibid.*, 1–2.

19. Both quotes from Dowd, "Winning One for the Gipper"; see also Andrew Sullivan, "The Bork Screw," *New Republic,* October 19, 1987, 16.

20. Lear quoted in *Daily Variety,* October 19, 1989, 3.

21. *Los Angeles Times,* February 10, 1990, 1; *Hollywood Reporter,* September 11, 1989, 1; EMA board members were listed in *EMA,* Volume 1, Number 1, June/July 1990, 2.

22. Quote on EMA's purpose from pamphlet, "Environmental Media Association: An Entertainment Industry Response to the Global Environmental Crisis," published by EMA, no date given; *Hollywood Reporter,* September 11, 1989, 1.

23. *USA Today,* February 5, 1990.

24. Neil Hickey, "TV's Campaign to Clean up the Planet," *TV Guide,* April 21–27, 1990, 21.

25. *Daily Variety,* February 14, 1990, 14; *Wall Street Journal,* October 3, 1989, B1.

26. *Daily Variety,* April 19, 1990; and April 20, 1990, 12.

27. On Ted Turner, see *Orange County Register,* April 15, 1990, N16; and Hickey, "TV's Campaign," 22; on David Zucker, see *Daily Variety,* June 21, 1990, 12; on David Simon, see *USA Today,* February 5, 1990, "Life" section, 1.

28. Robert Iger, "Guest Column" in *EMA,* Volume 1, Number 1, June/July 1990, 3.

CHAPTER 8

1. Sally Steenland, *What's Wrong with This Picture? The Status of Women on Screen and Behind the Camera in Entertainment TV* (Washington, D.C.: National Commission on Working Women of Wider Opportunities for Women, 1990), 55–58.

2. Howard Rodman, "Unequal Access, Unequal Pay: Hollywood's Gentleman's Agreement," *Montage,* October 1989, 4.

3. *Daily Variety,* February 12, 1991, 1.

4. Rodman, "Unequal Access," 4.

5. Author interview with Leonard Stern, June 28, 1990.

6. Author interview with Marvin Kaplan, August 21, 1990.

7. Kirgo quoted in *Los Angeles Times Calendar,* May 25, 1989, 1.

8. Author interview with Marcy Kelly, June 19, 1990.

9. Anonymously quoted in Steenland, *What's Wrong,* 61–62.

10. Steinberg quoted in *Los Angeles Times Calendar,* May 25, 1989, 1.

11. Author interviews with Marcy Kelly, June 19, 1990; Ernest Harada, July 23, 1990; and Elaine Pounds, July 10, 1990; *Daily Variety,* February 6, 1991, 3.

12. Author interview with Jean Firstenberg, August 13, 1990; Rodman, "Unequal Access," 5.

13. On actors, see Steenland, *What's Wrong,* 10; on women, see Steenland, *What's Wrong,* 66; on minority writers, see Rodman, "Unequal Access," 5.

14. Author interview with J. Nicholas Counter, December 21, 1990.

15. John Eisendrath, "The Making of the Hollywood Working Class," *Washington Monthly,* November 1988, 14.

16. *Ibid.*

17. Simpson quoted in Mark Litwak, *Reel Power: The Struggle for Influence and Success in the New Hollywood* (New York: William Morrow, 1986), 275.

18. Michael Goldfield, "Labor in American Politics—Its Current Weakness," *Journal of Politics*, Volume 48, February 1986, 23.

19. Quoted anonymously in Lawrence Christon, "Strike Reflections: A Pyrrhic Victory for the Odd Men Out," *Los Angeles Times Calendar*, August 14, 1988, 3.

20. This strike and its aftermath is dicussed in David F. Prindle, *The Politics of Glamour: Ideology and Democracy in the Screen Actors Guild* (Madison: University of Wisconsin Press, 1988), Chapter 5.

21. *The Wall Street Journal*, August 4, 1988, 23.

22. Joan Didion, "Letter From Los Angeles," *New Yorker*, September 5, 1988, 85.

23. Stefan Kanfer, *A Journal of the Plague Years* (New York: Atheneum, 1973), 284.

24. Curtis J. Matheaus, "Lights! Camera! Contract! The Impact of Technology on Entertainment Unions," Master's thesis, University of Texas at Austin, 1990, 49–50.

25. *The Wall Street Journal*, May 5, 1988, 32.

26. *Daily Variety*, June 24, 1991, 1.

27. *Ibid.*

28. Eisendrath, "The Making of the Hollywood Working Class," 16–17; *Daily Variety*, March 7, 1988, 1.

29. *Daily Variety*, August 3, 1988, 1.

30. *Daily Variety*, August 15, 1988, 1; *Wall Street Journal*, August 4, 1988, 23.

31. Eisendrath, "The Making of the Hollywood Working Class," 17–19; *Los Angeles Times Calendar*, August 14, 1988, 3.

32. *Daily Variety*, August 8, 1988, 1.

33. Author interview with J. Nicholas Counter, December 21, 1990; *Daily Variety*, December 3, 1990, 23.

34. *Daily Variety*, March 8, 1989.

35. *Daily Variety*, December 13, 1990, 1; December 18, 1990, 1; December 26, 1990, 1.

36. For a discussion of the differences between Anglo-American and Continental copyright law, see David J. Kohs, "When Art and Commerce Collide: Colorization and the Moral Right," *Journal of Arts Management and Law*, Volume 18, Spring 1988, 16–17.

37. George Stevens vs. National Broadcasting Company et al., 270 Cl App. 2d 886, 76 Cal Reptr. 106 (1969).

38. On time compression/expansion, see *Daily Variety*, August 31, 1990, 12; on panning-and-scanning, see the testimony of Eliot Silverstein before the Subcommittee on Technology and the Law of the United States Senate Judiciary Committee, May 12, 1987, reprinted in *Journal of Arts Management and Law*, Volume 17, Fall 1987, 90.

39. *Daily Variety*, October 30, 1986, 16.

40. *Daily Variety*, December 23, 1988, 1; *U.: The National College Newspaper*, March, 1989, 11; Dan Renberg, "The Money of Color: Film Colorization and the 100th Congress," *Hastings Comm/Ent L. J.*, Volume 11, Spring 1989, 396.

41. Testimony of Ginger Rogers before the Subcommittee on Technology and the Law, 87.

42. Reported in Steven Gibaldi, "Artists' Moral Rights and Film Colorization: Federal Legislative Efforts to Provide Visual Artists with Moral Rights and Resale Royalties," *Syracuse Law Review,* Volume 38, 1987, 988.

43. Anne Marie Cook, "The Colorization of Black and White Films: An Example of the Lack of Substantive Protection for Art in the United States," *Notre Dame Law Review,* Volume 63, November 1988, 311–322; see also testimony of Woody Allen, Milos Forman, Sydney Pollack, and Eliot Silverstein before the Subcommittee on Technology and the Law, 79–93.

44. For statements in favor of colorization, see the testimony of Roger L. Mayer, Rob Word, and Buddy Young before the Subcommittee on Technology and the Law, 64–78.

45. Testimony of Rob Word before the Subcommittee on Technology and the Law, 70–71.

46. Testimony of Roger L. Mayer before the Subcommittee on Technology and the Law, 69.

47. Testimony of Sydney Pollack before the Subcommittee on Technology and the Law, 85.

48. Scorcese quoted in Michael Landau, "The Colorization of Black-and-White Motion Pictures: A Gray Area in the Law," *Journal of Arts Management and Law,* Volume 19, Fall 1989, 74.

49. Fred Zinneman, "Colorizing Is Not A B & W Issue," *Daily Variety,* March 17, 1989, 42.

50. See, for example, testimony of Woody Allen before the Subcommittee on Technology and the Law, 81.

51. *Ibid.,* 80.

52. Directors Guild of America statement quoted in testimony of Eliot Silverstein before the Subcommittee on Technology and the Law, 90–91.

53. Kohs, "When Art and Commerce Collide," 23–24.

54. Renberg, "Money of Color," 419.

55. *Daily Variety,* September 28, 1988, 1.

56. *Daily Variety,* September 20, 1989, 1; September 27, 1989, 1.

57. Billington quoted in *Daily Variety,* November 20, 1990, 1.

58. ACLU quoted in *Daily Variety,* June 13, 1991, 1.

59. For example, see Cook, "Colorization of Black and White Films"; and Gibaldi, "Artists' Moral Rights."

60. For example, see Caryn James, "Fighting Film Coloring with a Label as Weapon," *New York Times,* November 6, 1990, B1.

CHAPTER 9

1. *New Republic,* February 8, 1988, 7.

2. This information on *The Birth of a Nation* comes from Richard Schickel, *D. W.*

Griffith: An American Life (New York: Simon and Schuster, 1984), 213–299; and Nickieann Fleener-Marzec, *D. W. Griffith's "The Birth of a Nation": Controversy, Suppression, and the First Amendment as it Applies to Filmic Expression, 1915–1973* (New York: Arno, 1980).

3. Quoted in Schickel, *D. W. Griffith*, 270.

4. Quoted in Michael Paul Rogin, "'The Sword Became a Flashing Vision': D. W. Griffith's 'The Birth of a Nation,'" in *"Ronald Reagan," The Movie, and Other Episodes in Political Demonology* (Berkeley: University of California Press, 1987), 219.

5. On lynchings and social science experiments, see Fleener-Marzec, *Controversy*, 8, 34; on KKK recruiting, see Rogin, "Flashing Vision," 233.

6. Dubois quoted in Fleener-Marzec, *Controversy*, 8.

7. This material on the "Maude" controversy is taken from Kathryn C. Montgomery, *Target: Prime Time: Advocacy Groups and the Struggle over Entertainment Television* (New York: Oxford University Press, 1989), 27–50.

8. Clark quoted in *ibid.*, 35.

9. National Council of Catholic Bishops quoted in *ibid.*, 36.

10. Quoted in *ibid.*, 37.

11. This information is distilled from many articles that appeared in *Daily Variety* during the summer of 1988.

12. Hayford quoted in *Daily Variety*, July, 13, 1988, 1.

13. *Daily Variety*, July, 21, 1988, 1.

14. Griffith's statement quoted in Schickel, *D. W. Griffith*, 282.

15. *Daily Variety*, July 27, 1988, 3.

16. Mutual Film Corporation vs. Industrial Commission of Ohio, 236 U.S. 247 (1915), quoted in Lucas A. Powe, Jr., *American Broadcasting and the First Amendment* (Berkeley: University of California Press, 1987), 29.

17. Burstyn vs. Wilson, 343 U.S. 495, 501–502 (1952), quoted in Richard S. Randall, "Censorship: From 'The Miracle' to 'Deep Throat,'" in Tino Balio (ed.), *The American Film Industry* (Madison: University of Wisconsin Press, 1976), 432.

18. Information on MPPDA from *Fortune*, "The Hays Office," in Balio (ed.), *The American Film Industry*, 295–314.

19. Information on the economic plight of the industry during the Depression from David F. Prindle, *The Politics of Glamour: Ideology and Democracy in the Screen Actors Guild* (Madison: University of Wisconsin Press, 1988), 16.

20. Breen quoted in *Fortune*, "Hays Office," 314.

21. Details on code taboos from Hortense Powdermaker, *Hollywood: The Dream Factory* (Boston: Little, Brown, 1950), 54–81.

22. Lewton quoted in Thomas Schatz, *The Genius of the System: Hollywood Filmmaking in the Studio Era* (New York: Pantheon, 1988), 196; for historical accounts, see Schatz, passim; and Nick Roddick, *A New Deal in Entertainment: Warner Brothers in the 1930s* (London: British Film Institute, 1983), 34–38.

23. Randall, "Censorship," 446.

24. The following discussion of the "X" rebellion is based on information from *Daily Variety*, July 25, 1990; August 3, 1990; September 19, 1990; September 25, 1990; September 27, 1990; and September 28, 1990.

25. Valenti quoted in *Daily Variety*, September 19, 1990, 1.

26. *New York Times,* September 27, 1990, A1.

27. William Grimes, "NC-17 Rating Declares a Film is ...What?" *New York Times,* November 30, 1992, B1.

28. For an overview of judicial doctrine on government regulation of broadcasting, see J. W. Peltason, *Understanding the Constitution,* 8th ed. (New York: Holt, Rinehart, and Winston, 1979), 146; for an example of the argument that broadcasting should not be regulated, see Powe, *American Broadcasting;* for a discussion of the "public interest" clause, see Erwin G. Krasnow, Lawrence D. Longley, and Herbert A. Terry, *The Politics of Broadcast Regulation,* 3rd ed. (New York: St. Martin's, 1982), 17.

29. Jaffe quoted by Todd Gitlin, *Inside Prime Time* (New York: Pantheon, 1985), 252–253.

30. Montgomery, *Target: Prime Time,* 6.

31. On CLEAR-TV, see *Daily Variety,* February 7, 1989, 2.

32. On ACT, see Marie Winn, *The Plug-in Drug: Television, Children, and the Family,* rev. ed. (New York: Penguin, 1985), 6; *Daily Variety,* July 13, 1989, 1; and October 18, 1990, 1.

33. Author interviews with Elaine Pounds of NBMC, July 10, 1990; Ernest Harada of AAPAA, July 23, 1990; and Marc Allen Trujillo of Nosotros, July 25, 1990.

34. Author interview with David Wolper, January 11, 1991.

About the Book and Author

Hollywood is an intense and unique culture of artists, producers, promoters, technicians, and managers. It is a community of superstars and extras, successes and failures—a place where, according to David Prindle, most "live in an emotional world characterized by paranoia, suspicion, resentment, and dread." *Risky Business* examines the politics and economics underlying the complex interrelationships and interior struggles that exist between Hollywood's principal players.

David Prindle takes us behind the facades of Hollywood and discusses the "existential truths" about Hollywood's totality as a monolithic culture and the stresses that the industry applies to all involved. Subjects covered include the anxieties at work within the industry, with a focus on Hollywood's industrial structure and distribution difficulties; the "sociological nightmares" of Hollywood that include interpersonal relations, the awards industry, and AIDS; Hollywood's liberalism; political activism and the "good citizen" celebrity; the internal politics of affirmative action, labor and management, and artists' rights; and the issues of censorship and self-expression.

The author has incorporated all the learning and theoretical sophistication of political science yet has written an accessible and colorful book. Full of details and anecdotes, *Risky Business* will appeal to anyone interested in a more comprehensive understanding of the Hollywood mystique.

David F. Prindle was born and raised in the Los Angeles area, where he first became interested in Hollywood as a social system. He earned two degrees at the University of California and a doctorate in political science at the Massachusetts Institute of Technology. He is presently associate professor of government at the University of Texas. His previous books include *The Politics of Glamour: Ideology and Democracy in the Screen Actors Guild* (1988) and *Petroleum Politics and the Texas Railroad Commission* (1981). He lives in Austin with his wife, Angalene, and his son, Matthew.

Index

Screen Actors Guild, 8, 62
  and affirmative action, 127
  attitude of, toward independent
    producers, 33
  and controversy over Hollywood
    Helps, 80
  efforts of, to acquire representation of
    extras, 136
  and fear of AIDS among actors, 78
  jurisdictional conflicts of, with
    AFTRA, 129
  1980 strike of, 132
  1989 agreement with AMPTP of, 136
  size of membership, 56
  See also Actors; Unions, Hollywood
Screen entertainment industry
  advertising function of, 15
  financing function of, 15
  production function of, 15, 16
  retail sale function of, 15, 16
  See also Distribution function of
    screen entertainment industry
Screenwriters
  and homosexuality, 75
  maneuvers of, under Production
    Code, 156
  position of, in Hollywood's status
    hierarchy, 133
  and women in the Hollywood labor
    force, 125
  See also Strike of 1988; Writers Guild
    of America West
Screen Writers Guild, 133. *See also*
    Writers Guild of America West
Sequels, 27
Series
  motion picture, 27
  television, 27–28
Sheen, Martin, 75, 111, 118
"Shmooze," to, 59–60, 61
  and awards ceremonies, 66
  and discrimination against women
    and minorities, 127
  and homosexual network, 71
  and political activism, 105, 112
  and political liberalism, 99
Simpson, Don, 24, 59, 131

Smith, Marcia, 79–81
Spielberg, Steven, 6, 63
Spinoffs, 27–28
Stallone, Sylvester, 25, 74
Star system, 25–26
Star Wars, 5, 28
Steenland, Sally, 126
Stein, Ben, 89, 96
Steinberg, Herb, 127
Stevens, George, 138–139
Streep, Meryl, 26, 112
Streisand, Barbra, 112, 114
Strike of 1988, 132–135. *See also*
    Writers Guild of America West
Studios, major. *See* Major studios
Studio system, old, 20, 25
  and colorization controversy, 141
  value of films made under, 156
  See also Star system; Vertical
    integration
Supreme Court, United States, 154,
    156, 159
Symbols, political, 10–11, 110–111
Syndication market, 21, 24
  and fin-syn rules, 39
  and independent TV stations, 17
  and "Star Trek" series, 28

"Teenage Mutant Ninja Turtles," 29, 30
Telephone companies, 49
Television industry, 16
  advent of, and labor relations, 129
  differences of, from motion picture
    industry, 138
  importance of producers in, 26
  labor relations in, 128–131
  lack of star system in, 26
  and potential censorship, 148
  and problem of residuals, 131
  self regulation of, to avoid
    censorship, 155, 159–161
Television programs, 20
Television stations, independent. *See*
    Independent television stations
Television stations, network affiliated,
    20